Flunking Chemistry Class

The Baseball Players

Jim Lynch

Copyright © 2014 Jim Lynch
All rights reserved.

ISBN: 0692210172
ISBN 13: 9780692210178

Dedication

This book is dedicated to the many professional baseball players who have chosen to compete honestly in their sport and who have demonstrated the courage to speak out against the deceit and dangers inherent in the abuse of illegal steroids and HGH. Brad Zeigler stands out among these players. He has had the bravery to challenge his peers and the baseball establishment to eliminate performance enhancing drug usage in baseball.

The book is also dedicated to the numerous sportswriters who have critically chronicled the growing dilemma that baseball has faced during the so-called Steroid Era and called for change. Among these writers, Tom Verducci stands out as having been instrumental in informing the public, not only about the risks to the integrity of the game but also about the risks to the health of the players who play the game and to those who follow in their footsteps.

Although I have never met either of these two men, I believe that they represent their professions honorably and with distinction. I salute them and their like-minded peers.

Contents

I: Is Jelly Coming to the Bronx? (Fall 1998) — Page 1
II: The Pool Party (Fall 1998) — Page 4
III: 'Roid Rage at the Earth Series (October 2000) — Page 19
IV: Arizona Clinic League (August 2001) — Page 36
V: The Earth Series Redux (October 2001) — Page 44
VI: Parade of Stars Game (July 2002) — Page 55
VII: Big Sky Country (July 2002) — Page 66
VIII: Going Postal in The Morning After (**October 2002**) — Page 78
IX: The Juice-Off by the Bay (April 2004) — Page 86
X: CoJo and Jelly Settling Some Scores. (June 2004) — Page 99
XI: The Texan Does the Carolinas (July 2004) — Page 103
XII: Expansion^2 (September 2004) — Page 115
XIII: The Congressional Hearings (March 2005) — Page 126
XIV: The Texan as a Jersey Boy (August 2005) — Page 135
XV: A Dork and the Three Stooges (October 2006) — Page 149
XVI: The Witchell Hunt Report (December 2007) — Page 158
XVII: The Last Cuts of Spring Training (March 2008) — Page 175
XVIII: Double Dating at the Ballpark (April 2008) — Page 183
XIX: The State of the Sport Address (July 2009) — Page 188
XX: Playing the Outfield (August 2009) — Page 193
XXI: Flunking Chemistry Class (January 2010) — Page 202
XXII: "Yeaoww!" (March 2010) — Page 207
XXIII: Dreaming on the Outer Banks (July, 2010) — Page 211
XXIV: Jelly's Travail (Spring 2011) — Page 220
XXV: The MVP and the Botch Job (Fall 2011) — Page 224

XXVI: Is It Over? (December 2011)	Page 231
XXVII: The 26th Man Law Suit (April 2012)	Page 233
XXVIII: Coopersville (June 2012)	Page 237
XXIX: Starting and Restarting (Summer and Fall of 2012)	Page 244
XXX: Spring Training in Miami (March 2013)	Page 249
XXXI: The *Myo-Nemesis* Mess (Summer of 2013)	Page 256
XXXII: Never-Ever? (Fall of 2013)	Page 259
XXXIII: The Beginning of the End (January 2014)	Page 269
Postscript (July 2018)	Page 279

I

Is Jelly Coming to the Bronx?

Fall 1998

"F*** that s***."

Will Morehead cringed – as he always did – when he heard Lester Postal utter his trademark three word commentary on just about everything.

The question that Morehead had posed to Postal was simple: "Do you think the Bronx Bloomers should sign Jelly Rogers?" Rogers was a free agent pitcher and the former ace of the Beantown Wallbangers. More recently, he had been the ace of the Toronto Thunderbirds. Now it was rumored that Jelly Rogers was heading to the Bronx.

Will Morehead never liked hearing those three indecent little words from his lead sports writer. In fact he always tried to tune them out like he was hearing "f*** that s***" instead of the actual off-color verbiage. However Lester Postal used his offensive rejoinder quite frequently with a variety of different meanings depending upon the question; the context of the question; the tone of his response and a host of other variables.

Sometimes, "f*** that s***" simply meant an emphatic "no," like now, when Morehead had just asked whether or not the Bloomers should sign Jelly Rogers.

Other times it meant: "I don't want to talk about it." This might occur if someone would ask Postal if he and his fourth wife, Mona

Flunking Chemistry Class

Morningstar, were quarreling again. The sportswriter would just answer: "f*** that s***."

He sometimes emphasized the *adjective* between his lurid verb and noun so that it also could express incredulity. (Ex. "Unbelievable, what a play!" = "F*** *that* s***!") This astonishment was usually accompanied by a nose squinting and a furrowed brow facial contortion.

Lester Postal sometimes said it *hastily* as "f***/that/s***," with no space between the words when he was being dismissive. (Ex. Question: "Do you want to go back to the office?" Answer: "F***/that/s***."); (Ex. 2 Question: "Are you going to take your wife to the opera?" Answer: "F***/that/s***." This meaning was complemented by a backward flip wave of his right hand as though he were trying to swat away the inquiry.

Only occasionally would Postal use the phrase to express sheer delight. (Ex. Question: "Did you see the knockers on that waitress?" Answer: **F*** THAT S***!!!**" The kinetic supplement for this connotation was a wide-eyed, eyebrow-raising, facial gawk.

Fortunately, Lester Postal was able to contain the usage of his pet phrase so that he didn't bring it to the office with him. There was an occasional lapse or two but for the most part he only used his colorful colloquialism in the barrooms of Manhattan which served as his home away from home.

Will Morehead was the chief sports editor of *The New York Roast* the city's most popular tabloid newspaper, and Lester Postal was his lead writer. Fortunately, Postal was much more elegant and insightful in his newspaper reporting than he was with his barroom banter. And because Postal had such a broad and loyal following in the Big Apple, Morehead put up with Lester's out-of-the-office lifestyle, which included other profligate habits such as gambling, smoking cheap cigars, and frequenting titty-bars.

Morehead and Postal had been working together for more than two decades, so the veteran writer enjoyed some latitude that was not accorded to younger members of *The Roast's* staff. But Morehead hated chasing Postal down in his favorite haunts just to make sure the writer hadn't gone over the edge some place and might miss a deadline.

Is Jelly Coming to the Bronx?

On this occasion however, Morehead had sought out Lester Postal in *Joey Dee's Tavern*. Morehead wanted to get an answer to the exciting rumor-laden question that was sweeping through the subway trains, the busses, the taxis and the limousines that rolled across the streets of the Big Apple. Postal had all sorts of inside sources within the Multinational Baseball League and Morehead simply wanted to know whatever his writer knew about the answer to the big mystery: *Was Jelly Rogers going to become a Bronx Bloomer?*

II

The Pool Party

Fall 1998

It was the first time that he had ever been there. However Jelly Rogers immediately liked CoJo Janesco's house. It had lots of mirrors; big mirrors, small mirrors, round mirrors, square mirrors and elaborate mirrors of every shape imaginable. And the mirrors weren't just in the three bathrooms on the ground floor. They were everywhere. There was a 5 ft by 3 ft oval mirror just inside the front door. There was an oversized 11 foot by 8 ft mirror in the ballroom and there were three smaller patterned mirrors on one side of the hallway. Past the ballroom, the study and the indoor barroom, there was a 20 foot by 20 foot home fitness center with a 15 foot high ceiling. The door at the far end of this gym led out toward the patio area surrounding the pool. The wall facing the far end doorway was covered by a floor to ceiling form fit mirror that made the room seem twice its actual size. Every one of these mirrors – with the obvious exception of the form fitting mirror in the fitness center – was adorned with an expensive and ornate frame.

The fact that these mirrors fit into no logical theme or decorative style didn't faze Rogers in the least. He thought the mirrors were very cool. Obviously Janesco must have felt the same way. Rogers was able to see himself in every room he entered. And Jelly Rogers could think of no one he would rather stare at than Jelly Rogers; the super stud

The Pool Party

starting pitcher for the Toronto Thunderbirds of the Multinational Baseball League.

Rogers arrived alone at Janesco's house in Miami because he had just finished an interview with a national sports network at their Floridian outlet. Rogers had confirmed the rumors that he had asked the Thunderbirds for a trade. Meanwhile Rogers' wife had come over a couple hours earlier to spend some time with CoJo's Janesco's wife, Chiquita.

After being given entry to the house of mirrors by Janesco's housekeeper, Rogers was surprised to see that the house appeared empty. Of course this didn't bother him one bit. He simply thought to himself: *look at all these fucking mirrors; how cool is that!*

Rogers walked slowly down the hallway passing one mirrored room after another. As he passed each mirror he took loving peeks at himself. *Damn I look good,* he thought. At one point just before he reached the home fitness center there was a section of the hallway with two mirrors at right angles to one another. This enabled Rogers to get a sidelong view of his own profile. He noticed a slight flaw! The pitcher was horrified to see that he was beginning to get just a little puffy at the jowl, slightly below his jaw. The imperfection was not noticeable at all from the head on view of himself that Rogers normally saw. *Shit, what the hell is that!* He wondered if this mini-jowl was readily visible to everyone – and to his own misery he believed that it was. He abruptly stopped walking down the hall. Then without taking his eyes off his double angle reflection in the mirror, he pushed his jaw forward so that it projected his lower teeth about half an inch in front of his upper teeth. *Whew. It's gone.* Then Rogers realized that projecting his jaw in that manner removed any possibility of smiling. *That's okay he thought. I'll manage.* Jelly Rogers was not much of a smiler anyway. There would be other ways to deal with this puffiness later. He simply wanted to get through the party that evening. So he determined that he would attempt to face people head on and do the best that he could to avoid exposing his profile. He knew that if it got too crowded at any point and there were people at his side, he could always opt to temporarily exercise his jowl reducing jaw-jut.

Flunking Chemistry Class

There were two separate egress routes from the house to the pool area. One was a door at the end of the hallway and the other was the door on the far side of the fitness center. Rogers chose to walk through the fitness center and get a look at all of Janesco's workout toys. Once he was in the room he turned toward the full length mirror. It immediately looked like there were twice as many toys in the room as he had originally noticed. But Rogers was more fixated on the full length view of himself than he was on the treadmills, the weight machines and the stationary bikes. His own image was more pleasing to the pitcher than all of the workout gear. Then, however he did notice two side-by-side floor to ceiling climbing ropes. These appeared poised for racing up to the ceiling near the large skylights that helped illuminate the room. However Rogers was dressed for the party in khaki shorts and a tight fitting sky blue collared polo shirt, and so he resisted the sudden urge to climb one of the ropes. Besides there was no one else in the room to race, and no one there to witness his rope speed or the muscular bulge that it would produce.

Rogers turned slightly as he looked at the wall mirror and gave his image a full body flex salute. He did it in a way that didn't require a lot of movement, just a slight bend in one knee and a hardening of his thigh muscle in his other leg. He didn't raise his arms but simply made two fists and bent these muscled arms slightly at the elbow while they remained hanging down from his brawny shoulders. In this manner he flexed his triceps rather than his biceps, while he also bulled his neck. However this final maneuver made the nascent jowl appear once again so he quickly relaxed his neck muscles. Then he returned his whole body to parade rest without ever looking away from the mirror. When his four seconds of self satisfaction were complete Rogers turned around and completed his journey through the rear door and out onto the swimming pool patio.

The large pool sparkled in the dazzling late afternoon sun. Tangerine colored tiles surrounded the bi-level free-form pool. The two sections of the pool were connected by an electrically powered waterfall that continuously cycled the water from one level to the other. The expanse of tiling was broken up in three different areas where three transplanted palm trees loomed. These trees provided a small amount

The Pool Party

of shade for those who were less inclined to be all out sun worshipers. Surrounding the farthest reaches of the pool area were tightly packed beach grass plants. These plants had grown to more than seven feet in height on either side of the pool house bar and cabana. Together with some fencing that was not visible through the lush landscaping, these grasses provided total privacy from the neighboring properties.

When Jelly Rogers entered the pool area he quickly noticed that there was no one in the pool. In fact there were only two people in the whole pool area. The sight of these two women immediately stimulated the pitchers' interest. Chiquita Janesco and Dolly Rogers had pulled their plush lounge chairs all the way up to the edge of the pool near the shallow end and had angled the chairs and their bodies toward the blazing overhead sun. Rogers noticed that his wife was topless and wore only the small bottom piece to her string bikini. The top was lying on the tile next to her chair. Chiquita Janesco was stretched out on the adjoining lounge chair and was totally nude, except for a Bronx Bloomers baseball cap. Neither the top nor the bottom of Chiquita's bathing suit was anywhere in sight. As Rogers moved toward the women he called from a short distance to alert them of his presence, but casually continued his approach in a counterfeit nonchalance.

"Hello ladies. I see you're enjoying the South Florida sun."

Dolly Rogers sat up when she heard her husband and smiled as he got closer. As she sat up she squared her shoulders and straightened her back because she knew what a stickler Jelly was when it came to posture. Chiquita Janesco didn't move at all.

"Hi Jelly." Dolly went from the stiff backed sitting position to a standing position of equal rigidity. How did the interview go?" The baseball pitcher made sure that he stood directly in front of his wife so that he could smile without utilizing the jaw-jut to obscure his recently discovered mini-jowl. Dolly Rogers leaned in toward her husband and kissed him on his lips lightly, in greeting, not passion, although she did press her naked breasts against his chest in the process.

"It went fine. Of course they wanted to know about the trade request. I did my best not to bash the Thunderbirds, but I did confirm that I would welcome a trade to a contender."

Flunking Chemistry Class

Chiquita remained quiet, motionless and nude. And although Jelly and Dolly Rogers were only five feet away she made no move to alter her sun soaking slouch on her padded lounge chair. Her posture was geared to maximize an all over tan rather than to offer any modicum of modesty whatsoever. Her legs were parted so that the inside of her thighs would get a truly total tan and there was absolutely nothing left unexposed from the bottom of her pencil thin eyebrows to the tips of her pink-painted toe nails.

Chiquita Janesco was half French and half Cuban-American, but that didn't matter to her husband, CoJo. She was only twenty-five years old but CoJo regarded her as a classic Cuban work of art. In fact he had recently hired a local sculptor to come to his home and try to create a life sized and life-like statue of his beautiful wife. That process was ongoing because Chiquita had grown bored and restless while posing as a model for the sculpture. Therefore it was a bit ironic that she was able to lay so motionless now with Dolly and Jelly Rogers looming nearly on top of her.

Meanwhile after her quick peck of greeting Dolly Rogers sat back down next to Chiquita and then stretched back out along her own padded lounge chair. The bottom of both lounge chairs was so close to the pools' edge that Jelly Rogers was not able to stand at the foot of the chairs without standing in the water on the first step. Therefore mindful of the fact that he wanted to avoid any sidelong views, he walked behind the women's lounge chairs. He was now standing behind their heads and looking towards their feet. At this point Chiquita Janesco finally parted her lips and spoke.

"Hi Jelly, *I'm-a* Chiquita. I *think-a* we *met-a once-a* before...*at-a* the club, maybe?" Chiquita's native language was a French and Spanish blend and her English was heavily accented. Further complicating her pronouncement was the fact that she was still attempting to remain motionless as though the slightest movement might yield uneven exposure. Even more galling was the fact that Rogers had met Chiquita on at least three or four separate occasions in the past and had even danced with her at one of the previous parties that the Janescos and Rogers had attended together prior to an Parade of Stars game a couple of

The Pool Party

years back. Chiquita just always seemed to be on her own planet, so Rogers didn't let her comment unnerve him. He stayed cool.

"Sure Chiquita we've met before." Rogers was now staring down upon Chiquita's naked body from a standing position above her head. Her body was glistening with tanning oil that had been evenly but generously applied over Chiquita's entire body surface a few minutes before Rogers had arrived.

Rogers in essence was viewing his hostess' naked body from an upside down vantage point as they talked. Being an aficionado of great bodies, the pitcher simply took it all in. Chiquita's eyes were closed but they were hidden anyway under her Bronx Bloomer's baseball cap. Everything else was right out there. Her mouth and lips were slightly upturned in a frozen half smile, but from Jelly's reverse vantage point, they appeared to form a slight frown instead. Her torso was an evenly toned light bronze with no hint of a tan line anywhere in sight. The expanse of well toned bronze was interrupted only by a tiny tuft of black pubic hair. And there wasn't much of that to see. Chiquita had availed herself of a Brazilian wax treatment on a regular basis, but rather than opting for the full fledged Sphinx type, she had left a tiny two inch by one inch trapezoidal tuft of pubic hair right above – *below* from Jelly's vantage point – her, ahem, not-so-private pudendal region.

As Jelly Rogers visually consumed the image from his reverse angle he couldn't help but stare at the tiny trapezoidal tuft. It was vaguely reminiscent of the face of Harry Puissant, one of the Thunderbirds' outfielders, who had sported a soul patch below his lips.

It was not as though it was the first time Jelly Rogers had ever viewed a woman's body in a reverse juxtaposition of heads and feet. However in the normal course of these events his eyeballs were in significantly closer proximity to the subject matter than his current standing position permitted. All of this simply caused Rogers to shake his head to clear it of unseemly images of Harry Puissant and to convince himself he wasn't beginning to feel some sort of instant sunstroke from the blazing yellow sphere that delivered unfettered radiation through the cloudless Miami sky.

Flunking Chemistry Class

"Where's CoJo, Chiquita? I expected he would either be in your fitness center or out here at the pool."

"The *feetness* center doesn't *get-a* used *all-a* that much. I *theenk eet's more-a* for show. Some of the *eequeepment in-a* there has never *been-a* used at all. Anyway, I *theenk that-a* CoJo should be home soon. He's been driving into town to get all of *hees* cars washed before the party. Don't *ask-a* me why. He rarely drives anything but *hees* Ferrari."

This was more than Chiquita wanted to say from the prone position. She finally sat up. Then she stood up and walked around to the deep end of the pool where the diving board was located. She walked in a carefree manner as though she were strolling through the Garden of Eden. Jelly Rogers watched carefully and Dolly Rodgers watched her husband's Adam's apple bob up and down in serpentine acknowledgement of how perfectly formed Chiquita's wrinkle free tanned torso was. Before Dolly could make any comment that suited the situation, Chiquita's banana brained husband appeared out of nowhere.

"Hey Dolly, Jelly, how are you guys?" Even though his hedonistic Caribbean wife was now bouncing provocatively on top of the diving board, CoJo's eyeballs zoomed in on Dolly Roger's jollies, while Jelly's interest began to rise in salute to Chiquita, wife of banana brain.

Dolly Rogers could feel the heat from CoJo's lurid stare and tried to nonchalantly grab the top piece to her bathing suit and hoist it up to cover the jollies Roger. The top was miniscule consisting of five thin strings: two of which tied at the top; two of which tied behind her back; and the last short piece connecting two triangular patches that covered her breasts, or at least part of her breasts.

Jelly Rogers looked away from the diving board just as Chiquita launched herself into the pool and responded to his host's greeting. "We're doing fine, CoJo. I guess we should all put some clothes back on before all of your guests arrive."

"Yeah, probably not a bad idea, although parties here frequently turn into clothing optional affairs before too long." Then he shouted across to his wife who was just resurfacing in the pool. "Wrap it up, Chickey. Jelly thinks we ought to be more prim and proper before the rest of the party guests arrive.

The Pool Party

Chiquita climbed up the side wall ladder and out of the pool. She immediately walked over to a stack of oversized towels that were lying on top of a stone warmer. With the temperature in the low 90's, there was really no need for the stone heater, but Chiquita appreciated the warmth the towels provided nonetheless. She wrapped herself carefully in one of the lily white towels. Then she flashed a look back at her husband and at Jelly Rogers as if to say, *what a bunch of tired old prunes.* Finally she turned back toward Rogers's wife and said, "So Dolly do *you-a wanna ta* join me *een-a da* sauna before *we-a* get ready *for-a da* party?"

Dolly Rogers was uncertain how to react and took the easy way out, "Sure Chiquita that sounds like a pleasant way to unwind." In order to emphasize the fact that she could make decisions for herself, she also re-loosened and then untied the back of the bikini top which she had tied only three minutes earlier. She didn't take it off right away but merely left it provocatively hanging from the neckline strings. Then she followed the towel draped Chiquita toward the opposite end of the house. A stairway led downward to the recreational amenities of the residence which included; a game room; a sauna; a steam room; a video arcade and *his* and *hers* bathroom facilities. Dolly kept her eyes open to see if the Janescos had any particular household extras that she should encourage Jelly to buy for their own home in Texas.

Poolside the two baseball players began to converse amiably but aimlessly. They weren't particularly close friends although they had spent the last season playing together for the Toronto Thunderbirds. In reality they were drawn together more frequently by their wives' friendship than any kind of shared interests – other than baseball, of course – of their own. Once the women left, the ballplayers started walking slowly in the direction of the cabana bar, beyond a duet of palm trees but still within the perimeter of the poolside tile decking. The cabana wasn't significantly sized but it was quite functional, including a wet bar, a small changing area and a rest room. Four bar stools stood in front of the bar, with the seat backs leaning toward the top tier of the pool.

"So Jelly baby, what's all the noise about you going back to the Wallbangers? There are more than a few Beantown fans down around here and they're all over the radio saying they want to reclaim the Jelly Man."

"We're open to a deal, if it's the right one. I'm not sure Boston will be the spot, but I certainly wouldn't rule it out. How about you, CoJo? Are you going to re-sign with the Thunderbirds?

"Doesn't look that way. I want to play nearer to home anyway. My agent is talking to the teams here in Florida. This is where I'd like to play."

The moment they made it up to the cabana bar, a bartender materialized seemingly out of nowhere and began priming a margarita making machine. It was getting close to party time. Jelly Rogers also noticed that the laid-back Jimmy Buffet music that had provided a backdrop for Dolly and Chiquita's earlier sunbathing had been displaced by a bouncing reggae sound. This change also appeared to have been effortlessly effectuated. Rogers began patting his thigh to the beat as soon as they sat down at the bar. As soon as the ballplayers had drinks in front of them, other guests began to arrive. Among the guests were a few ballplayers; some from the South Florida based Miami Minnows and a few others who played for the Tampa Bay Groupers. The wives and girl friends of the ball players were every bit as competitive as the players themselves. For the most part they wore low cut sun dresses or tight fitting backless tank tops or halter tops that exposed more than they halted. The women also displayed expensive jewelry and exotic shoes and sandals of all types. It was billed as a pool party, but no one brought a bathing suit.

The guests included some other celebrities besides the ballplayers. The rapper Iced Kream came accompanied by two toppings known only as Cherry and Sprinkle. The three of them were totally sizzled on cocaine. Also among the earliest party arrivals was gay Republican Congressman Clark Flatley who had not yet outed himself, but came to the party with a wispy young male aide who helped swing the closet door open more than just a tad. The proprietors of two trendy local restaurants were also guests although neither of their establishments was catering the party.

The Pool Party

The guest list also included several people who were not counted among the rich and famous of the Miami jet set. One member of this proletarian group was Billy Pillary, CoJo Janesco's personal trainer, nutritionist and druggist. Pillary's multi-occupational talents had helped shape Janesco's body and his career. And as Janesco's playing days were winding down he was contemplating going into the drug supply business with Pillary. No, CoJo didn't want to risk his personal freedom by dealing coke, cannabis or other illegal recreational drugs. Instead he thought that he might be able to build his reputation among his ball playing peers as a dispenser of magical elixirs that could cut and ripple their bodies and elongate their careers. Anabolic steroids, human growth hormones and customized concoctions of performance enhancing substances were of significant interest to many ballplayers now that St Louis Scarlets first baseman, Popeye Maloney, had shattered the homerun record. CoJo Janesco was already experimenting in this regard along with his twin brother, HoBo Janesco, who was another of the recently arrived guests at the party.

Within a half hour or so more than eighty people had arrived at the Janesco residence. It was almost as though they had all parachuted into the back yard from some flying dirigible that had floated down the Miami shoreline.

The Janesco brothers and some of the male guests were still crowded around the cabana bar and someone had flipped on the large screen TV that hung ominously overhead from a couple of steel rods at the end of the long rack of liquor bottles on the back shelf of the bar section. Suddenly the image of the President of the United States, Clint Blanton, appeared overhead. He was making a statement to the American public in an effort to explain his relationship with a suddenly infamous young intern, Veronica Cummings-Dresser. By now everyone in the world was totally intrigued by the story of Blanton and Cummings-Dresser; the presidential kneepads; the sexual dickering and the semen-stained blue dress. Most people were well aware that Cummings-Dresser had testified before a federal grand jury saying that Blanton had taught her new and interesting things to do with a cigar. And now they were fascinated by the fact that the president had come on TV to appeal to the American people to stop obsessing about what went on in the oval office, and to allow his family some privacy to work through his dilemma of dalliances and indiscretions. In spite of his admission of "inappropriate behavior" with a female member of his staff, toward the end of his plea, a red faced President Blanton rebelliously wagged the index finger of his right hand and defiantly asserted "I did not have sexual relations with that woman." This immediately revved up the conversation among the male guests at Janesco's party.

"I can't believe that he just said that," Billy Pillary intoned."

"To tell you the truth, I'm not exactly sure what he said," Jelly Rogers answered. "He said there was some inappropriate behavior, but denied that there was any sex. It sounds like he doesn't want to admit that he turned the executive suite into the oral office. That shithead lied right in our faces." Rogers was using his jaw-jutting, jowl camouflaging manner of speech as he was now facing Pillary and CoJo, but had his profile exposed to HoBo.

"No, I don't think that's the case." CoJo Janesco argued. "He was just being diplomatic."

"Diplomatic!!! What could possibly be diplomatic about that statement?"

"You're not being very fair, Jelly. I think he was very diplomatic. He certainly didn't want to lie to the American people or apparently to his family, and he didn't. First of all he fessed up to some 'inappropriate behavior,' essentially admitting that in some way he has cheated on his wife. But he was careful not to mention Cummings-Dresser by name ... very diplomatic, I'd say. Remember there are some other women lined up who also claim to have west wing stories of their own, but apparently without the hard DNA evidence. Anyway ... Blanton then truthfully denies that he has had any sexual relations with *that woman* ... obviously, but not overtly, referring to Veronica Cummings-Dresser. I think he was quite diplomatic actually."

A second or two passed. The pounding of the reggae music had been turned up slightly and the general din of laughter and animated bi-lingual frivolity in the background semi-obscured the political debate

The Pool Party

around the bar. However now Jelly Rogers, a registered Republican, was more incensed than ever.

"How can you say that Blanton was *truthful* about not having sexual relations with this intern bimbo? You just acknowledged what everyone now knows ... that she has DNA substantiation. Thank God she didn't swallow the evidence."

"Come on Jelly. Don't you get it? He's simply saying that he didn't have *vaginal* sexual intercourse with her. That's what he means by 'sexual relations.' *Blow jobs don't count.* See what I mean? Therefore he *was* telling the truth." He wagged his right index finger in the same manner that Blanton had done in order to underscore his point.

HoBo then seconded his twin brother's assertion. "Besides, how can you blame the guy? He's got a really tough job, being the President of the United States and all. I think that most guys would agree that he deserves to get a BJ every once in a while ... you know, to reduce stress and all."

Jelly Rogers thought about all of this and was beginning to be swayed by the brothers Janesco. They had seemed to make a credible point or two. He wondered if the rest of the American public would agree with their assessment. He even began to wonder why he had been a bit disingenuous himself with regard to his criticism of Blanton. After all it wasn't like he had been entirely faithful and dutiful to Dolly when he was on the road with the Thunderbirds. For that matter there was a young country singer that he had been seeing on occasion who probably did a much better job at stress reduction than Cummings-Dresser in that the entertainer never left any evidence.

The group of a half dozen or so men at the cabana bar now had their attention grabbed by the distribution of super-soaker water guns by some of Janesco's household staff. Apparently this had been Chiquita's idea of how to jump start a party that didn't need any additional stimulation. But by now Chiquita and Dolly had reappeared after their sauna and were dancing with each other on the veranda just outside the massive kitchen area of the house and overlooking the tiled pool area. Before redressing for the party the women had shared a couple of joints and were now feeling just fine.

Flunking Chemistry Class

The whole rear of the house was structured on three different sloping levels and was landscaped artistically so that there was plenty of sunshine but there were also small alcoves of privacy on each level. Both Chiquita and Dolly were armed with super-dooper-super-soakers which were the best water guns of all, being able to hold a gallon of water and capable of firing a fat stream of H^2O on a level distance of 35 feet. Other less powerful water weapons had been distributed to other guests at the party and the squirting began promptly with none other than Dolly Rogers firing the first water volley at Sprinkle, one of the two tasty toppings who had accompanied the rapper, Iced Kream. Sprinkle was wearing a thin loose fitting cotton pants suit that was long sleeved but very light weight. It managed to hide most of the needle marks that ran up and down her arms. Her upper limbs were also adorned with a mish-mash of multi-colored tattoos. But these were also hidden by the her pajama style attire.

The men at the bar watched a shot or two being fired back and forth between the wet water contestants, but then CoJo had one more cogent thought that he wanted to add about President Clint Blanton. "You know, in many ways, Blanton is a great role model for all of us. You wait and see this whole flap with Cummings-Dresser will blow over soon enough. Blanton realizes that people can forgive a cheater, but they'll be in no hurry to forgive a liar. There's a big distinction. And they are even less likely to forgive someone who lies about cheating. That's why he's a smart man to have told the truth."

"Not only that, he's cleared the way for all of us to get a hummer every once in a while without having to think about it as cheating." HoBo Janesco slapped his brother's back as he agreed with his twin. "You're right CoJo, Clint Blanton. He's the man!!!"

Jelly Rogers no longer argued. He was beginning to understand that the Janesco Brothers might be a bit savvier than he had realized. He didn't want to forget that it was CoJo who had introduced him to Billy Pillary, who in turn had introduced him to his own trainer, Ryan McGhee. And McGhee then helped him build his body up to the point that he was able to win 20 games two seasons in a row, even with the lowly Thunderbirds. Maybe he should pay

The Pool Party

more attention to the Janescos. If nothing else they could apparently throw a great party.

By now everyone was squirting everyone else. There was a lot of laughter as people were getting drenched even without going in the pool. The men at the cabana bar soon received their own water weapons and went out and joined the fray. Inevitably a couple of people, who were already quite soaked and quite intoxicated, began stripping off wet clothing and began jumping into the pool in various states of dishabille. Jelly Rogers found this a little discomforting, but he couldn't help but notice that his wife Dolly Rogers had reloaded her super-dooper-super-soaker and was once again one of the main culprits of the deluge of delirium.

Most everyone seemed to be enjoying the craziness. A few ...very few actually ... of the guests who were not overly excited about the prospects of becoming participants in what was rapidly resembling a high end wet T-shirt contest, had made their way back into the house. One or two guests had actually left. Meanwhile Billy Pillary began to take pictures of all the excitement with his new pocket sized digital camera.

This didn't mean that *everyone* was thoroughly enjoying the madcap mood. In fact, Iced Kreme and the toppings had begun to come down from their cocaine high and were no longer passive participants in the water wars. For whatever reason, Dolly Rogers had taken particular delight in saturating Cherry and Sprinkle and they were now moodily protesting the fact that Dolly Rogers was somewhat drier than many of the other partiers. As Iced Kreme and the toppings began to approach Dolly Rogers, her husband was simultaneously making his way over to her side. Meanwhile Clark Flatley, the closeted congressman, and his thin beard were already standing nearby.

Jelly Rogers had begun to worry that the party was getting out of hand and he was beginning to think about his own reputation and what that meant with respect to his contract status in Toronto. He had always tried to maintain a personal posture that would garner respect from the general public without seeming too staid and unadventurous to his teammates and other ballplayers. He thought that it was about time for him to grab Dolly and leave. However by the time he had gotten close

Flunking Chemistry Class

enough to his wife, Iced Kream and the toppings had grabbed a large plastic tub that was filled with ice water and about a half dozen cans of beer. They snuck up behind Dolly Rogers and dumped the contents of the tub over Dolly like a couple of football players dumping Gatorade over the winning coach's head. Not only did Dolly get totally soaked but she also got clobbered by a couple of the remaining beer cans that had been in the plastic tub. Jelly Rogers lost his cool quickly and took a swing at the laughing Iced Kream. However, besides being a rapper, Iced Kream was an amateur boxer as well. He quickly side stepped Jelly's wild haymaker and hit the pitcher with a short right uppercut to the solar plexus. The pitcher doubled over in pain but recovered enough to take another wild swing at Iced Kream. The rapper again dodged Rogers' wild pitch and the pitcher's fist followed the natural trajectory of his arm and crashed into the ass of the Congressman Clark Flatley. Within moments peacemakers and mayhem mongers alike started swinging wildly at each other without really choosing sides. Twenty minutes later the police came to quiet things down, but Jelly and Dolly Rogers had already left the party. No one was arrested; the music was toned down a couple of notches but the party kept rolling along.

The following day tabloid headlines for the *New York Roast* summed up the previous day's events quite succinctly. The front cover had a picture from the presidential briefing of a flush faced President Clint Blanton with his right index finger raised in admonition. The picture sat below *The Roast's* headline: **BLANTON GIVES US THE FINGER**.

The back pages of the *New York Roast* were dedicated to coverage of sports and sports figures. There was a picture that was taken at the Janesco's party that showed the effect of Jelly Rogers swing and miss at Iced Kreme. The result had been the punching of Congressman Flatley's derriere as the legislator had turned to run to avoid the fracas. *The Roast* had a full page picture that captured the moment of contact and the tabloid chose to headline it as: **JELLY FISTS CONGRESSMAN FLATLEY**.

III
'Roid Rage at the Earth Series

October 2000

Commissioner Buzz Selout looked across his office at Timmy Burr. The nerdy-looking assistant statistician was a constant source of new data on Selout's beloved International Pastime. Although he didn't like to admit it, Selout was emotionally dependent on Burr and his daily update of player statistics and on the relative financial health of the MBL, the Multinational Baseball League. Buzz was addicted to his business and his business was all about statistics.

On this fine October morning however, Commissioner Selout was not a happy camper. He was very worried that before long the cat would be out of the bag forever. He worried that soon the naive sportswriters would finally figure it all out. And that was not a good thing. While Selout was personally dependant on support from Burr and his fellow statisticians and accountants, Selout's business, the MBL, the globally treasured International Pastime, was even more dependent on the emotional support of the MBLWA, the Multinational Baseball League Writers Association.

The MBLWA was the group that most ardently kept the fan base abreast of developments in the sport. The writers' association members were also the final arbiters of all the statistics of the game. Each year they would look at the total compilation of statistics of the players and vote for the annual award winners. The awards included: the Most

Flunking Chemistry Class

Venerated Player Award; the Sly Jung Award (for pitching excellence); the Newbie of the Year Award, and the Field Supervisor of the Year Award.

But now Selout was more worried than ever that the burgeoning group of baseball fans throughout the far reaches of the world would finally realize the truth; that the MBL was no more of a legitimate sport than was professional wrestling. It was fixed. Some of the wrestlers... err ballplayers... err chemically altered competitors ... were destined to win and others were destined to retool their skill sets and try again the following year. Competitive balance was a sham. Recently championships were becoming a virtual certainty. The Bronx Bloomers would win the Earth Series almost as certainly as wrestler Bulk Rogan would defeat perpetual loser Cowboy Rob Gordon. However the winners and losers in baseball were determined in a slightly more scientific manner – by the selection and use of certain performance enhancing drugs. In a bizarre way this somehow gave the game of baseball slightly more verisimilitude than pro wrestling enjoyed.

But now Selout was facing a big problem. The night before, in Game Two of the Earth Series, superstar pitcher Jelly Rogers threw a split bat at superstar catcher, Matt Palazzo. On the back page of the *New York Roast* there was a vivid picture of the two players grimacing angrily at each other under the headline: **'ROID RAGE**.

"Look at this header," Selout said smacking the rear page of *The Roast* with the back of his hand. "Last night was a disaster. Everyone is talking about Jelly Rogers' 'roid rage. Our whole sport seems to be hanging in the balance because of those two selfish clowns." Burr knew that his boss was referring to Matt Palazzo and to Jelly Rogers. But he was startled to hear the commissioner acknowledge that the proliferation of steroids was a bad thing for baseball. All those homeruns that had been hit over the last few years were causing the stadiums to be packed once again. The flak caused by the steroid confrontation the night before was widespread. However Timmy Burr knew that the flak would only draw more interest and dollars into the game of baseball, so he was a bit surprised to hear Selout react the way he did. Public pronouncements aside, Selout rarely was this critical of steroid abuse

'Roid Rage at the Earth Series

when talking to his staff. He normally tried to minimize or refute the impact of these chemicals on the game.

"I can't believe Rogers actually went at Palazzo with a splintered bat. That's why everyone is talking about roid rage," Burr opined. "If the umpire didn't step between them, I'm sure Rogers would have shown no clemency whatsoever. The man was totally out of control." Burr was inclined to blame the whole incident on Jelly Rogers.

Selout never took the position that because he was the boss he was always right. In fact, much to the contrary, he often suffered through the outspoken opinions of his staff simply because he had a hard time deciding on almost everything. Therefore the more opinions he got the more likely he was to get one that he could agree with.

After pausing a moment or two Selout responded to Burr. "You may be right. I've watched the replay video a half dozen times and it looked to me like Palazzo was scared shitless. He wanted no part of Mr. Rogers' neighborhood. It probably was mostly Rogers' fault. Maybe Palazzo just hadn't taken his vitamins lately."

"Well what would you expect?" Burr ignored his boss' implication that Palazzo was also a juicer. "Palazzo wasn't going to take the first swing. He would have been thrown out of the game. Besides Jelly Rogers is no gentle giant. And Rogers still feels that his manhood was affronted by Palazzo on numerous occasions over the last few years. Palazzo is hitting something like .550 off Rogers and Palazzo has taken him deep several times as well."

"I'm aware of that." Selout was matter of fact.

"Rogers already beaned Palazzo earlier this season. Apparently Rogers' steroid cheating wasn't enough to make him a better player than Palazzo so he had to bean him. And now this ...in the Earth Series ... no less. I think that Palazzo was so scared that it was enough to make his back break out in a full-fledged case of acne."

Burr was simply planting a plausible excuse for the plethora of puss filled pimples that adorned Palazzo's shoulders and upper back. Burr was in denial about the possibility that his hero, Palazzo, was pumping steroids just like Jelly Rogers, and that that indulgence might have allowed Palazzo to pummel Rogers in the past.

Flunking Chemistry Class

"What's this manhood thing you're talking about, Timmy? You know that Jelly Rogers has no balls."

"Why do you say that?

"We all know that he's been taking steroids for a few years now. One of the sportswriters told me that his junk looks like a peashooter and a couple of grapes. His eyes are bigger than his balls for Christ's sake. No wonder he always looks pissed off at the world. He's been a feral flamethrower ever since his Toronto days. Look at that mess that he got into at CoJo Janesco's party a couple of years ago. People are starting to catch on and headlines like this don't help."

"Why don't you suspend him for juicing, Mr. Selout?" Timmy Burr was a wisp of a little man. He was 24 years old but looked half that age as he sat in a large leather chair in Selout's office. However Burr had been around Selout long enough to know that the Commissioner often needed a little push to take action on almost anything. Still little Timmy Burr was the only one in the office who called the commissioner, Mr. Selout. To everyone else he was just Buzz.

"Well, we have no unshakeable evidence that Jelly's a juicer. We have a contract to uphold with the players association and until we begin to negotiate the next contract with MBLPA, there's not a whole hell of lot that I can do about his juicing and this so called 'roid rage. So I might as well just sit back and enjoy the Earth Series. There's nothing more important than the Earth Series."

Selout got up and walked around his office in private thought. Then after a few moments he decided to share his thoughts for Burr's sake.

"So far this has turned into a wonderful season. We haven't had a subway series since the Brooklyn club moved out west and became the Hollywood Hedgers. Now we have the Bronx Bloomers and the Metropolitan Mutts going at it full tilt. The Bloomers are the best draw in all of professional sports and they're the team that everyone loves to hate. That's why it was so good for the sport when they signed Jelly Rogers away from the Thunderbirds."

Timmy Burr had grown up on Long Island and had been an avid fan of the Metropolitan Mutts throughout his life. But he wanted to

'Roid Rage at the Earth Series

come across as non-partisan. He didn't want to appear to favor the Mutts in the dispute between Rogers and the Bloomers on one hand and Palazzo and the Mutts on the other hand. He secretly loathed Jelly Rogers and everything that he stood for. Meanwhile he refused to believe that the Mutts' catcher/first baseman and clean-up hitter, Matt Palazzo, was taking steroids. In fact he could honestly attest to the fact that he had never heard anyone remark about the size of Palazzo's bat or the gravitas of his balls. However he was slightly worried about the rumors that the Italian-American slugger was in fact a switch hitter.

"It's hard to understand why folks haven't been more critical of the Bloomers over the last few years. Every time they sign a free agent with an inflated average, the player seems to have an inflated physique as well. Lester Postal, that sports writer for *The New York Roast*, says that every year in October it seems like the Bloomers sport a roster full of ball players that could participate as *floats* in the Thanksgiving Day Parade a month later. He says that Rogers is just the latest *float*. They have signed others in the past."

"Like who?" Selout asked the question with slight indignation. They both knew the answer to the question but for appearances sake Selout wanted to sound uninformed.

"Well it's no big mystery why the Bloomers picked up David Lawless from the Cleveland Featherheads at mid season. The guy cranked out 41 dingers this year. That's nearly twice as many as he hit in each of the last two years. That certainly hasn't hurt the Bloomers much. It seems like every season at the trade deadline they pick up a new float and then they go on to win the Earth Series every year. And as we both know there's nothing more important in life than the Earth Series." Burr finished his argument with Selout's pet proclamation.

"It's amazing how fast Jelly Rogers's body changed. You know Timmy, before Rogers pitched for the Thunderbirds; he was a pretty decent pitcher for the Beantown Wallbangers for a few years ... even with narrow hips and normal balls." Selout was now conversing with Burr like a fellow fan. He was not talking like Burr's boss.

"Yea, you're right, Mr. Selout, and now the Wallbangers' fans are complaining that Rogers should have inflated earlier. They haven't

Flunking Chemistry Class

won anything since the Revolutionary War. Meanwhile they dump pennants into the Boston Harbor like the patriots dumped tea bags. The Boston fans are beginning to clamor for their own floats."

"That's understandable. The Wallbangers might not have lost so often if they had signed a few free agent floats." Selout seemed oblivious to how he must have sounded to Burr. There was almost 40 years difference in their age and yet they sounded like two teenage boys in a schoolyard.

"But Rogers is relatively small potatoes compared to the biggest float of them all, the Bay City Mammoths' own Harry Bombs. He's been doing so much juice that he's now nearly as big as those cable cars out there. Can you imagine just how amazing the stats for Willie, Mickey and the Duke would have been if they had juiced?"

"Yeah so now instead of Willie, Mickey and the Duke, we have Jelly, Harry and the Floats." This thought brought Selout back down to earth and he was trying to decide on a course of action, if indeed one was needed. Selout simply shrugged his shoulders and hit the intercom button for his secretary, Marguerite. She answered quickly, "You buzzed, Buzz?" There was also an audible sound of the snapping of her bubble gum.

"Yes, what kind of calls are we getting on the Palazzo – Rogers confrontation?"

"Depends." More smart ass gum snapping.

"Depends on what?"

"Depends on whether you root for the Bronx Bloomers or the Metropolitan Mutts."

"Give me the Bloomers fans' version, first."

"They believe that Palazzo had it coming. He's a wimp ... got soft playing all those years for the Hollywood Hedgers. That kind of stuff."

"What about the Mutts fans?"

"They're saying that Jelly threw at Palazzo on purpose and that he ought to be suspended for the rest of the Earth Series. They are also using the dreaded term, 'roid rage.' This could be the start of some real juicy problems."

"Okay, okay, Marguerite, keep the wise-ass editorializing to yourself. We'll get by this just fine like we always have in the past. The fans will realize that this is simply two future Corridor of Conceit studs going at it with everything they have. Let's see if we can get the Bloomers owner on the phone."

"Actually Mr. Sledgehammer has already called." Marguerite informed her boss. "He sounded like he was in a good mood ... probably because our Bloomers are leading the Mutts two games to none already." Marguerite was a Bloomers booster and she knew that Burr, a Mutt toady, was seated in Selout's office. She couldn't help the urge to rub in the score, while announcing the call from Larry "Bass" Sledgehammer, the volatile principal owner of the Bronx Bloomers.

"Bass Sledgehammer never calls just to gloat. He does that in the press. When Sledgehammer calls my office, there usually is an ulterior motive."

"I'm sorry Buzz. However, Mr. Sledgehammer never discusses such matters with me." Marguerite now sounded indignant and both Selout and Burr cringed at Selout's secretary's disrespectful tone. "He simply demanded that you call him back and then he hung up. Mr. Sledgehammer sounded like it was important. You know? It was like he wanted you to call, you know, like right NOW." Marguerite actually raised her voice as she pronounced the last word.

"That's typical of Bass. Sometimes I think that squat little turd thinks that *he* is the commissioner." The Commish himself was 6 feet 4 inches tall and enjoyed referring to Bass Sledgehammer as though he were a pipsqueak.

Burr simply sat in the commissioner's office listening to the exchange between Selout and his secretary. However he couldn't help but feel that maybe Selout was right; From time to time Bass Sledgehammer certainly did act like *he* was The Commish. Burr wondered if Selout ever wished that he was still just a team owner rather than enduring all of the headaches of being "The Commish."

Ironically there had been a time when Selout *was* simply a team owner. In the past Selout owned the Wisconsin Cheeseheads; a small market

Flunking Chemistry Class

team that actually made it to an Earth Series in the 1980's when Selout owned the team. The Cheeseheads also produced two terrific ballplayers; Jay Yank and Hal Monitor who later went on to be enshrined in the Corridor of Conceit. But now Selout was making real money as The Commish. His sport had been in danger of losing its fan base rapidly, the way professional boxing had done and Selout had been credited with saving the game simply by maintaining labor peace over the last half decade.

In 1994 the MBLPA had voted to strike against the MBL. The season was truncated and they didn't even play an Earth Series for the first time in over 90 years. After fumbling around with the mess for far too long, Selout finally got the two sides together and ended the strike. And now there had been labor harmony for six full years. In fact there was reason to believe that baseball was now more popular than ever. The game's resurgence had even allowed it to shake its nickname as the *International Past Prime*. It might still have a ways to go to catch football as the world's favorite spectator sport but it was once again flourishing. Two huge factors in this reinvigoration of baseball were the renaissance of the Bronx Bloomers, who had now won three of the last four Earth Series and the revival of the homerun ball as evidenced by Popeye Maloney's eclipsing of the homerun record in 1998. It was widely suspected that both phenomena were directly aided by steroids.

When Selout finished his intercom exchange with his secretary he still looked worn out. He subconsciously adjusted his toupee, and then pushed his wire rimmed glasses back up on his steep sloping nose. He wasn't sure what Bass Sledgehammer wanted to discuss, but he had suddenly lost his urge to call him so quickly. Instead he went back to his mundane conversation with Burr.

"About the steroids thing, Timmy ... how many players do you think are actually using stuff? Do you think it's as high as 10 percent?"

"Higher."

'Roid Rage at the Earth Series

"Higher? Did you say, 'higher?' How much higher? Fifteen percent, maybe?

"Higher."

"Come on, Timmy. How much higher could it be? Not twenty percent ... that would mean one out of every five players is juiced."

"My guess ... from what I can tell statistically ... and from anecdotes from some of the players that I have spoken to ... the number is probably more like thirty-five to forty percent and rising every day." Burr had some valid statistical analysis, but he had never discussed any of this with any ballplayers. It was merely his weasel minded little attempt at exhibiting some bravado in the hope that Selout would take him more seriously.

"That's crazy. It can't be that much. At that point we might as well just distribute the stuff ourselves to *all* of the ballplayers. Then at least we'd have competitive balance."

"No. Now *that's* crazy. That's like that TV show from the seventies ... that's in reruns – *Gall in the Family* – you know ... the Starchy Bungler theory of how you stop all the airplane hijackings ... arm all the passengers."

Before they could get any further in their discussion, Marguerite buzzed back in. "Bass Sledgehammer on line two, Buzz."

Lester Postal had been covering local sports for the *New York Roast* for more than thirty years. His employer was a widely read tabloid that was infamous for the headlines that adorned both the front and back covers of the daily publication. Lester was on his fourth marriage and rarely returned home to the bed of his new wife until after he had covered every sporting event that the electronic media could deliver to the bars that he frequented. Lester was a veritable sports historian. He could tell you who made the last out in the 1942 Earth Series; who was the first hockey player to sip champagne from the Stanley Cup and how much time was left in the fight when Emile Griffith killed Cuban welterweight Benny "the Kid" Paret in the ring in 1962.

Flunking Chemistry Class

Lester's favorite sports were boxing and baseball. He didn't care much for golf, tennis and Olympic equestrian events. In fact, Lester had never ridden a horse in his life and yet he had wagered more than a year's salary on horses at various racetrack venues during his sports writing career. Oh yes, and Lester had a temper. He had been thrown out of more watering holes than he could count, but was usually allowed back into these venues after a reasonable "time out" had passed, simply because ... well simply because Lester Postal was Lester Postal.

Lester had no real friends but for various lengths of time he could be friendly with nearly anyone and everyone. It was almost as though he was borrowing people for periods of time. Or maybe it was more like he was *renting* them. Mostly these people were folks who had an insight on some sporting event that Lester wanted to know about. Lester had convinced the editors of *The Roast* that he needed to cultivate these contacts in order to do his job appropriately. Therefore he had managed to wangle an expense account that covered his boozing it up with these contacts or *rental friends*. Some of these *rental friends* were surprisingly forthcoming in their imparting of knowledge on particular sports topics and Lester had an uncanny ability to extract value from his discourse with these *rentals*."

The Earth Series was designed to provide a travel day for the participating teams after the first two games of the series to allow the teams to get from one venue to another. The 2000 Earth Series however required no such travel day because the participating teams played their home games in two different boroughs of the same city. If a pigeon decorated a windshield on a car in the parking lot at Stray Stadium, home of the Queens County based Metropolitan Mutts; the same pigeon could drop off a calling card turd on the center field monuments in Bloomer Stadium during the same excretory event without energetically exercising itself in flight. Nevertheless the players were not pigeons and therefore they were deemed to need a day of rest in between games. So

'Roid Rage at the Earth Series

as Lester Postal sat in the midtown gin mill known as *Joey Dee's Tavern*, there was a whole day and evening left to discuss the 'roid rage event that took place during Game Two.

Joey Dee's Tavern was not named after the wunderkind player who roamed center field for the Bloomers in the 1940's; nor was it named after the former lead singer of the Starliters, the group who gave us the spearmint twist in the 1960's. *Joey Dee's* was simply named after Joey Dee Junior's father, Joey Dee, Senior. The Dees had owned their midtown Manhattan gin mill for over half a century and never bothered to tell any of their patrons that they were not related to either the ballplayer who was enshrined in Coopersville's Corridor of Conceit or the musician who should have been enshrined in the Rock and Roll Corridor of Conceit in Cleveland.

They were seated at an inconspicuous booth toward the back of *Joey Dee's*. Lester Postal was treating his latest rental friend to a cheap burger and fries luncheon. Timmy Burr was nervous enough to order a Beefeater martini to go with his burger.

"So from what you told me on the phone, Sledgehammer and Selout have talked today. That's important to know. Tell me more. Is Selout going to take any action against Rogers?"

"No apparently the incident passed Buzz' red light test."

"What is that?"

"If it doesn't affect the integrity of the game then there is no red light. Nothing gets stopped. The games go on as usual. Buzz doesn't want his office to do something that will affect the outcome of the Series. He believes that nothing is more important than the Earth Series."

"But what if Jelly beans Palazzo again? He could actually kill him. That certainly would be even more serious than the Earth Series."

"Buzz' position is that it's not going to happen. He thinks that you can't interrupt the Series just because someone might get hurt."

"You can't be serious."

"Yes, I'm being perfectly serious. No one has been hurt. No one will get hurt and so the Series must go on. We have a business to run you know." Spindly little Timmy Burr, who was 5'8' tall and 140 pounds after Thanksgiving dinner, had abruptly grown courageous with his first two sips of his Beefeater martini. He now was talking like he himself was The Commish, rather than just the commissioner's assistant statistician. Lester was very pleased with this development. Over the past few weeks he had noticed that his latest rental friend provided a good bit more insight after the alcohol hit his brain.

"Okay, I understand that. What else did Sledgehammer and Selout discuss?"

"I'm not sure of all of the details but I know that they discussed the upcoming MBL contract with the MBL Players Association. Sledgehammer is particularly concerned about the other owners' discussion of some kind of salary cap or possibly raising the luxury tax to keep the Bronx Bloomers salary spending in check. The other thing that worries Sledgehammer is possible contract language concerning steroid testing. Sledgehammer is siding with the Players Association on both of these issues and against the other team owners. But he has been trying to curry favor with The Commish so that Selout can help tip the scales in his direction."

"Exactly where does Selout sit on these issues?"

"Start with the fact that Selout can't stand Sledgehammer personally. Yes, we all know that it was Selout who overturned Sledgehammer's lifetime ban from the MBL. But trust me these guys are not asshole buddies or anything. Now temper that with the fact that Selout is a businessman and you have a very interesting dynamic. Revenues are rocketing up in almost all markets. However the Bloomers are making a disproportionate amount of that revenue which conceivably gives them a competitive advantage. With no salary cap or meaningful luxury tax in place the Bloomers can simply continue to sign just about every free agent float out there. Selout knows that's a problem. But the luxury tax issue is small potatoes compared to the swelling problem with the floats."

"Well not every good player is a *float*." Postal was pleased to hear Burr use his descriptive caricature nomenclature for steroid swollen ballplayers and so he readily reinforced the use of the term.

"Don't be so sure of your assessment. I've been doing some statistical regression analysis on the batting average, home run/RBI totals

'Roid Rage at the Earth Series

and OPS for the players who are most widely considered to be floats. I can't go into detail but the results are startling. Same thing is beginning to hold true for the pitchers."

"So tell me. What's your opinion? How did baseball get into this mess?"

"Rumor has it that it has been going on for at least a decade. But people never paid much attention. When the homerun totals started rising people thought that it was *the ball* that was juiced. They started doing all kinds of tests on the ball manufacturing process. But there were never any reliable results. Some people think it was simply a Selout red herring. But a lot of writers, like you, remained suspicious of the *ball* rather than the *ballplayer*. Then two years ago when the St Louis Scarlets' first baseman, Popeye Maloney, started launching baseballs into outer space, people finally got suspicious. The same was true about the Chicago Gumballs' outfielder, Corky Samuels. Before he started taking the stuff he was only a so-so player. Then both of these guys passed the homerun record in the same season and wow, people took notice. In fact one of your brethren sportswriters spotted a bottle of androstenedione in Popeye's locker and asked him about it. Maloney correctly told him that the stuff was a legal over the counter vitamin supplement. What he *didn't* tell him was that andro has been banned by the NFL and the International Olympic Committee and the NCAA. It is what is known as a performance enhancing drug or in the new vernacular for this kind of discussion … a PED."

"But the fans still haven't paid much attention to this PED stuff. Maloney was still widely celebrated after he broke the record." Lester Postal was fishing around a bit now but he thought he still might have a significant story in there somewhere.

"That's because they don't understand the extent of the problem. These vitamin supplements and steroids and all the other crap these guys are taking, can kill you. Some of the stuff is not even meant for humans. It's meant for animals. And we can't have humans competing with animals on the diamond. Besides some guys are taking this crap in ridiculous overdoses." Burr's voice was now taking on an unnatural aggressive timbre.

Flunking Chemistry Class

Postal countered: "But there have always been some players who are in better condition than others; have better diets and nutritional supplements; or who simply take better care of their bodies. You know; they lift weights; do cardiovascular exercises and all that. These are the body builders. The other ball players call them 'gym rats.' And then there were guys like the Babe or the Mick, who could party all night and just roll out of bed and hit a three run homer. What's so different now? From what I can see the partiers still far outnumber the gym rats."

"You're not getting the gist of the issue, Lester. The partiers are now taking the party to the gym. Body building is no longer done the old fashioned way. Think about it: What would you rather do, pump iron all day or simply pump a few pills after a night out on the town? These floats have fast tracked the body building process big time. Yeah they spend a little time in the gym, but for the most part their bloated biceps are as phony as the blown up boobs of the baseball bunnies that follow them around. They're just not real."

"That's a very juicy perspective."

"You might say that."

"So tell me Timmy, about this regression analysis stuff. Can't players simply get better over time and with experience?"

"Sure ...to a point. But baseball is a game that is driven by numbers. And we have statistics that go back a whole century and in some cases even longer. When you eliminate certain variables and adjust for major changes in the game – like the deadball era; the lowering of the mound in 1970 and the inception of the designated hitter in 1973 – the statistics just don't lie."

"Give me an example."

"You have to be blind not to see this stuff, Lester." Burr had barely taken a bite out of his hamburger but was already signaling for another martini. His pronunciations were getting bolder. "During the regular season this year 47 players hit 30 or more homeruns! Got that? FORTY FUCKING SEVEN PLAYERS!!! To give you an idea how crazy that is, ten years ago in 1990 there were only 12 players in all of baseball with 30 dingers. 10 years before that in 1980 there were a total of 9 players with 30 long balls. Before that going back to the end of World War II there were a similar number of 30+ homerun hitters – generally 10 or less each year. But this year: FORTY FUCKING SEVEN PLAYERS!!!"

Timmy Burr was getting loud and Lester Postal didn't want to share the information from his rental friend with others around him. He also knew that it was a lot easier to simply verify the assertions that Burr was making rather than try to dig up this kind of data by himself. Therefore he had been making copious napkin notes throughout the conversation. He was getting a little worried that Burr was getting pretty plastered so he encouraged his rental friend to eat his burger. And he waited a few seconds to make sure that Burr was indeed eating before he posed a direct question.

"And of course, you have shared *all* of this data with the commissioner?"

Burr had his mouth full so he attempted to nod his answer, but Lester couldn't determine what the nod meant. First it was a slight up and down affirmative answer. Then Burr quickly followed that with a slight head tilt and nose wrinkle that appeared to say "on second thought..." and then he ended with the quick left-right head nod that appeared to be an ambivalent negative.

Lester Postal didn't like playing charades but Burr had now redoubled his eating speed and once again had his mouth full when Lester pressed forward.

"Does that mean you've shared *some* of your analysis with Selout?" Postal subconsciously nodded his own head up and down affirmatively in order to attempt to secure concurrence. But he quickly realized his own stupidity, realizing that the truth was more important than mere concurrence, so he abruptly stopped kinetically leading the witness and simply watched for an answer.

Amazingly Burr repeated his up-down; tilt-wrinkle; left-right answer. This time it was accentuated with up turned open left palm, while he used his right hand to scoop the last part of his burger. Lester decided to simply wait in silence for his rental friend to finish his meal. This actually took a minute or two longer because Burr also wolfed

33

Flunking Chemistry Class

down all of his fries and then fastidiously rolled his tongue around his lips teeth and mouth in completion of his dining experience.

Knowing that the meal would be on Postal's expense account, Burr quickly signaled the waiter for a third martini. He didn't directly answer Lester's question but rather he simply gave him some additional thoughts on the matter of floats.

"If you want a great example of a statistical outlier for an individual player, a great example is Andrew Brady of the Maryland Blackbirds. The guy hit a total of 14 homers in his first four years in the big leagues. Then he has a few years in the low teens. And then out of nowhere, in his ninth season in the MBL, he comes back from the offseason as big as a house. Would you believe it? The damn float pops fifty big flies, like he's been doing it for years. Amazing!"

"Wow, f*** *that* s***!" Postal paused to let his statement of amazement sink in and then added, "But he hasn't come close to that number since then. Was that year just an anomaly?"

"Again I'll refer you to the century of data that we have been rolling through. What it tells us is that on a level playing field those kind of statistical anomalies just don't exist. But actually the concept of a level playing field is the wrong metaphor for me to use. The playing field is the same – just like the baseballs themselves are the same. However once a player opts to become a float he becomes so much larger in most ways – testicles aside – that it is like a leviathan competing against a child. The outcome of that contest would never be in question and the statistical evidence of that competition will reflect the mismatch.

"The thing that makes this travesty all that much more egregious is that in the sport of baseball, players and teams don't only compete against one another, they also compete against the record book. It's a large part of the game's popularity and extremely important to its long term viability. That's why Buzz Selout is so upset about this steroid thing."

"Wow, well said my friend," Naturally he didn't call him his *rental* friend. "So then Selout really *does* understand all of this. And he has tasked you with the statistical research to bring this all out in the open. Have I got that right?"

'Roid Rage at the Earth Series

"No not at all. In my job as assistant statistician, I'm usually called upon to provide numerical insights of a more positive nature. A lot of this other research and analysis I have been doing on my own."

"What do you think Selout would do if he knew you were having this conversation with me right now?"

"Probably fire me for starters."

"Then why are you telling me all of this?"

It was a fair question and one that Timmy Burr was not quite sure how to answer. But he knew it was more than just a free three martini lunch. Finally he gave a simple answer, "Because I'm a baseball fan."

Now it was Lester Postal's turn for a thoughtful pause as he accepted the young statistician's answer. Then he pursued a follow on question in the form of two statements; "And so this is what's got him so worried about the confrontation last night between Jelly Rogers and Matt Palazzo? He's worried that everyone will finally start paying attention to this steroid thing?"

"You've got that right."

"So then what's he going to do about it?"

"Same as usual."

"Which is?"

"Play ostrich. Put his head in the sand and hope all of the noise goes away. If he waits long enough there will be something else to distract the fan base. That's the strategy that's been employed so far, and I don't see any signs of a change in the works unless the sportswriters also get their collective heads out of the sand and yank Selout's head up along with them."

IV
Arizona Clinic League

August 2001

Seventeen year old Samuel Monroe Crockett could throw a baseball faster than anyone in the State of Texas as a high school senior. Sam Crockett could also hit a baseball further than anyone in the state of Texas during his senior year. And Crockett had the prettiest girlfriend of any baseball player in the Lone Star State as well. The only difficulty that faced Crockett was that his sixteen year old girlfriend, Betsy Jo Boone was five months pregnant, and her father was prepared to underline the definition of a shotgun wedding.

Sam's parents were both school teachers. They had hoped that Sam would use his baseball skills to earn a college scholarship. In fact Sam had received more than two dozen scholarship offers. Betsy Jo's father worked in the drilling bits business and had pressured Sam to take the $200,000.00 in bonus money that was being offered by the Wisconsin Cheeseheads. He wanted Crockett to support Betsy Jo and their baby. Not very many people knew about Betsy Jo's pregnancy, and that included all of the local MBL scouts.

The Bloomers, Mutts, Hedgers and both Chicago teams, the Gumballs and the Pantyhose, had all shown interest in Crockett. And Sam's home state teams, the Houston Arrows and the Dallas Drillies were constantly calling on the Crockett family as well. Even the two new international expansion teams the Tokyo Carp and the Sydney

Arizona Clinic League

Kangaroos had shown some significant interest. Most of the MBL teams believed that Sam Crockett was worthy of a first round selection in the draft. However when the scouts visited with Crockett's parents, they were informed that Sam would be taking a college scholarship ... no ifs ands, or buts about it. So when the June amateur draft came around, Sam slipped to the third round because of "signability issues." In fact Sam Crockett hadn't even hired an agent at the time of the draft. So when the Wisconsin Cheeseheads drafted Crockett in the third round, almost all of the other clubs thought that they had thrown away a pick. But as it turned out, the Cheeseheads had gotten the sleeper pick of the draft.

After the original euphoria of signing a right-handed pitcher who occasionally registered triple digits on the radar gun, the Cheeseheads began to understand that Crockett would be a *project* over the next several years as they harnessed his raw talent and taught him the art of pitching as a professional. On the other hand, the kid could really hit and he seemed to have great timing as well as a superior understanding of the strike zone. And even though Crockett was drafted as a right-handed fireballer, the debate in the organization began almost immediately as to whether or not the young Texan would make it to the major leagues faster as a corner outfielder rather than as a pitcher. When he was sent out to the Cheeseheads Arizona Clinic League team in July, those that viewed Crockett as a pitcher won out over those who supported his impact bat.

Betsy Jo Boone had become Betsy Jo Crockett three weeks after the June 2000 Amateur Baseball Draft. She was still living in San Antonio, Texas with her parents while Sam Crockett, now known as Sudden Sam Crockett was lighting up the radar screens in the Arizona Clinic League. It had been a long hot summer for Betsy Jo and she had celebrated her 17th birthday without her husband, who was also a bit lonely. Sudden Sam was trying to hold onto as much of his bonus money as he possibly could and so he roomed with a teammate in a small apartment just

Flunking Chemistry Class

outside of Glendale, Arizona. The apartment was a dump that actually was set down three steps from the walkway surface outside of the rundown apartment building.

Sam's roommate, Lance Leathermore was from Las Vegas, Nevada and was in his second year in the Clinic League. Leathermore was both a catcher and a first baseman, but he was beginning to look more like a designated hitter with every passing game. He led the league in hits, doubles, homeruns and errors. And when he wasn't on the diamond he led the whole state in games played with the baseball bunnies, who were constantly at his beck and call. The two room apartment that the two players shared had one paper thin wall between the two bedrooms and Sudden Sam frequently heard Leathermore touching all the bases in the room next door.

Near the end of August on her birthday, Sam called his wife Betsy Jo to wish her happiness on her big day. He made the call early in the evening because he thought that he would have some privacy while Lance was out on the prowl. He didn't expect Lance back from his bunny hoping escapades for at least another couple of hours. Normally it took catcher/first basemen about an hour to designate someone to hit upon. Then he had to take some time to liquor up the baseball bunny before he dragged her back to his side of their shared little dugout of an apartment. That was usually followed by more booze and a good bit of giggling before Lance undressed his baseball bunny and began playing ball.

"Hello Baby Doll. I'm just calling to say 'Hi' and to wish you a Happy Birthday. I wish I could be there with now, you know."

"Oh, Sam ...I miss you. When is the darn season going to be over so that you can come back here to Texas?"

"Soon, Baby Doll, soon. We just have one more week to go."

"So what are you doing tonight? Are you going out with some of the other guys?"

"No. I'm just going to stay home and read a book. I just got a copy of George Will's book, <u>Men at Work</u>. My new agent gave it to me. He said that if I read it and develop a work ethic like the guys in the book, that I'll have a long successful career and make millions of dollars."

"That sounds good to me. Isn't it great now that we know that we'll be having a boy? He will be so proud of his father. You're going to make a great Dad and a great husband. Did you know that?"

Betsy Jo had no sooner gotten the words out of her mouth when Sam heard the front door open and Lance come barging through the front door prematurely with a question of his own.

"Sammy brother, where the fuck are you? I got me more than I can handle. I don't know if I can turn an unassisted double play." Lance Leathermore was laughing uproariously and had a baseball bunny under each arm. He had his Tommy Bahama Hawaiian style shirt unbuttoned almost down to his navel. The girls were giggling along with one another and joined in with Lance in sing-songing, "Sammy, where are you?"

"Who is that??" Betsy Jo sounded very hurt.

"Oh it's no one. My roommate, Lance ... remember I told you about him ... he just came home with his girlfriend." Suddenly, Sudden Sam was silent. He didn't know what to say next, and his speech impediment wasn't helped a whole lot by the fact that one of the two young women who had come back to the apartment with Lance had decided to sit right square on his lap, with her ample cleavage parked right in front of the young hurler's nose. Sam might have been speechless but that didn't stop his mouth from salivating. He could feel his interest rising but he was conflicted with arousal and horror as the young lady on his lap said, "Hi I'm Loretta and that there's Lucille. We're the Ball Girls at Sunny Valley Stadium. We watched you pitch yesterday."

Sam had managed to cup his hand over the speaker on his cell phone but he wasn't able to drown out the hubbub entirely.

"It sounds like there's more than one girl there, Sam. Are you sure you'll be reading that <u>Men at Work</u> thing tonight. I don't want you reading any of that <u>Four Balls</u> book by that guy Jay Bouncer who used to pitch for the Bloomers. I just read that book. My Aunt Isabelle sent it to me. She said she used to date a baseball player and that I should know what I'm getting into by letting you go off to Arizona."

Flunking Chemistry Class

Sam held his index finger to his lip to silence the Ball Girl who was now nibbling at his neck. "Yeah there's some more people comin' in. I wasn't planning to have a party or nuthin' like that. These are just Lance's friends. Well, anyway, happy birthday, Baby Doll. I'll call you again tomorrow." With that Sam abruptly ended his conversation with his wife so that he could deal with the situation at hand.

Betsy Jo loved it when Sam called her Baby Doll. It made her feel sexy. But lately she wasn't feeling sexy at all. She was feeling motherly. She couldn't wait for her man to return. She was determined to trust him and not to worry. So when Sam ended the conversation abruptly, she simply put her hand on top of her growing midsection and sighed. *I trust my man*, she thought. *But he better not be calling anyone else Baby Doll.*

Meanwhile, back in Arizona, Sudden Sam was becoming Sullen Sam. He didn't know what he wanted to do. Lance had already claimed that he didn't feel up to the unassisted double play, but Sam wanted to remain faithful to his wife back in San Antonio. He had yet to remove lovely Loretta ... her descriptive nomenclature not his ... from his lap and she gave every indication that she wanted do more in his lap than just sit in it. She began licking her lips in a lascivious manner the moment Sam hung up with Betsy Jo. Meanwhile Lucille and Lance had moved quickly to Lance's bedroom and the sounds of rustling removal of clothing were quickly followed by muffled and cursory assessment of the various parts and tools that each of them had brought to the bedroom.

"I hate tattoos," Lance began. "But then again I've never seen one there before."

"Looks to me like you don't *feel* that way ...entirely. Apparently at least part of you has no problem with my tat."

Then there was more giggling and a quick bit of squishy kissing and sucking noises followed by a series of loud grunts and a final male sounding, "Aaahhh." The female sounds were more like "unhh," and "pheph," and then an unlabored exhaling noise that included a slight reverberation of Lucille's lips. Apparently Lucille would have desired more foreplay but Lance didn't take any batting practice. He simply waded in there and took his cuts.

Arizona Clinic League

All of this could be heard in the room next door and there was no mystery to any of it. Crockett was saved momentarily when his cell phone rang and he saw the number of his new business agent, Brad Scott. He pushed lovely Loretta off his lap saying, "Sorry, I've got take this call. It's my agent."

"Hello Brad. Good to hear from you." Scott was one of the premiere talent agents representing many of the best ball players in the MBL. He also had a handful of top draft choices and minor league ballplayers, whom he looked to groom for business down the road. Scott had as good an eye for baseball talent as any of the MBL teams' head scouts. He took care to nurse the few minor leaguers that he represented through the labyrinth of minor league baseball so that when they were ready for "The Show," he would be ready to get them the best possible financial terms and conditions on their contracts. Sometimes that meant starting the process before the players were even drafted. In the case of Sam Crockett, Brad Scott didn't pick him up as a client until after he had signed with the Wisconsin Cheeseheads. Brad knew that if he had gotten to Crockett earlier he would have convinced him to go to college and pitch for a year and then reenter the draft. Barring injury, that would almost definitely have ensured a high first round selection and a lot more money for Sam Crockett...and for Brad Scott.

"How's it going Sam? I saw the numbers from the game you pitched yesterday: four innings, one hit, seven strike outs, four walks and two earned runs. It doesn't matter at all that you didn't get the win, but they were crazy to let you throw 87 pitches. We have to get that pitch count down."

"Yeah well I was getting pretty tired there at the end. I didn't realize I threw that many pitches."

"Too many curve balls also ... Back off that stuff. The guys in Milwaukee only want to hear about the heat. If they think that you can bring triple digit cheese to the Cheeseheads, they'll move you up the line that much faster. The coaching is better in the upper minors also. No one is going to let you throw 87 pitches in four innings."

Sam was slightly put off by Scott's tone and attitude. Was this all he was calling about: to complain that Sam was throwing too many

Flunking Chemistry Class

pitches? His question was answered forthwith as Brad Scott simply continued what had quickly become a one way conversation.

"You've got one more start down there and they're only going to let you throw 75 pitches or five innings whatever comes first. Then you will have a month off and then report down to the Dominican Republic Fall League."

"What do you mean, Brad? I don't know anything about the Dominican Fall League. I thought I was supposed to shut it down right at the end of the Arizona Clinic League season. And what about all those pitches that everyone is so worried about? How many more innings are they going to want me to pitch down there?

"None, actually. When you get down to the DR you will be playing right field for the Dominican Dandies. You'll have lots of fun. Maybe you'll even learn to speak Spanish."

"I don't want to learn to speak Spanish. I'm an American from the great state of Texas. Why in hell would I want to speak Spanish? Besides, my wife is expecting our first child in December. I don't want to miss that. And I will need to get a job in the offseason. The bonus money won't last forever."

"You're going to need to support that child when he's growing up, Sam. There's no money in the DR gig but the Cheeseheads will cover some of your expenses. Just think about it as investment in your son's future. The real payoff will come over the next few years."

"Will they let me play every day?"

"It depends upon performance, of course. But right now the Dandies are thinking about you as their everyday right fielder."

"What do they think about this idea up in Milwaukee? I thought that the brass wanted me to be a pitcher."

"Don't worry about that. This will ultimately work in your favor. There are still some people in Wisconsin who like your bat."

"I'll think about it, Brad."

"Pitch your game next week and then give me a call. We'll need to confirm your participation and get the paper work done before Labor Day. Love ya, Babe." Brad Scott's clients were familiar with his signature signoff to every phone call. He always gave the impression that he

Arizona Clinic League

was in a big time hurry and that there was another equally important call waiting for him on another phone. This also afforded Scott the last word in all conversations and gave him a leg up on compliance with his suggestions. For that reason, Sam was quite surprised when the phone rang again almost immediately and the LED identified that it was Brad Scott calling right back again.

"Hi Brad, you didn't give me much time to make a decision." Sam was proud of himself for being quick witted enough to verbally joust with his powerful agent. He heard Scott give a quick laugh of recognition on the other end. However then the agent jumped quickly into a different topic.

"I forgot to ask you ... did you get to the gym I told you about in Scottsdale? Carlos is great on conditioning, strength training and nutrition. He knows all about vitamin supplements and developing young bodies. I called him yesterday and he said he hasn't heard from you." Scott was obviously answering his own question before allowing his client time to answer.

"I haven't had ..."

"Don't worry about it. Just make sure you see him and get to know him before you leave Arizona. Talk to you after the game next week. Love ya, Babe." This time the click was audible and definitive almost as if the phone was telling him Scott was not going to call back again.

By the time he got off the phone, lovely Loretta had joined Lance and Lucille in the other bedroom. He could hear Lance's voice as clear as a bell.

"I didn't know that you two were both sisters as well as Ball Girls. That's crazy ...like good crazy." Incredibly the rustling removal of clothing noises started up again and Sam heard Lance remark, "Well look at that, no tat. That's how I like it ...clean as a whistle." Then came the squishy kissing and sucking noises again and Sam simply walked over and locked his door, while he marveled at the fact that Lance was going to accomplish his unassisted double play after all.

V

The Earth Series Redux

October 2001

New York City was in shock. The United States was in shock. Most of the world was still shaking. It was a little more than five weeks since the terrorists had attacked the World Trade Center. The United States and the rest of the world were far from approaching a return to typical day to day life. However the MBL, the Multinational Baseball League, was trying to do its part to resurrect normalcy. After the 9/11 attacks MBL had suspended play for about a week and then resumed the season eventually playing a complete season by making up the suspended games in early October and pushing the playoffs back a week.

Once again the Bronx Bloomers were league champions and would be playing in the Earth Series. They would be opposed by the Arizona Asps and there were several intriguing side stories to the Series. The most intriguing issue was that the Series *wasn't* all that intriguing this year. Sporting events were taking a secondary or tertiary (at best) place in the interests of a public that was horrified by being at war against a concept rather than a nation. But the Earth Series would have been lackluster in a normal year. The Earth Series wasn't even the biggest event in baseball this year. It wasn't even the biggest event in baseball since 9/11. The biggest event in baseball took place in San Francisco on the first weekend in October, with the Bay City Mammoths hosting Hollywood Hedgers.

The Earth Series Redux

Neither the Mammoths nor the Hedgers made the post season in 2001 but each team had a rather prominent float on their respective rosters. The Hedgers had Gorey Schlepfield, a right handed slugger who was known to take one of the hardest swings in the game. He was nicknamed the "Assassin" because he swung so viciously that it appeared that he would rather smash the ball in a thousand pieces than hit it over the fence, but he still managed to do the latter more than 35 times that season.

The Bay City Mammoths star player was none other than the biggest float of them all, Harry Bombs. Unlike the "Assassin," Harry Bombs had a short compact swing and when he hit the ball out of the ballpark he soft-shoe-strutted around the bases. Whenever he was interviewed Bombs exhibited an almost eunuch-like voice and demeanor. The fans of San Francisco loved their soft-spoken superfloat and whenever he drifted up to the plate they cheered wildly.

In the other ballparks around the league the reception for the Mammoths superfloat was not nearly as hospitable. Whereas the Hedgers float was nicknamed the "Assassin," the Mammoths balloon had garnered the simple sobriquet of "Asshole," from the fans in other ball parks. These fans regarded him as one part ballplayer, two parts balloon and three parts buffoon. And the fans in other ball parks had begun repeatedly sing-songing his nickname whenever he visited their park.

These adverse receptions were hard for Harry Bombs to understand, because only three years earlier, when Popeye Maloney, the Scarlets' first baseman, broke the homerun record, he was adored everywhere. That exact adulation was what Bombs had craved, so right after Maloney set the record, Bombs decided to take some magic creams that would turn him into the greatest float of all. And then on that first weekend in October with the Hedgers in town, Harry Bombs obliterated Popeye Maloney's home run record and set the new record at an astounding 73 dingers. By contrast the Hotshot's "Assassin" had less than half that number. And in the process the "Asshole" had defecated all over the major league record book.

Flunking Chemistry Class

The New York Roast's readership was not subscription based at all. Newsstand sales at subway stations and street corner vendor locations drove the circulation of the paper, and the front and rear headlines drove the newsstand sales.

The Roast was a tabloid that essentially was divided in half. The front half of the paper was devoted to headline news; wars, politics, natural disasters, and the like. The back half of the paper was devoted exclusively to sports, with a heavy emphasis on professional sports. All other stories, columns and other newspaper fodder – such as cross word puzzles, word games and gossip bylines – were stuffed somewhere near the middle of the paper. The centerfold of the newspaper was usually devoted to photographic back up to either the news headline or the sports headline or both. Like its rival tabloids, *The Roast* had a keen eye for the sensational story or the salacious scandal and would further dramatize such occurrence by creating large bold print headlines. Either in deference to the space needed for the large size of the headline print or because a good part of its readership was incapable of reading long phrases, *The Roast* put a premium on the brevity of its headlines. This was true of both the front page news and the back page sports. The editor-in-chief of the paper was particularly proud of his team's work on two separate occasions when they had managed to have the same headline on both the front and the back of the paper. He referred to this as a "Frontsy-Backsy."

One year when the Olympics coincided with the final push of a presidential election, a USA decathlon winner outscored his nearest competitor by setting a personal best in the pole vault event. On the same day, a sex scandal involving one of the presidential candidates allowed his rival to jump seventeen points in the approval ratings. The next day the creative editors of the *New York Roast* came up with the same headline on both the front page and the back page of the paper: **STUNNING POLL VAULT** on the front page and **STUNNING POLE VAULT** on the back. However the editor-in-chief said that this didn't count as a perfect Frontsy-Backsy because of the variation in the spelling of the word *poll* or *pole*. He pined for the day that they could pull off a flawless Frontsy-Backsy. Several years later they got their opportunity when there was a local scandal about a waste management company that was allegedly tied to organized crime. The company had apparently double billed on some government contracts and was kicking back dollars to a government official. In retaliation for breaking the story, the waste management company had apparently dumped fifty tons of garbage on the whistleblower's two cars in his driveway at his home in the middle of the night.

In an unrelated sports/news story on the same day, The Metropolitan Mutts centerfielder incurred a DWI arrest. *The Roast* had dispatched reporters and photographers to cover both events. They managed to get a robust picture of the whistleblower's vehicles covered in smelly garbage and they also managed to get a copy of the Mutts centerfielder's mug shot looking totally bewildered right after his arrest. These two pictures covered the front and rear pages of *The Roast* that day under the same one word headline: **TRASHED**.

The editor-in-chief was thrilled: a flawless Frontsy-Backsy!

The Earth Series was about to begin in two days and Lester Postal was back at the offices of *The New York Roast*. He was glad that the Bronx Bloomers had once again floated their way into the fall classic. While in the office, he was on his best behavior of late because he didn't want his editor to rescind the approval for his trip to cover the opening two games in Phoenix in person. Having recently divorced his fourth wife, Lester was once again a single man. This meant that there was very little that could be done to curtail his boozing and Lester had been taking full advantage of that liberty of late. However the side effects of all the late night boozing included horrific headaches and hyper-dehydration. Each day he tried to combat the latter problem by almost living on top of the office water cooler during the business day and desperately trying to be as friendly as possible to all of his co-workers. The former problem was fixed each night by substituting booze for water thereby re-anesthetizing his brain against the painful hangover from earlier in the day. But he hadn't gotten that far in the process on this particular Tuesday and he was greeted at the water cooler by one of the senior sports editor, Will Morehead.

"Hey, Postal, how's the noggin?"

"Just fine, how's your head, Morehead?"

The verbal exchange between the two newspapermen would have seemed *more or less* ridiculous to others, but was actually a coded confrontation between the two veterans of *The Roast*. They had long supported each other's success without particularly enjoying each other's company. Both men were heavy drinkers and both men regarded this as a personal problem that the other man needed to work his way through.

As a senior editor with responsibility for the sports pages of the tabloid, Will Morehead was particularly attentive to gutsy but glib back page headlines. He had final responsibility for these carefully chosen words and phrases and was proud of his work in this regard over the past twenty-three years. Morehead also felt some keen intramural competition with the senior news editor who held final responsibility for the front page headline.

Morehead was still staring at Lester Postal over at the water cooler. He wanted to complement his writer on the piece that Postal had done comparing the starting pitching staffs for the Bronx Bloomers and the Arizona Asps, but he couldn't find a good way to do it without sounding patronizing. The article had also included an interview with Bloomers manager Joe Trophy. It was a bit on the rah-rah side but wasn't quite a puff piece. Postal had managed to straddle the line between hometown favoritism and objectivity.

"Good piece on the starting staffs, Postal." Even though they had worked together for more than twenty years they always called each other by their last names except on the infrequent occasion that they were out drinking together. "How did you manage to get the interview with Trophy?"

"Thanks, Morehead. I ran out to the airport and caught Trophy in the VIP lounge. What a royal pain in the ass it was getting past security. The dopey security guard didn't even notice that my plane ticket was for a flight tomorrow morning …some fucking security that is …

The Earth Series Redux

scares the hell out of you ... doesn't it? By the way getting into that VIP Lounge alone cost me a Franklin. You'll see that on my expense account." If not friendship there was at least some legitimate trust and respect between the two newspapermen and Morehead knew that Postal never padded his expense account, simply because it was liberal enough to begin with.

"We're going to lead with your piece right under the back headline."

"Whatcha got on that?"

"The headline? I think we're going to go with: '**LET'S KICK SOME ASP**.' "

"Catchy."

"Thanks. Thought about shortening it by leaving out 'some' to make it a bold one liner, but the Series is just beginning. We can play with the 'Asp' thing as the Series goes along."

"Like you did earlier in the year when Arizona played the Mutts?"

"Yeah, we still get some chatter about that one on the talk radio shows." Morehead was proud of his rear headline on a dull midsummer sports day earlier in the year. The Asps were trouncing the Mutts out at Stray Stadium when a *Roast* cameraman caught a magnificent shot of a pretty young lady wearing a jersey for the visiting team leaning over the first base line railing trying to corral a slow rolling foul ball. The three-quarter angle allowed the cameraman to catch an identifying part of the Arizona Jersey, although it was now upside down. But more importantly it was a great shot of the young lady's taut derrière in tight bright red shorts as she leaned over to snatch up the cowhide sphere. The next day that picture of those tight red cheeks filled the back page of *The Roast* under the simple headline: "**NICE ASP**."

Both men moved away from the water cooler like two sated buffalos moving away from a river bed. They didn't want to wander too far because they knew they would soon wander back. But they at least moved out of ear shot of the other men and women who were hustling to make their respective deadlines.

"By the way, Postal ... did you get a chance to ask Trophy about that trainer contact of yours ... the one that told you he was sticking Jelly Rogers in the ass with a needle full of PEDs?"

Flunking Chemistry Class

"Well I couldn't exactly ask Trophy that question point blank. But I did find out that Trophy at least knows McGhee."

"How did that come about?

"We were just talking about the Series and I kind of got around to saying I ran into someone who claimed that he knew him. When I mentioned the name of Ryan McGhee, Trophy said he didn't know him well but that McGhee just hung around the clubhouse a lot because he was friends with Jelly Rogers and Randy Elfin."

"Wow, Randy Elfin too! I would never have expected him to be a juicer also. He doesn't even look like a float."

"Let's not jump to conclusions. All we have is the fact that Joe Trophy knows this guy and that he says that McGhee hangs with Rogers and Elfin. Honestly I seriously doubt Trophy knows any more than that."

"Clueless Joe. That's about right."

"Hey, don't come down on the manager. Everybody loves Joe Trophy! And guess what. If Joe knew anything strange was going on, do you think that he's going to give it up to me? Come on. Trophy is dumb like a fox. Look how he has managed to ride the Sledgehammer bull. That bull would have thrown any other manager by now. Remember he threw Wee Willie Martian three separate times."

"So why does this guy McGhee want to leak all of this steroid stuff about the Bloomers? I thought he was supposed to be a regular old jock sniffer."

"I'm not sure about that. I think he's looking for a job though. But I can tell you this much. I haven't given him a nickel, other than springing for a few meals. He did ask for Series tickets for one of the games at Bloomers Stadium next week. I told him that I would see what I could do."

"If he's such good friends with Rogers and Elfin, you'd think that he could score some seats from those guys."

"F*** that s***. That's the point I'm trying to make. I think they've had a falling out."

"Did this guy ever come right out and tell you he was sticking this steroid crap in Jelly's ass?"

The Earth Series Redux

"Absolutely he did. Do you want me to go over this again? As I told you before, McGhee was totally shitfaced when he told me this. And the last time I saw him, he refused to confirm or deny his previous disclosure. He's not exactly backpedalling but I have nothing else to go on right now except what he told me that one time."

"You need to keep working him, Postal. This could be the kind of story that rarely gets broken by the tabloid press."

"I'm working it, Morehead. I'm working it." Lester Postal turned and walked back away from the editor. He went back to his desk and called a ticket broker. He knew that if he wanted to maintain Ryan McGhee as his latest "rental friend" he would need to score some Earth Series tickets.

Timmy Burr was poring over the statistical data for the Bloomers and the Asps. He had been working for Buzz Selout and MBL for nearly three years and he was beginning to get frustrated. *It's all about the money*, he thought. The team owners were all interested in maximizing profits. The players were interested in maximizing salaries. Even "The Commish" wanted to keep his own ever burgeoning salary in place. The rising price of ballgame tickets was a good indication of who was bearing the burden of the ever escalating cost of watching one group of men cheat another group of men in an exhibition called baseball. The telephone in his office rang and he ignored it at first as he continued his efforts to glean insight from information. When he finally looked up and saw the caller ID specifics, he quickly grabbed the phone.

"Hello, this is Timmy Burr speaking." Burr already knew who was on the other end, but he wanted to act more officious and unimpressed by the caller.

"Hello Timmy ... Lester Postal from *The Roast*. How have you been? It's been a while since we talked?"

"Oh yes. Hi Lester. I've been just fine. I'm surprised that I haven't heard from you since before 9/11. I hope that your family, friends

Flunking Chemistry Class

and loved ones made it through the crisis okay." It was a typical statement from one New Yorker to another if they hadn't spoken since the attacks. However what Burr didn't realize was that Postal didn't have any real family, friends or loved ones before 9/11 or since the tragedy for that matter. His 7 month old divorce ended his fourth childless marriage and no one really cared one way or another about Postal's personal life, not even his rental friends.

"Yeah, yeah my people came through okay." Postal had no idea what people he was talking about but it seemed to be the right thing to say. "How 'bout you? Everything alright."

"I guess so. I've been busy with the job and I've just started my first semester of law school at night."

"Law school? What's that all about? I thought you were an accountant. You're a numbers guy. Right? Why do you want to go and screw that all up by being a lawyer?"

"It's not important. You just asked how I was doing so I gave you an answer."

Timmy Burr didn't want to pursue this line of discussion any further and he was sorry he brought it up in the first place. He knew that he wanted a law degree because it fit in with his new occupational goals in life. He knew that he had never been much of an athlete – crap he knew that he had never been an athlete period. So he thought that the only way he was going to get some of the big time bucks that the elite athletes made, was to become a big time player agent. He believed that becoming a lawyer would help a great deal in that pursuit. He never stopped to ask himself how many of the most successful agents were actually lawyers. He didn't really have a clue as to what the best skill set for player representation might be. He didn't realize that many of the big time agents hired a whole passel of attorneys to do all the grunt work. A law degree was a nice thing to have but certainly not a requisite to represent ballplayers as a player agent. But Timmy Burr was never one to let this kind of logic stand in his way and so he had enrolled in law school anyway. It was somewhat ironic that someone who could be so methodically precise and realistic in his everyday job, could be so impractically idealistic with respect to his personal ambition.

The Earth Series Redux

There was an awkward moment when neither of them said anything and Lester Postal almost forgot why he had called. He wanted to get an update on the commissioner's thinking about steroids especially in light of what everyone had been saying since Harry Bombs had floated past Popeye Maloney's three year old homerun record. But he knew that he would have to take his young rental friend out for lunch or dinner soon and that was what he had called to arrange. It was important to get an insight into the commissioner's latest perspective and it would be particularly important if he would be able to blow the lid off the Jelly Rogers – Randy Elfin story with the help of his newest rental friend Ryan McGhee. But before he got around to asking Burr for a luncheon date, Burr restarted the conversation.

"I read your story on the starting staffs for the Series. Nice piece."

"Thanks. Looks like it should be a competitive Series because of the pitching alone."

"So do you think we'll have another 'Roid Rage' incident in the Series like last year?"

"I sure hope not. The country's got a lot more to think about this year than last year. I think that right now people are more worried about anthrax than about what chemicals Jelly Rogers is taking."

"Yeah. I get it. But Buzz did get a call from the White House. The president is hoping for a real good Earth Series. He's confident that it can help get things back to normal. No one is announcing this yet because of security concerns but it looks like President Shrub will be throwing out the first pitch when the Series comes back to New York next Tuesday."

"That's the game Jelly Rogers is going to start. I hear that Rogers is a big fan of Shrub. I wonder if Shrub feels the same way about the Jelly Man."

"I can't help you there."

"Maybe someone should ask Shrub what he thinks about the steroid mess. He's a baseball man. He should have an opinion. I wonder if he had any floats when he owned the Dallas Drillies."

There was a slight pause and Postal could hear Burr making some quick key strokes on his computer. Then the statistician replied. "Shrub

Flunking Chemistry Class

only owned about ten percent of the team and he liquidated that holding when the team was sold in 1998. But during the previous ten years there were a few floats that played for the Drillies ...the right fielder Lon John Zalez and the catcher Igor Dorquez for sure ... but the first baseman they got from the Maryland Blackbirds; Daffy Palmgreed is a classic float. They got him after Shrub sold the team but he's been cranking balls out at a steroidal rate ever since."

"Wow. It seems like there are so many players on the juice. It's almost like the whole sport is juiced."

"Duh!"

Lester Postal hated it when the younger generation used that sarcastic one word phrase. But abruptly he realized that he deserved it. He had been chasing the wrong story. The story wasn't about who is juicing and who isn't. The real story was that the whole damn sport is juiced. Or better yet: *the whole damn sport is juiced ... duh!*

VI
Parade of Stars Game

July 2002

Buzz Selout waited for Marguerite to close the door. He took out the cheat sheet that his staff had prepared for him. He wanted to look it over one more time before he got on the owners conference call which was scheduled for 2 PM. The financial results for all 30 teams were highlighted in several different ways. There was a depiction of profit and loss for 2001. There was also a graph demonstrating the escalation of television revenues over the past ten years. There was another chart that showed a similar trajectory for the escalation of players' salaries over the same period. The positive slope of the salary chart was even steeper than the positive slope of television revenues and the slope of the chart for overall revenues. However each chart showed a very steep incline.

Player salary expense was now equivalent to about 55 percent of total revenues for the sport, compared to about 38 percent ten years earlier. One player alone, the shortstop for the Dallas Drillies, Alan Dorquez, was making more than $25 Million a year, after signing a 10 year contract for more than a quarter of a billion dollars!. In fact, the Drillies were also paying their catcher Igor Dorquez – no relation to Alan Dorquez – about $10 Million a year. Therefore they were collectively paying A Dork and I Dork – as they were commonly called – more than $35 Million a year. In addition the Drillies were also shelling out an additional $20 Million to their other two big name floats, right fielder Lon John Zalez and first baseman Daffy Palmgreed. It was quite apparent that swelling salary inflation was keeping pace with the ballooning bloat of the floats themselves.

The annual Parade of Stars Game was only a week away and Selout realized that his business had several issues that needed to be solved as soon as possible. He was almost certain that he would be asked a boatload of questions by the media when they all converged on Milwaukee for the Parade of Stars Game the following Tuesday.

Recently the owners had voted on the possibility of contracting the numbers of teams in the MBL from 30 to 28 by dropping the Montreal Olympians and the Minneapolis Clones. Selout's office let it be known that the vote passed 28 to 2 with the two negative votes coming from the ownership groups for the Olympians and the Clones respectively. The players union immediately dismissed this vote as saber rattling by the owners in an attempt to put a non-issue on the negotiating table to obscure some of the real bargaining concerns.

Selout's biggest problem was that the players had been playing the first half of the year without a new master contract in place. There could be a strike at any time and negotiations on the new contract were not moving swiftly. The basic agreement between the players and the owners still had many topics to be resolved because the two sides were moving slowly. The one saving grace in the negotiations was that neither side wanted to look too greedy to the public at a time when the country was in the troughs of its war against terrorism. On the other hand that was very difficult to do because both sides *were* gluttonously greedy and it was excessively apparent. Still a handful of people were having a hard time deciding how to split up 3.5 billion dollars in annual revenue. Meanwhile the average value for each team in the league had doubled in the last five years and the teams were now worth more than a quarter billion dollars apiece. The MBL was looking insatiably rapacious, and Selout knew it. After all, his personal salary was now approaching eight figures.

And then there was the issue of performance enhancing drugs. Eughh!! *This topic makes me want to barf,* Selout thought. He felt

Parade of Stars Game

comfortable dealing with expansion and contraction of the league and its number of teams, but he was at loss of how to deal with the expansion of the players themselves. He knew that baseball had had its drug problems over the years. The cocaine epidemic of the 1980's destroyed the careers of many players, and probably cost the Metropolitan Mutts an Earth Series or two because of the addictions of two of their more prominent players, Blight Badass and Darnell Raspberry. But cocaine only destroyed players; PEDs were destroying baseball. He sheepishly acknowledged that while addicted players ignorantly dismissed the long term consequences of cocaine in favor of the incredible short term rush it provided; baseball's ownership group had ignorantly disregarded the enduring consequences of PEDs in favor of the attendance swelling impact caused by the increase in homeruns.

Now Selout had two more dramatic revelations in the steroid controversy to deal with. Tim Veracity, a well respected sports writer for the weekly magazine *Games Thrillistrated* had recently interviewed Cam Commitadoosey, the former San Diego Chaplains third baseman. Commitadoosey confessed to Veracity that he had ballooned up in the mid nineties. He also admitted that his use of steroids was a major factor in allowing him to win his league's Most Venerated Player Award at the peak of his career. Commitadoosey was now retired and apparently fighting several different addictions but his confession still held a certain amount of weight, because he didn't implicate any other players, and was not benefitting in any way from his admission. In fact his frank discussion of the topic included an assertion that because he was adding so much synthetic testosterone through his shoot-up of anabolic steroids that his body had stopped producing testosterone on its own and consequently his testicles had seemingly gone into hibernation. Furthermore Selout was horrified to see that Commitadoosey had told Veracity that steroid use in MBL could be as high as fifty percent, but The Commish was even more aghast at what another recently retired player had to say.

CoJo Janesco was now claiming that eighty-five percent of MBL players were using steroids and that he was going to write a book about his career and how it was enhanced by steroids. And whereas

Flunking Chemistry Class

Commitadoosey had refused to directly implicate any player other than himself, Janesco promised that his tell-all book would name numerous players past and current who were "certifiably juiced."

Selout was further irritated by the cheap secondary rip-off article that was published by *The New York Roast*. *The Roast* had focused on two particular parts of the *Games Thrillistrated* exposé: the high percentages of suspected steroid users and the physiological evidence of the supposedly rampant PED usage. Lester Postal's article repeated many of the same assertions that had been made in the *Thrillistrated* piece and then added the conjecture that possibly *all* of the players in the upcoming Parade of Stars Game might exhibit similar testicular shrinkage to that experienced by Commitadoosey. *The Roast's* back page headline shrieked: **GONADS ARE GONERS!** Now Selout was worried that the reporters, who would be covering the upcoming Parade of Stars Game from the locker rooms after the game, would be sneaking sidelong glances at the genitalia of ballplayers to assess the gravitas of their gonads.

Selout had stopped reading the financial report while he was caught up in reverie about the PED problem but he came back to life and put down the report as Marguerite buzzed him on the intercom with her heavy New York gum-snapping accent. "Two minutes *befaw ya* call, Buzz." The commissioner took off his wiry glasses and wiped them clean with a handkerchief. He could only wish that it would be as easy to clean up the image of baseball. Regardless he determined that the new contract would be the place to start.

Since the late 1930's the MBL had paused in the middle of every season to play its exhibition contest known as the *Parade of Stars Game*. It was also colloquially referred to as the Midsummer Masterpiece. The first few games of this annual event were taken quite seriously by the participants but in recent years the contest had taken on the characteristics of a true exhibition game with little regard for the outcome. The Masterpiece was played between two teams who fielded the best

Parade of Stars Game

players from each of the two leagues who made up the Multinational Baseball league or the MBL.

The Native League, had been in existence since the latter half of the 19th Century, Each year it played against the Amerind League, which was formed as an upstart competitor to Native League at the beginning of the 20th Century. Although the Native League was considered the senior circuit, the Amerind League had some of the marquee franchises in the game including the Bronx Bloomers; the Beantown Wallbangers; the Cleveland Featherheads and the Dallas Drillies. The Native League had its share of big name teams as well including: the Hollywood Hedgers; the Metropolitan Mutts; the Cincinnati Crazy Legs; the Wisconsin Cheeseheads and the St Louis Scarlets.

The Native League currently had sixteen teams and the Amerind League had fourteen franchises. Each league had a Canadian franchise; the Montreal Olympians in the Native League and Toronto Thunderbirds in the Amerind League. As a concession to the "going global" trend of all businesses, just prior to Y2K, the MBL had outsourced half of the home games of Native League's San Diego team so that they were played in Sydney Australia. The same was true of the Amerind League's franchise in Seattle. It now played half of its home games in Tokyo, Japan. These moves, which were orchestrated by Commissioner Selout, had caused some schizophrenia on the part of the fans of these two franchises. It was not the relocation of half of the home games that caused the problem. The quandary for the fans was caused by the fact that when the San Diego Chaplains played in Sydney they actually changed their name to the Sydney Kangaroos. Likewise when playing in Tokyo, the Seattle Seafarers became the Tokyo Carp. The actual players were the same but the locale and the team name changed to suit the venue. All of this was apparently Selout's "toe-in-the-water" approach to going global. If nothing else it helped to sell a lot of new baseball caps and other memorabilia with the new global logos.

Flunking Chemistry Class

The 2002 Parade of Stars Game was a homecoming of sorts for Buzz Selout. It was being played in Spiller Park in Milwaukee, home of the Wisconsin Cheeseheads, a franchise once owned by The Commish and now owned by his daughter. It was also a franchise whose fans had recently been jerked around by Selout as well, when he moved the team from the Amerind League to the Native League in 1998.

The state of Wisconsin is widely known for its cheese and its beer. Even though the team was named after the former product, local brewery owners had a large say in the development of the new ballpark that had opened in 2001. Brewers throughout the country had been growing concerned about the inroads that the wine industry was making into the customer base of alcohol drinking sports fans. The fact that the combination "wine and cheese" was a more commonly recognized duet than "beer and cheese" was not lost on the beer brewing profession, which had some of its most powerful industry leaders located in Milwaukee. Therefore the Milwaukee beer makers were glad to have the opportunity to pair their product more closely with the Cheeseheads.

The stadium itself was constructed with a retractable dome and was built with nearly $300 Million of public funds that were raised through a 20 year sales tax surcharge placed on purchases made in Milwaukee and the surrounding counties in Wisconsin. Around the park there were several displays that celebrate the combination of beer and cheese and many of these displays also recognize the importance of beer in celebratory situations. Pictures from the 1982 Amerind League Pennant winning celebration, for example, show players spraying beer rather than champagne in the locker room.

Initially some of the biggest names in Milwaukee's brewing industry fought for the naming rights to the Cheeseheads' new stadium. Finally a compromise was reached by taking the letters "S" and "P" from two different breweries and the secondary letters "iller" from another large locally headquartered beer company. Thus the name Spiller was formed. The combination created not only a new name for the park but also an ambiance of frivolity around the product itself. This allowed fans to consume the product freely and occasionally spray the product liberally whenever there was an opportunity

Parade of Stars Game

for celebration or occasionally when there was rank disagreement with an umpire's call. The Cheeseheads management team embraced these ideas and fostered them by creating an outfield extravaganza featuring Barney Brewmaster, a team mascot who alternatively dives, slides or cannonballs into a huge barrel of beer beyond the centerfield fence whenever a Cheesehead unloaded a homerun. When the opposition hit a dinger, Barney Brewmaster could be seen spilling a beer over the head of another mascot wearing the jersey of the opposing team. This activity was known to provoke similar antics throughout the stadium and some fans had taken to wearing raincoats to the games even though with a retractable roof, there was never a threat of rain.

The 2002 Parade of Stars Game was a sellout as had been almost all of the previous Midsummer Masterpiece games. And there was nothing that Buzz Selout loved more than a sellout. The games *biggest* stars – in the truest sense of the word – were all lined up along the base paths for the introductions before the game began. It was a swell time for baseball.

The Amerind League stars were the first to line up taking their position along the third base line. The reserve players and pitchers were announced first and then the Amerind League's starting lineup was broadcast to the fans. The crowd cheered or jeered depending upon what they thought of the various participants. Several Asian fans began snapping pictures immediately when the name of Japanese star Itchy Kazuti of the Seattle Seafarers/Tokyo Carp was announced. The rooting for Kazuti was drowned out a bit by the subsequent booing when three members of the Bronx Bloomers in the starting lineup were announced. The biggest booing was saved for Mason Jambino, the Bloomers first baseman who was signed by Sledgehammer and the Bloomers as a free agent float during the past off season. However two other prodigious floats, Boston leftfielder Manboy Ramendez and shortstop Alan Dorquez – also known as A Dork – of the Dallas Drillies were also booed lustily.

Flunking Chemistry Class

When the Native League stars were announced, the loudest cheers were for the hometown's two representatives on the team, reserve infielders, Rex Sixten and Joe Homonez. The crowd also had polite cheers for Matt Palazzo of the Mutts and Sean Brown of the Hedgers. But when the public address announcer said the name of Harry Bombs of the Bay City Mammoths, the crowd broke out in the now typical reaction to the player. His reputation in San Francisco was now even larger than that of "Rice-A-Roni: the San Francisco Treat." But his physique had gotten so big that he was now sometimes called "Harry Bombs: the San Francisco Fleet."

However, other monikers aside, around the league Harry Bombs was constantly serenaded with a single word nickname that was sung over and over in a manner that made it sound like two words. The first syllable ended up in the air and the second syllable came back down to earth and the single appellation was then slowly but repeatedly sung: "asS-Hole, asS-Hole, asS-Hole, asS-Hole" and the singing got louder and louder with each repetition. The public address announcer at Spiller Park must have shared some of this sentiment, because he waited for almost twenty seconds for the cascading serenade to crescendo before moving on to the next player on the list.

The Spiller Park serenading of Harry Bombs was not lost on Buzz Selout. He was now hearing about the dissatisfaction with the steroids everywhere he went. He knew that this insidious menace was destroying his sport, but he was at a loss as to what to do about it. It was bad enough that steroids were destroying the *sport* of baseball, he was now genuinely worried that steroids might actually destroy the *business* of baseball. That would mean it could cost an awful lot of money. With that threat in mind he was sure that he would now have to intervene. Once again he came to the conclusion that he might have to make this a real issue in the contract negotiations. Or at the very least, he would need to get the public to believe it was a significant issue in the contract negotiations.

Parade of Stars Game

Once the introductions were completed and the other ceremonies had wound down, the Native League took the field and the game began. In the early innings, the Native League took a 4 – 0 lead after Harry Bombs blasted a two run dinger in the third inning. The Native League still led by a score of 5 – 2 at the end of six innings. The two managers, the Asps Bob Bentley for the Native League and Joe Trophy of the Bloomers for the Amerind League, substituted players liberally trying hard to get everyone in the game – like managing a Little League team – rather than trying to win the actual contest.

The scoring went back and forth until the Amerind League tied the Native League at 7 – 7 after scoring a run in the top of the eighth inning. The Native League team was retired quickly in the bottom of the eighth and neither team scored in the ninth inning.

That's when the trouble began. As they went to extra innings each team only had one pitcher remaining who hadn't already appeared in the game. Incente Dapilla of the Philadelphia Philistines and Fanny Arcadia of the Seafarer/Carp then each pitched two scoreless innings. But prior to the bottom of the eleventh inning, the two managers met on the mound and in an unprecedented move, Buzz Selout came out of the stands and joined them on the hill. After a short discussion, The Commish decree that the bottom of the eleventh would be the end of the game, whether it was tied or not, because the teams were out of pitchers.

The game remained tied following the bottom of the eleventh inning and The Commish declared a draw. When the announcement was made over the public address system the crowd went wild, demanding refunds and calling for Selout's resignation. When the pitchers finally stopped throwing baseballs the fans began throwing beer bottles, a few of them crashing near the commissioner, who was in the process of trying to make a quick exit, and getting a bit beer soaked in the process. The mascots in the outfield popped up and began spilling beer over one another and general mayhem prevailed.

All eyes remained on Selout, who was now deemed the appropriate villain in the catastrophic ending to the Parade of Stars Game. From behind the plate a shrill voice intoned "What kind of host runs out of

Flunking Chemistry Class

pitchers before he runs out of beer?" From centerfield came, "You suck, Selout." And down in the leftfield corner a voice proclaimed, "Take you floats and go back to New York, Selout, you asshole." That last taunt was the tipping point and from somewhere down the third base line the chant started welling up. The crowd began giving the commissioner the sing-song salute that they normally employed only for Harry Bombs.

The back page of the *New York Roast* was relatively tame, There was a close up picture of a couple of beer soaked Cheesehead fans screaming in Buzz Selout's face as he was pulling back from them with his toupee slipping down over his wet forehead. The headline read simply: **WIGGED OUT**. However the accompanying article, by Lester Postal, which started in larger print on the back page and spilled into smaller print in the innards of the back section of the paper, was a blistering attack not only on the tie ballgame but on the growing problem of steroid abuse:

"The Multinational Baseball League's Midsummer Masterpiece turned into a nocturnal nightmare for Buzz Selout, the MBL ownership group and their flotilla of superstars. Collectively they turned the Parade of Stars Game into a beer soaked three ring circus that was preceded by a freak show as the steroid swollen superstars lined the basepaths for introductions. It appears that the game is slipping into a circus atmosphere faster than Selout's toupee can slip off his head and over his eyebrows.

Last night the fans finally began to fight back. After Commissioner Selout allowed managers Trophy and Bentley to frivolously exhibit all of their players in a non-competitive fashion, he decided to halt the disturbing display of distended dumbbells after an exhausting exhibition of quick exits of overpaid egos in the Parade of Stars. Buzz Selout made it quite clear that this was not the Parade of Stars Game; it was simply the Parade of Stars period. And the fans were furious. They showered Selout and his entourage with beer and boos as he decided to halt the game after eleven innings in a 7 - 7

Parade of Stars Game

tie. They even called him by the same nickname they usually reserve for their excretory orifice or for Harry Bombs.

Never before had a game ended in such a manner. But then again, never has a commissioner been so blinded by financial success. So while the value of franchises; the salaries of ballplayers; the salary of the commissioner and the price of a beer at the ballpark, continue to escalate exponentially, the fan in the stands gets less and less for his dollar. Instead of a baseball game he gets a parade of floats. Selout should just cancel the Midsummer Masterpiece or move the mindless menagerie to the end of November and have his floats follow Snoopy, Mickey Mouse and Curious George in the Macy's Thanksgiving Day parade...."

The commissioner couldn't read any further. Selout didn't know Lester Postal all that well, but he was aware that the sports reporter had a huge following among the strap-hanger fans of New York City. He also felt that occasionally Postal seemed to know a little too much about the inner workings of the commissioner's office. Regardless he knew that he would have to do something to stem the groundswell of indignation and resentment that Postal was provoking. Postal and other writers were now taking every incident that occurred in the game of baseball and turning it into a story about steroids. *Whatever happened to the benign neglect of the nineties? I need to talk to talk to Danny Fowl, the Executive Director of the Players Association. We might have to do something about it in this upcoming contract after all.* As these thoughts rumbled through Selout's mind he also had another thought about the Parade of Stars Game. *Maybe we can make it count for something. Maybe the league that wins can get home field advantage in the Earth Series. That would certainly change things. Everyone knows that there's nothing more important than the Earth Series.*

VII

Big Sky Country

July 2002

Sam and Betsy Jo Crockett were expecting their second child. In fact they had just learned that it would be their second *son*. However the Crocketts felt as though they were at opposite ends of the earth. In truth they were only 1500 miles apart. Seventeen year old Betsy Jo was at her father's San Antonio Texas home caring for her eight month old son Sam Jr, while she was carrying their yet to be named second son.

Eighteen year old Sam Crockett was pitching for a half-season low single A team in the Big Sky country in the state of Montana. The season had started in mid-June after Sam had spent April and May at the Cheeseheads clinic in Arizona. It was now the end of July and Sam had just made his fifth start for the Little Cheesies. Sam had reason to be happy with his baseball performance. In his five starts he had pitched a total of 33 innings struck out 43 batters and his walk total was down to just 12 – not great but a big improvement over the previous year. He had also hit four batters but had given up only 1 homerun and he was sporting a nifty 1.78 ERA and a 1.12 WHIP. He was dealing. His fastball had been clocked consistently at 96 - 97 MPH and although he didn't have great command over his curveball, it still had two feet of break on it most of the time.

However Sam Crockett was also in a bit of a funk. There was absolutely nothing to do in Montana but play ball. It seemed as though the

Big Sky Country

same 125 or so people came to the ball games each night and after the games, most of the players would go out to one of the two bars that made up the town of Moose Butt, Montana. The town was in the middle of nowhere, halfway between the town of Jawbone and the foothills of Montana. His one close friend on the Moose Butt Little Cheesies was his catcher and roommate from the previous summer. However just to make matters worse for Crockett, Lance Leathermore had just been promoted to the full-season affiliate of the Cheeseheads, the Wausau Wedgies, back in Wisconsin, after a startling performance in his one month in Moose Butt. Leathermore had come back from the off season with an extra 25 pounds of sinewy size and had almost immediately muscled his way out of Moose Butt by hitting 13 homeruns in the first 25 games of the short season.

Crockett was happy for Leathermore but he was surprised at how fast he had grown. Leathermore was two years older than Crockett but appeared older than 20. In some ways Crockett felt that maybe he should be more dedicated to his profession like Leathermore was. He knew that Leathermore had played winter ball in Mexico and that he had also worked extensively with Carlos, the Scottsdale Arizona strength and conditioning trainer that Brad Scott had recommended. He could almost hear his agent's words about Carlos ringing in his ears: *He knows all about vitamin supplements and developing young bodies.*

Originally Leathermore wasn't even one of Brad Scott's clients, but he had heard about Carlos through the grapevine and it appeared as though he was able to work some physical miracles. During the 2001 season Leathermore had been big boned but a bit fleshy. But before the 2002 season, Leathermore had managed to develop a physique that looked a bit like that of the now retired CoJo Janesco. Leathermore had confided in Crockett that his new body building process had included some HGH injections, but he said that there wasn't much to it and that once the stuff was in his blood stream it was virtually undetectable.

Crockett was not enthralled with the idea of putting these foreign substances in his body. He had heard that the side effects were somewhat horrific. Besides he was already throwing the ball in the high nineties. How much good could that stuff do? However there was ample

Flunking Chemistry Class

temptation anyway because Crockett had only hit two homeruns and if he still wanted to consider the option of being an everyday player, he would have to show a little more power. The trouble was that he wasn't getting much guidance from his agent, Brad Scott. He hadn't heard from Scott in four weeks and he was beginning to wonder if he should get a new agent. He decided that he would do what he always did when he was confused, he would call Betsy Jo.

"Hello, Baby Doll, How are you feeling? And how is my little boy, JR?"

"JR is fine, just fine." She emphasized the word "fine" as though it merely a passing grade. "And the little one on the inside is doing just fine also. And I'll be doing fine also as soon as your season ends and you get back to San Antonio."

"That's real good Betsy Jo. I'm glad everyone down there is doing just *fine*." He emphasized the adjective in mock dismissal of her obvious irritation.

"You don't sound *fine*, Sam. What's happening with you and the Little Cheesies?"

"Baseball-wise everything is *fine*." He paused for a second and decided it was time to stop playing the word wars. Maybe his wife could emphasize with his loneliness. "I told you last week that Lance got called up to the Wausau Wedgies back in Wisconsin. Most of the other guys on the team here are either real hicks or they're from somewhere in South America. There's not a lot to do and I miss you and JR."

"The season will be over soon, Sam. Tell me about the baseball stuff."

"I've been throwing the ball damn near as best as I can, Baby Doll. And the manager here, Trab Simpson, says that I've got *big league stuff*. He told me that I just need to work on getting a *big league head*."

"What's that mean?

"He says that lots of guys have big league stuff but the only ones who make it to The Show these days are the guys with big league heads."

"I don't get it. Is he calling you dumb?"

"No, I don't think that's it. I just think he's telling me that I need more experience. That's all. He's said the same thing to some of the other guys."

Big Sky Country

"And what do those guys think when he tells them that they need big league heads?"

"Most of them kind of think like I do … that he's just telling us we need more experience. Except Lance had a different idea of what Simpson was talking about."

"I don't know if I like this Lance guy very much."

"Come on, Baby Doll, you've never even met him."

"I'm just sayin' …"

"Sayin' what, Baby Doll?"

"You know, Sam. Remember what you told me about Lance Leathermore and his double plays?"

"Aw hell, Betsy Jo. I shoulda never gone and told you 'bout that."

"Don't you go hidin' anythin' from me, Sammy. Remember I'm your wife."

"Come on Betsy Jo. You know I ain't ever hidin' anythin' from you …else I wouldn't have told you about Lance's double plays and all that. Besides, Leathermore is a single guy. And for good measure, he ain't even here anymore. Come on Baby Doll, cut me some slack. I didn't call you to get ragged on."

"I don't like that expression either, Sam Crockett. But I'm goin' to let it go this time." Sam could hear his wife's anger rising on the other end of the phone. He realized that their long distance relationship wasn't any easier for her than it was for him. He was content when she changed the subject even though he could still hear her ire. "So what does your friend Leatherhead …?"

"Leather*more*, Betsy Jo. It's Leather*more*."

"Okay, Leathermore. Anyway, what does Leathermore think that this Simpson guy means by a *big league head*?"

"Lance said that he was talking about PEDs."

"That's steroids right."

"Well yeah, steroids are part of it. But there's also something called HGH, human growth hormone. In fact there are all kinds of PEDs."

"What does that stand for?"

"Performance Enhancing Drugs …these are drugs that make you play better."

Flunking Chemistry Class

"Isn't that cheating?"

"Maybe ... but maybe not ... if everyone's doing them."

"I don't know Sammy. It sounds like cheating to me. You can't just do something like that because you think someone else is doing it. It's like your mother used to tell you when you were a little kid. 'If everyone else is jumpin' off the Rainbow Bridge, it still doesn't mean that you have to be stupid too.' I think it's just dumb ... and furthermore it's cheating. So what about this manager of yours, the guy who told you that you need a *big league head*. Why does Leathermore think that he was talking about PEDs?" "

Lance says that Simpson is a good guy. He wants his players to succeed. But he believes that they have to get juiced in order to compete effectively. And all of the juicers seem to grow at least two hat sizes the moment they start on the program. You should see Lance. He's bigger than a house and he went up to a size eight hat."

"That's crazy Sammy. Why would anyone want a big head? Just last week when I went to see my obstetrician, she asked me whether I was hoping for a boy or a girl and I told her that I didn't care and that all that all I wanted was a small head. Then of course she told me that I was having another son." Betsy Jo paused for a second and then went back to the topic at hand. "Don't you go messing around with any of that steroid stuff. Do you hear me Sammy? I like your head."

"I like your head too Baby Doll. But making a living for our kids is not dependant on your head."

"It's not dependant on your head either, Sammy. You've got a great fastball. You don't need a big head."

"That's not what Leathermore was telling me. Besides, I don't want to be a Little Cheesie for the rest of my career. I want to be a Wedgie and then a Munster and then eventually I want to get to The Show as a full-fledged Cheesehead. What's wrong with that?"

"You know I love you, Sammy. And I have been very supportive of your baseball career. We're both making sacrifices for your ultimate goal ...our ultimate goal. But I don't want to be married to a cheater. If you're cheating in baseball, what's to stop you from cheating on other things as well? You can get to be a Cheesehead without being a meathead. Just keep pounding your heater, Honey. That's what makes you *sooo* good." In order to turn the tide a bit, Betsy Jo half whispered her last line in an attempt to get her husband to feel virile and sexy and she knew just how to play his chords.

"Ooo, that sounds good, Baby Doll. I wish you were here. I'd be pounding my heater like there's no tomorrow." Crockett always felt better after he talked with Betsy Jo. She seemed to know just how to get him thinking straight again. However he had another topic that he wanted to broach before they got further into their phone flirtation and whatever else popped up.

"But I wanted to ask you something else, Betsy Jo. I haven't heard much at all from Brad Scott and when I do hear from him, he always wants to talk more about my conditioning than about my pitching or hitting. I was thinking about dumping him and getting a new agent. What do you think?"

"That's fine by me. I never liked the guy in the first place."

INCOMING CALL: BRADLEY SCOTT. Sam Crockett's new cell phone lit up with an announcement that his agent was calling. It was almost as if Scott's ears were ringing.

"Let me call you back, Baby Doll. You won't believe this. The devil himself is calling. Let me pick him up and I'll get back to you later."

"Okay Sammy. And whatever you decide about your agent it's fine with me. I love you."

"Hi Brad, what's up?" Crockett had already learned that it was best to get right to the point with his agent.

"What? Are you in hurry or something? Not, hello Brad. How are you doing? How's the family?" Scott was toying with his client. He knew that Crockett was upset with him because he had heard that from Lance Leathermore. Leathermore had just signed with Brad Scott as a new client after the catcher made it to the Wedgies with the help of Scott's specialist trainer, Carlos in Scottsdale.

Flunking Chemistry Class

"Sorry, Brad. It's just that I haven't heard from you in a while and I thought that you might be in a hurry. I'm not in a hurry at all. So how are you? How's the family?"

"Now that's better. Well, everybody's fine thanks." This was an easy answer for Scott because he had no family to speak of other than the twin pit bulls, Dionysus and Bacchus, that he had guarding his palatial estate in Monterey, California. But he also wanted to regain Crockett's confidence. "How are you and Betsy Jo and the little one doing?" Scott was reading the names from an index card that his secretary had prepared before he called, but he couldn't read the name of Sam Crockett's child.

"Everyone's doing all right. As you know Betsy Jo and I are expecting again in January. So she's a little anxious for me to get out of Moose Butt and back to San Antonio."

"Well I've got some good news for you. It looks like you won't be stuck in Moose Butt much longer."

"Does this mean I'm getting bumped up?" The excitement was hard for Crockett to hide. Finally he would be able to extract himself from Moose Butt and become part of the Wedgies.

"Well it's a little more complicated than that. You've got a little more than five weeks left to the season in the Big Sky Association, so when league play ends, your time in Moose Butt will end along with it."

Sam Crockett's heart sunk as fast as its beat had risen. This was just more double talk from his agent. When was Brad Scott going to help him in any positive way? He answered Scott with a voice dripping with sarcasm; "Tell me something I don't already know, Brad. I wasn't going to come back here next year no matter what."

"Well sometimes these things are beyond your control. However, fortunately we do have a plan. Apparently the Bloomers have had their eyes on you. Off the record – because they really aren't supposed to mess with another team's players – although it happens all the time – they are impressed with the fact that you're throwing in the high nineties, even without any help *yet* from my specialist trainer, Carlos."

"Did they actually ask you that? Did you actually talk with someone from the Bloomers?"

"Yes and yes …to answer both of your questions."

"So then the Bloomers are interested in me because I'm throwing hard even *without* doing any PEDs."

"Exactly."

"Wow that's great to know that there is some integrity in the game. It's great to know that a franchise as storied as the Bronx Bloomers likes the idea that a young guy can bring natural heat in the upper nineties."

"No, not exactly. What they really like is the thought of how hard you might throw if we got you on our specialist program. We're talking easy cheese in the triple digits. Now Sledgehammer's gang likes *that* idea a lot!"

"Look, Brad, I don't know where you're going with this. All I know is that I'm still under contract to the Cheeseheads. Why are you bringing up all of this Bloomers stuff? They've got scouts just like everyone else. The other teams can see my WHIP and my ERA and the scouts can get my fastball on the radar gun. Why are the Bloomers any more interested in me than any of the other teams?"

"Because they know you're not juicing. They know you can still take it up a couple of notches. Most of the other teams just assume that you're already on the stuff and that's how you're hitting 97 on the gun. The Bloomers trust me. I've delivered a lot of big leaguers to their door step. So when I'm telling them that you're clean, they believe me."

"So tell me. What's this have to do with my current contract status? Why should I care what the Bloomers think?"

"Here's the deal. You play out the string there in Moose Butt. Just stay healthy and keep throwing hard. Work on your other pitches if you want, but throw heat most of the time. There will be scouts watching. You're young enough that the results don't matter as much as your stuff. Then at the end of next month, the Bloomers are going to make a bid for your contract. They'll include a lot of cash and there's probably going to be a few other players involved. Don't pay attention to any of that. After that you'll be a part of the premiere organization in all of the MBL. But there's one catch. They're going to want you to play fall ball in Mexico."

"We talked about this before, Brad. After the season. I want to go home to Texas. I've got to get a job to make a few extra bucks. Like I told you, I've got another kid on the way, and my wife has been plenty patient with me. I'm only making $1,500 a month playing for the Little Cheesies. It's not even a living wage. I'm eating into my bonus money."

"I know I've already explained some of these things to the Bloomers. So here's even more good news. The Bloomers are willing to ante up an additional five grand if you'll play for their Mexican affiliate. That's five grand plus whatever the Mexicans will pay you. That's a lot of money for two and a half months work. And you'll be back in Texas for Christmas and the arrival of your new kid in January. What a deal!!! But don't thank me yet. Just go out and pitch in August and we'll see how things go."

"Okay, Brad. You're sure this is all going to work out just like that? I'm not so sure though. I can make more than that working with my father-in-law in the drilling bits business back in San Antonio."

"Yea but this is five grand for *playing a game*. A lot of these guys don't get paid at all. They don't call me Big Bucks Brad for nothing."

"And one more thing. The Bloomers have a conditioning program in Arizona right before Spring Training begins in Florida at the end of February. It will be great for you. It will start you on your way to the really big buckeroos."

"What do they do at the conditioning …?"

"Oops, there's another call coming in. Got to go for now Sam. Love *ya*, Babe. And remember just keep pounding your heater." Somehow it wasn't at all the same as when Betsy Jo said it.

It was his sixth start for the Little Cheesies and Sam Crockett was once again pitching a great game. Through six innings Moose Butt was leading the Helena Hellcats by a score of 2-0. Crockett had only given up two hits in the first six innings and he hadn't walked anyone until there was one out in the seventh. Along the way he had struck out ten Hellcat hitters. After striking out the third basemen to open the seventh, Crockett had walked the next two hitters to bring up Helena's left fielder, Troy Odysseus, a right-handed hitter who was built like a Greek god. The Little Cheesies manager Trab Simpson came out to the mound to see how much gas Crockett had left in the tank.

"How you feeling. Sammy boy?"

"I'm feeling great. I'll get us one ground ball. We'll turn two and we'll be back in the dugout."

"Sounds good. Throw him soft stuff. He'll be sitting on the heater."

"Struck him out twice already with the four-seamer," Crockett argued.

"That's why he'll be sitting on it." Simpson spit out a wad of chewing tobacco and then stared into Crocket's blue eyes with his own red-lined orbs, to ensure that his pitcher got the message.

"I've been working him in. I'll paint him on the outside and keep it low. He'll miss it or bang into a double play. Don't worry Trab, I've got this guy."

"Read my fucking lips, Sammy boy, just throw soft stuff. Throw him that yacker of yours and keep it tight. Trust me on this one. Odysseus won't know whether to shit or go blind when he sees that curve from you."

The debate was over. Simpson turned around without allowing his pitcher to have anything else to say. The Little Chessies' new catcher had just stood out on the mound the whole time without saying a word. The catcher, Pablo Rosario, didn't understand a word either man had said because he had just arrived from the Caribbean Island of Curaçao and only spoke Papiamentu and Dutch. Every other member of the team spoke either English or Spanish. Rosario knew that the conversation between the manager and the pitcher had been a bit terse so he just smiled at Crockett and jogged back behind the plate.

Regardless of language deprivation, the catcher was responsible for at least making the signals to suggest a pitch and Rosario thought that this would be easy. He put down one finger and aimed it toward the outside of the plate, knowing that they had been coming in on Odysseus the whole game.

Crockett stared in at his catcher's sign and thought; *Great minds think alike*. However he remembered the steely eye stare of his manager and he shook the catcher off. Immediately the catcher signaled for a fastball inside. Again Crockett shook him off. The catcher put his hand up in a sign asking the umpire for "time," and jogged rapidly to the mound. When Crockett saw him coming he was amazed because he had no idea how they would possibly converse. Meanwhile the tiny crowd began to yell at them for delaying the game. When Rosario made it to the mound he simply uttered something that sounded like; "What the fuck?" Apparently he had begun to learn some English after all.

Crockett showed him two fingers hidden behind his glove so that the catcher would understand that the manager wanted a curveball. The catcher shrugged and ran back behind the plate and flashed the two fingers and set up on the inside corner of the plate.

But now Crockett had changed his mind. If he was going to get beat, he was determined to get beat with his best pitch so he shook off Rosario for a third time. The catcher was confused. He didn't normally signal the location for the curve ball but rather simply set the target after they had gotten concurrence on the type of pitch. Then he thought maybe he wants me to set up outside, so he put down two fingers once again and slid towards the outside corner. To his utter amazement Crockett shook him off once again. Crockett didn't have a change-up so Rosario thought that maybe Crockett didn't like him and was just messing with him. In a piqué of anger he again flashed a single finger, but this time it was his middle finger and it was turned upward to signify his displeasure with his teammate.

Crockett simply nodded his assent and went into his stretch. He fired a ninety-eight mile per hour fastball on the outside corner of the plate. Troy Odysseus swung from the heels and hit the ball about halfway across the Big Sky State.

Simpson was out of the dugout and halfway to the mound before Odysseus had completed his odyssey around the base paths. Rosario

Big Sky Country

joined him at the mound. "What the fuck?" was the immediate reaction of the manager upon arriving at the mound. *So that's where Rosario is learning his English*, was Crockett's first thought. His second thought was equally succinct: *No one hits a ball that fucking far without being on the juice.*

VIII

Going Postal in The Morning After

October 2002

Now in early October, 2002, Timmy Burr was sitting on a barstool next to Lester Postal in a bar called *The Morning After*. Actually this was the same 8th Avenue bar that used to be called *Joey Dee's;* the same gin mill that Lester Postal had treated as his home away from home. However Joey Dee Jr had taken a repeated beating on the tote card of a local sports bookie and was forced to sell a fifty percent interest in his place to a partner who insisted on renaming the place before he would close the deal. So now *Joey Dee's Tavern* was saddled with its new sobriquet, *The Morning After*. Nothing else about the place had changed.

What had changed was the rapport between Lester Postal and Timmy Burr. Their relationship had evolved a bit over the last couple of years. They no longer sat in the dim perimeter of the watering holes where they met. And now the information flow was no longer one directional. Postal was leaking some information to Burr about some of the trainers and body builders that he had met since he started to dig into the performance enhancing drug debacle. Meanwhile Burr had provided a certain amount of insight into the inner workings of the commissioner's office as it pertained to the steroid fiasco. Weasel-looking Burr fashioned himself as some sort of double agent, although he was not deriving any particular financial or social benefits from this line of work. Sure Postal still considered him a *rental* friend and always paid for every drink and every meal, but double agent Burr didn't really know how to benefit from the information that was flowing through him. There were no Bond girls and no fancy cars to drive. Regardless Burr simply continued to operate as a conduit of intelligence without an iota of recompense for his efforts. He sometimes wondered how he could enhance those circumstances without breaking any laws.

Burr was now in his second year of law school and his fourth year of working for the office of the commissioner of baseball. As he sat next to Postal in *The Morning After*, he began to realize to his own horror that he actually had less of a social life than Postal. His life seemed to consist of school and work and a few drinks with Postal whenever they exchanged viewpoints on the evolution of the International Pastime. If nothing else at least Postal had been married and now divorced four times. Burr realized that he hadn't had a date since he was fixed up for his high school prom.

"I hear that Bass Sledgehammer is really pissed at Joe Trophy for getting beat in the Division Series by the Anaheim Afterthoughts. What do you know about that?"

"Probably not a lot more than you do, Lester. Mr. …*uh*… Larry … *uh* Bass, Sledgehammer honestly expects to win every single year. He paid big time bucks to bring over Mason Jambino from the East Bay Bees and he expected another Earth Series Championship."

"Well he can't blame Jambino. He smacked more than 40 dingers during the regular season and another one in the Division Series. He also had a boatload of RBI's and hit over .300. There's not much to criticize there. That's why I think that Trophy is under the gun. Sledgehammer always has a scapegoat. Trophy looks like a logical candidate."

"Who knows with Sledgehammer? He could be ticked off at the way Trophy used the bullpen. They gave up 6 runs in the eighth inning of the three games they lost. There was no bridge to Riviera

Flunking Chemistry Class

Sandmando. Or he could be ticked off at Jelly Rogers who got bombed in the opener even though it was the only game they won."

"So what's he going to do about it?"

"Bass? ... Hard to say. But I'll bet you almost anything that his guys are now assessing whatever free agent floats will be out there in the offseason. It was bad enough last season when the Bloomers lost the Series to the Asps. This year Sledgehammer's team won't even be *in* the Series. And as Mr. Selout always says: There's nothing more important than the Earth Series."

The bartender came over with another shot and a beer for Postal and another martini for Burr. The newspaperman and the statistician made an odd couple of sorts. Burr was 26 years old but looked like he was 12. Postal was 53 years old and looked 10 to 15 years older than that. But the age difference faded over their mutual interest in baseball. And now that it was in the middle of October, the playoffs and the Earth Series were the talk of all the sports bars. Postal had already written his column for the following day and so now he was ready to do some serious drinking. And for a young nerdy statistician Burr was holding his own with his martinis. He had also finished work for the day.

"I've got another question for you, Kid."

"Shoot." Burr tried to hide the fact that he hated it when Postal called him "Kid."

"Who do you think got the best of the situation in the new contract ...the players or the owners? It's been more than a month since they announced the settlement, and all the fans seem to care about is that there won't be a strike. What do you think? Who won?"

"I'd probably have to say the same thing that Mr. Selout has been saying. The contract is a win-win. Both sides got a lot out of it and most importantly, as you said there was no strike."

"Okay then, aside from the money issues and the labor peace, what about the steroid stuff. Selout is trying to tell everyone that they are finally doing something about steroids like he's really proud of the agreement. But it's really nothing at all. It's total horseshit. They will continue the testing in the minor leagues with no penalties other than

Going Postal in The Morning After

drug counseling ... as if that's some kind of penalty. And the major league testing doesn't start until next season and it's on a trial basis. What the fuck does that mean? A trial basis?"

"The union insisted that the testing would be on a trial basis and that it would only be testing for specific steroids, not for other stuff like cocaine, marijuana or amphetamines. The testing is only for the so called 'performance enhancing drugs.' It contends testing for that other stuff would be an invasion of privacy."

"F*** that s***. Now there's a croc ..."

"It is what it is ..."

"Didn't we once have a president who said something like that?"

"No. Slick Clinty said: 'It depends upon what the definition of is, is.' He was arguing *tense*. Regardless, Clint Blanton and The Commish have a lot in common."

"What do you mean?"

"They were both outed for trying to hide something. The public found out that Selout was *going* bald when the fans dumped beer on him in Spiller Park. The public found out that Blanton was *getting* balled when he dumped Veronica Cummings-Dresser and she spilled the fact that he spilled."

"Do they teach you all that double talk at the commissioner's office?"

Burr looked at Postal with a sense of pride at having the newsman actually treat him like an equal. He was able to take the conversation in another direction if he wanted to and didn't have to simply always answer Postal's questions about the commissioner in order to get a free dinner out of it. He ignored Postal's jab and got off the topic of politics and went back to their earlier discussion of the contract and PEDs.

"You're probably right about the bogus testing for PEDs. The new contract doesn't really do much. But I guess you have to start somewhere"

"But this new 'trial testing' is being put in place so that Selout and the owners know more about what's happening. They're not going to punish anyone for cheating. They're not even going to publish any

Flunking Chemistry Class

of the names of the cheaters. It's hard to believe that Selout's actually trying to sell this horseshit to the public as progress."

Postal flipped back his shot of bourbon and took a full gulp of his beer. He shook his head vehemently and then continued by adding another cryptic assessment.

"Maybe Selout's doing the right thing. Just *act* like you care. That might satisfy the few of us who actually give a shit about the integrity of the game."

"More than a few people care about …"

"F*** that s***." Lester Postal cut off his rental friend in mid sentence. "Especially here in New York. Do you think any of the Bloomers' fans care that their team is a veritable armada of floats?" He then answered his own question without waiting for the scrawny statistician to reply. "Of course they don't. They just want Sledgehammer to go out and buy another winner. They could care less how juiced the players are."

"The Bloomers aren't the only team that employs floats."

"Yeah, but nobody knows for sure who is cheating and who is playing it straight. That's why they should have real testing, and publish the names of the cheaters and then throw them the fuck out of the game. Then we could have our fucking game back."

As the booze was getting to Postal he began to get more foul and cantankerous, which was never a good sign for Joey Dee, the bar owner. Three bar stools away from them an equally irritable and inebriated patron of *The Morning After* decided to join the conversation.

"Hey dipshit, what are you saying about the Bloomers? Are you trying to tell me that they don't deserve to win? Every team has floats, man. We just have the best floats. So take that cheating crap and shove it up your ass."

The belligerent man joining the conversation was wearing a Bronx Bloomers hat with a 2000 Earth Series insignia on the side of the cap. He apparently wanted to ensure that no one doubted his allegiance. However he remained seated while he delivered his diatribe. He was a large man who was wearing clothes that were two sizes too tight for his ample girth. He was at least twice the size of Timmy Burr and a good

Going Postal in The Morning After

bit larger and much younger than Lester Postal. He was clearly obese but appeared to be a stout person beneath the evident layers of human lard. However the *New York Roast* reporter never backed down from a barroom squabble.

"Who asked you asshole?"

The large fleshy Bloomers fan looked startled that Postal would offer any verbal rebuttal whatsoever. He was obviously used to having the final word in this kind of situation. And he had no idea who the reporter was or why he cared any more than the next baseball fan.

"Who are you calling an asshole, you worthless little shitbug? Besides if you think that the Bloomers are the only team with floats, I'll quote you a price on the Brooklyn Bridge."

The big man uncorked his dissent in a flustered manner and then as though his rebuttal needed verbal backup rather than mere physically menacing support, he added, "Look at the Asps, man. They've got lots of floats on that pitching staff. Those fucking guys are like a hundred years old, man. Look at Sandy Jackson. The guy may be 7 ft 3 inches tall, but he's also almost 40 years old. How the fuck can a guy that averages a little over 200 strikeouts a year through most of his career crank it up in his late thirties so that he averages 340 K's a year for the last five years. The rumor is that they call Jackson the Big Eunuch because his johnson doesn't like the juicin'. That's a pretty tall price to pay for a few extra strikeouts. And that other clown they have out there on the Asps, Kirk Shrillage. He keeps flapping his jaws about other people juicing, while pretending that people don't notice how buff he has gotten. What an asshole! Or maybe I should call him an *Asphole*. The pitcher doth protest too much, methinks."

Besides being surprised to hear the fleshy Bloomers fan end his string of expletives by paraphrasing a quote from Hamlet, Timmy Burr began to worry that this dispute was beginning to heat up. Once before he had witnessed Lester going postal and the scene wasn't pretty. He tried to intervene before things got out of hand. He got off his barstool and walked between the two verbal combatants in an attempt to mediate. "What my friend was simply trying to say ..."

Flunking Chemistry Class

"Who the hell are you, Henry fucking Kissinger? Get out of my way you little twerp." He put his meaty hand on Burr's shoulder and began to move him out of the space where Burr had planted himself.

Lester Postal was moved. He wasn't at all scared. But he was emotionally charged. He had heard Timmy Burr call him "his friend." Since grammar school he had been called "asshole" thousands of times. He had been called "shithead," hundreds of times. And he had been called "a drunk," "a dirtball" and "a deadbeat" by four ex-wives. But it had been an awfully long time since someone called him "a friend." He leaped out of his barstool with his right fist firmly wrapped around the handle of the beer mug of an innocent bystander (*bysitter?*) who happened to occupy the stool between Postal and Fleshy Bloomers Cap.

Overhand right ... beer mug hits Fleshy ... beer splashes Bysitter ... Bysitter goes after Sportswriter ... Fleshy's bleeding from broken tooth through lip ... Bysitter grabs Sportswriter as Fleshy wipes lip ... Fleshy swings roundhouse at Sportswriter while Bysitter holds him from behind ... Fleshy whiffs with roundhouse... follow through from whiff hits Bysitter #2, a Cute Young Thing, heretofore minding her own business ... CYT's Boyfriend AKA Bysitter #3 hits fleshy in back of neck ... Fleshy goes down hard just as Fleshy's buddy returns from men's room ... Fleshy's buddy clobbers CYT's Boyfriend... CYT's BF goes down hard next to Fleshy on the floor ...meanwhile ... Statistician pulls Bysitter #1 off Sportswriter ... Sportswriter defends honor of CYT by belting Fleshy's buddy with the remnants of beer mug ... more blood ... *The Morning After* bouncers arrive late to the melee ... Lester goes postal ... Bouncers bounce Postal.

After the police arrived, everyone agreed the fight had started outside the bar. Postal's most fervent readership consisted of cops and firemen. It was nice to have fans, and now Lester Postal even had a friend. Five weeks later Joey Dee allowed Postal back in *The Morning After*. No harm no foul. Postal's young friend, Timmy Burr was busy at nights at

Going Postal in The Morning After

law school, but the baseball season was over anyway. Things were slowing down for the winter at the commissioner's office.

The friendship between Timmy Burr and Lester Postal continued to grow over the next season as they commiserated with each other about the state of the sport of baseball. Meanwhile they each began spending as much time at *The Morning After* as they did at their respective jobs. Remarkably Timmy Burr somehow earned his law degree at the end of 2003.

IX

The Juice-Off by the Bay

April 2004

The closer for the Hollywood Hedgers was having a remarkable *run at* the record books. In fact he had already *run over* the record book. Derrick Goodyear had closed 63 straight games without blowing a save opportunity. (He would eventually take the record to 84 straight games.) It was by far the longest streak of its kind in all of baseball. Not even the Bronx Bloomers closer, Riviera Sandmando, had a streak that could come close to Goodyear's run. It was a freaky streak to say the least. Even Goodyear himself was surprised by how easily he was mowing down the opposition.

And Goodyear had a crafty cover for the fact that he was a juicer. The concealment came from the fact that he was a pitcher. For whatever reason, the general public did not suspect pitchers of juicing nearly as much as they suspected hitters of "roiding up." There were some exceptions. No one had much doubt about Jelly Rogers. And there was more than a little suspicion about a few other pitchers that were beginning to throw harder in their late thirties and even in their early forties than they did as twenty year olds. However, for the most part, pitchers had somehow managed to escape the scrutiny that now seemed to accompany every at bat of the game's power hitters.

Meanwhile Goodyear was the talk of Hollywood. He had come up with the Hedgers in 1999 and pitched parts of three years with

The Juice-Off by the Bay

the Hollywood club as a starting pitcher with a fastball in the low to mid nineties and with a still developing changeup. He came to spring training in 2002 after spending the off season transforming into a float. The ballooning process miraculously added about 6 to 8 mph to his fastball and he became the Hotshot's closer. Combining his new found four seam fastball that frequently was clocked in triple digits with a disappearing changeup and a bad ass curve ball, games were essentially over the moment Goodyear came into the game. From the end of August of 2002 through the entire season of 2003 *(He won the Sly Jung Award in 2003)* and into the first month of 2004 Goodyear had not blown a single save. He had already passed the old record of 54 with his streak of 63. It appeared as if he would never fail in a save situation.

The 2004 baseball season was merely three weeks old. The Hollywood Hedgers were playing the Bay City Mammoths in San Francisco. This was a century old rivalry that had moved across the country in the 1950's along with the teams that used to play in the Brooklyn and Manhattan boroughs of New York City. Some people argued that the rivalry between the Beantown Wallbangers and the Bronx Bloomers was the biggest rivalry in baseball. However in reality the Wallbangers hadn't won an Earth Series since Woodrow Wilson was President of the United States and the Bloomers had won 26 of the damn things. So the case could be made that the rivalry between the Hedgers and the Mammoths was the most intense, although neither team had won much lately.

Normally games in April don't mean a lot in the stretch of a season that goes more than 160 games. But whenever the Hedgers and the Mammoths laced up their spikes to do battle against one another, the game meant something to the fans. Neither the Hedgers nor the Mammoths had won an Earth Series in quite some time. In fact the Bay City Mammoths hadn't won an Earth Series in 50 years. Their last Series Championship came in 1954 during their days in the city of New York when they were known as the Manhattan Mammoths. In the interim the Hedgers had won six Earth Series Championships, but they had not won one since 1988. And as everyone associated with the

Flunking Chemistry Class

MBL was now well aware; there was nothing more important than the Earth Series.

So between championships the fans of the Mammoths and the Hedgers had to be satisfied with the individual performance records of their players. And currently the two most exciting players were Harry Bombs for the Mammoths and Derrick Goodyear for the Hedgers.

The mid-April game progressed rather routinely through the early innings. The Hedgers built a 3-0 lead in a rather pedestrian fashion scoring single runs in the first inning and then again in the sixth. Meanwhile the Hotshot's starting pitcher, Otis Paralysis, was mowing down the Mammoths. Paralysis, a journeyman left hander, had been careful throughout the game when he was pitching to Harry Bombs, the notorious Mammoth float. But now in the bottom of the ninth, the Hedgers decided to bring on their closer, Derrick Goodyear to face the 2, 3 and 4 hitters in the Bay City Mammoth's lineup. The cleanup hitter was none other than Harry Bombs.

The crowd of more than 42,000 fans was on its feet after Goodyear walked the first batter, but there was a collective groan when the next batter popped out to the center fielder. That meant that Bombs could not tie the ball game with a "Bombshot to the Bay." A homerun would only make the score 3-2. Goodyear could allow a long ball to Bombs and still retire the next two hitters and gain his 64th straight save.

Goodyear quickly got Bombs into an 0-2 hole with a change-up that Bombs got a little piece of and a curve that Bombs bunted foul. That's when something very weird began to play out.

On the mound – Right-hander Derrick Goodyear was 28 years old, and had inflated his physique up to 220 pounds. He wore his uniform loose and blousy. If he was at a venue other than a baseball diamond he could have easily been mistaken for a bag lady. He also was hygienically

The Juice-Off by the Bay

challenged. His cap was filthy and his fingernails had a quarter inch of dirt under them. Large ugly looking goggles hid his wild-eyed 'roid-ridden facial features.

At the plate – Lefty-swinging long ball hitter Harry Bombs was the "float of floats." At 40 years of age, no one could believe that he was officially listed as 6'1" tall and 195 pounds. The fact of the matter was that there was a PED induced layer of humanoid stuffing that surrounded the bottom of his feet and the top of his scull that added an inch to the top and bottom of his body now making him 6'3" tall. The port and starboard sides of this ship were also swelling with waves of steroidal bulk. He tipped the scales somewhere around 235 pounds.

These two ogres were standing 60' 6" apart when Goodyear stared in at Bombs after his bunt attempt. *What was that all about? Was Bombs trying to make fun of him for throwing off-speed stuff? Wasn't he taking this game seriously?* The thought seemed to occur to Bombs and Goodyear almost simultaneously. It was no longer about playing baseball. It was time for a JUICE-OFF!!!

Goodyear removed his goggles momentarily and wiped his eyes with the back of his disgustingly dirty sleeve. It was almost as though he was adding camouflage dirt to his face to make the Juice-Off all the more dramatic. With the goggles back in place, he stared in at the catcher and immediately shook off the call for another off speed delivery. There would be no more of that stuff. This would be simply juice-against-juice. This was not the time for chicken-shit off speed pitches. The next pitch registered 99 mph but was high and wide and Bombs lay off it. The following pitch was 100 mph but again it was high and wide and again Bombs let it go. Then he stepped back out of the batter's box with the count even at 2 and 2.

The crowd was now into it. They could see what was happening. They too became much more enamored with the Juice-Off than with the game itself. Goodyear was paying no attention to the runner on first and for that matter the runner on first was paying no attention to Goodyear. Like the other 42,000 people watching in the stadium and millions of fans watching on TV, the runner on first was far more interested in the unfolding Juice-Off.

Flunking Chemistry Class

Bombs stepped back into the batter's box and did away with all sense of pretense as he dared Goodyear to throw his best heater once again. He waved his hand across the plate about chest high. The goggled Hotshot hurler would not be intimidated. He kicked at the dirt around the rubber and then flared his nostrils like a raging bull ready to charge. The fielders behind him stood relatively motionless. If Bombs actually wanted to try to bunt again he could have walked into second base before a fielder would react. All eyeballs were glued on Goodyear as he went into his stretch and reared way back and threw his best four seam heater. The radar gun said 101. Bombs got a little piece of it to stay alive. Goodyear was aghast. *How the hell did he hit that – 101 mph heater with hop on it? Are his 'roids that much better than mine?*

Bombs stepped out of the box again. But this time he stepped right back in and then he once again motioned for Goodyear to take his best shot. Everyone in the stands was standing and screaming. It was almost as though the crowd itself had taken an injection of something.

Goodyear reloaded quickly. His nostrils flared wider than ever. He was being transformed from a closer to a colossus by the crowd. He reared back and fired. In that fraction of an instant it appeared as though everything and everyone in the park was stopped – freeze-framed in a rare moment of time. There were only three moving entities. Goodyear's arm, Bombs' bat and the tiny white cowhide sphere of a baseball that had been instantly launched where no ball had ever gone before. The sound of the bat on the ball could clearly be heard above the awed silence of the crowd. Goodyear's *103* mph heater had been deposited way back in the Bay, in a section called McWillie's Cove some 580 feet from home plate but foul by more than 75 feet.

The players on the field and in both dugouts stared, stupefied by the stupendous shot by Harry Bombs. Every single player had the same thought simultaneously. *WHAT KIND OF JUICE ALLOWS YOU TO PULL A 103 MPH HEATER FOUL BY 75 FEET!?!?*

On the mound, Goodyear had given up. He knew that fair or foul it didn't matter. He had just lost. There was no fair or foul in a Juice-Off. Bombs had squeezed him fair and square and splashed him to

The Juice-Off by the Bay

second place in the contest that would long be remembered as the "Juice-Off by the Bay."

Goodyear resigned himself to the fact that he had lost the Juice-Off and went back to trying to simply close out the baseball game. He backed off on the next pitch, the seventh of the at-bat and threw his fastball at an even 100 mph. Bombs deposited it in the center field bleachers, and then Goodyear retired the next two batters for the save as the Hedgers took the opening game of the series 3-2. It was a small consolation prize for Goodyear and the Hedgers.

Lester Postal and his fifth wife Georgette were on their honeymoon in San Francisco. Georgette was the first woman who wasn't a stripper before she became Mrs. Postal. Lester Postal's first four marriages had spanned 31 years but he had only been married a total of 7 years and 7 months during that time frame. He had now been married to Georgette for a total of 7 days and he was actually hoping that this marriage might last longer than his record to date of 2 years and 9 months of marital bliss (*er... marital misery.*) It wasn't like Postal hadn't learned from his mistakes. Marriages numbered two, three, four and now five, were all preceded by a prenuptial agreement. Marriage number one, to Lola Doveface was the longest in duration. Marriage number four, to Mona Morningstar was the shortest, barely lasting a full baseball season. But Lester's latest nuptials seemed more promising to him. His new wife was a young lawyer and the best man at his wedding was a young lawyer as well. Not only did Lester think that this afforded a certain degree of respectability, but it also demonstrated that he now had a *true* friend, Timothy Burr, Esq.

There was a good reason why Georgette was a lawyer and not a pole dancer. Georgette weighed nearly 310 pounds and that would have made for one weighty lap dance. But Georgette was a woman of goals and ambition. It had been her goal to make it under 300 pounds for their wedding and she fell a mere 8 to 10 pounds short of her

Flunking Chemistry Class

goal depending on whether the weigh-in occurred before or after her lunch hour.

Georgette and Lester had some things in common. They both loved to eat and drink and they both loved baseball. Lester was 24 years older than his wife and 124 pounds lighter than Georgette, but neither of these separations were of any consequence to either person. Lester Postal was Georgette's first and only lover and she enjoyed his company immensely. She thought of her sportswriter-husband as a very clever and talented scribe. Lester knew that Georgette was largely different from women he had known in the past. She had backbone ... in there somewhere.

Before Marty Cimonelli, Georgette's obese father, died of a heart attack at an early age, he used to read Postal's column to his daughter every day until Georgette was old enough to read it herself and then later they would argue the merits of whatever point Postal was trying to make in his column. Father and daughter would often take opposite sides in these debates just for the fun of arguing. Georgette's father believed that this would be great preparation for the ultimate occupation in wait for his daughter: lawyer.

Now after graduating from law school and being admitted to the bar in New York State, Georgette still loved to debate just about anything. However she was not disarmingly disagreeable. In fact she was usually comfortable taking either side of a debate. And although she would dispute just about anything at any time, she rarely actually cared about the position she staked out, even though she would defend her position vociferously. It was the argument itself that was important, not the principle or position that was being defended.

Her cantankerous character and challenging disposition made Georgette Cimonelli the perfect match for Lester Postal. In fact her argumentative skills actually charmed Postal because Lester also enjoyed arguing. And like Lester, Georgette would sometimes argue just for the hell of it. In any case it was about the only exercise she ever got.

Georgette had been in Timmy Burr's law school class and met Postal through Burr. Burr had set up the date by telling Postal that

The Juice-Off by the Bay

one of his classmates was a big fan of his and in fact might actually have a crush on him. But he never told Lester how *big* a fan Georgette was until they actually met one another. For once Postal was actually speechless when he saw her. Postal hadn't been expecting a beauty queen, but he might have anticipated a scholarly looking young woman, who might approximate the nerdy appearance of a female version of Burr. He might have even tolerated a zit or two. But Postal's original impression of Georgette was Roseanne Barr on steroids. This was not only a woman who had a crush on him. It was a woman who could crush him period.

It wasn't exactly love at first sight. Georgette was a bit surprised at how old Postal looked. She too had anticipated a somewhat different looking date. These expectations were brought on by the picture of Lester that accompanied his column in *The Roast*. The picture was fifteen years old and Lester had aged twenty years since it was taken. But Burr had done an effective job of playing matchmaker. Lester and Georgette only argued for seven months before they got engaged and then they happily argued, debated, disputed and contested their way to the altar two months later.

Lester had wanted to go to Las Vegas for their honeymoon. Georgette argued for Hawaii. They compromised on San Francisco only after Lester had surreptitiously checked out the baseball calendar to see if the Mammoths were playing home games that week.

Lester and Georgette were on hand for the Roid-Off between Goodyear and Bombs and when it was all over Georgette wanted an explanation from Lester as to why the Bay City fans were leaving the stadium in such good spirits.

"I don't quite get it, Lester. The fans here in San Francisco don't seem to be at all upset by the fact that the Hedgers took the game."

"Think of it as the game within the game."

"What does that mean?"

"Bombs basically proved to Goodyear that he could beat him whenever he wanted to. There's a lot more games left in the season. Tonight was only one game. Until we get further into the season people don't get as uptight about wins and losses. When these young players make

Flunking Chemistry Class

it to The Show, they are expected to deliver on significant individual performances and then as the season moves along they put together a run as a team. The performances within the team are what I mean by the game within the game. So the Hedgers won the game but Bombs won the Roid-Off against Goodyear."

"We keep hearing more and more about steroids and how many players are using them. Don't you think it's unfair ...I mean ... just because Goodyear and Bombs are both juiced up?"

"Sure it's unfair. In a strange kind of way these guys also compete against players that are dead and gone. The true joy of following baseball is in the statistics. Our mutual friend Timmy Burr must have told you that."

"Of course, but I don't need Timmy Burr to tell me that. Remember I've been a fan since I was old enough to eat a doughnut, and long before I was able to swill a beer. Lest you forget, Lester, I was also the one who told you to bet on the Miami Minnows last year in the Earth Series against Joe Trophy's Bronx Bloomers."

"And I did. I took your advice about good float pitching stopping good float hitting on most occasions. But it's too bad the Minnows owners let some of their floats off the tether after the season. Heck, they sign I Dork to catch for one season and then they let him go. Anyway after the Bloomers got A Dork in the trade this winter, they have to be the favorites once again. They'll have some left side of the infield with A Dork at third and Jared Leader at short."

"Don't be so sure. A Dork is ready to take over for Harry Bombs as the game's most notorious float. And how many championships have the Mammoths won while Bombs has been on the team?" Georgette raised her eyebrows in anticipation of an answer and when one didn't come immediately she added, "Try none. You see? Floats are nice to have but it takes more than just floats to win the Earth Series."

"Don't lecture me on this topic, Georgette. Believe me I know the score. It's just like the spectacle we just witnessed. These floats are just out for themselves. Let the team be damned."

"You're making my point for me, Lester. If Bombs and Goodyear only care about their own stats, then why would A Dork be any different?

The Juice-Off by the Bay

That's why I think that the Bloomers shouldn't be the favorites. And who knows about the chemistry between Leader and Dorquez. For my money, I'd have to say that the Wallbangers are overdue and that this will be their year."

"Come on Georgette, the Wallbangers never win anything."

Mr. and Mrs. Postal continued to enjoy their little argument as they waddled away from the stadium and back toward the Hyatt Hotel where they were staying. It was a bit of a long walk, about a mile and a half, but it was difficult to catch a cab after the game. It would have been even more difficult for Georgette to climb into the back of the cab if they were able to catch one in the first place. So they simply walked. Georgette thought for a second about her husband's declaration about the Wallbangers' futility. She caught her breath and then stopped in the middle of the sidewalk and stated her own conviction.

"Trust me Lester this is their year. They have some terrific floats. Manboy Ramendez, Peppy Orbits and the shortstop Roman Raggarappia all had more than 100 RBI's last season. Ronny Jamon also had ridiculous power numbers for a leadoff hitter. It looks to me like they've got their chemistry just right on that ball club."

"All right Georgette. I'll lay a few bucks on the Wallbangers in your honor. But I'll tell you this much. If you're right with your prediction, Bass Sledgehammer will go nuclear, and I wouldn't want to be in Joe Trophy's shoes."

"You've got to wonder about that man, Sledgehammer. Does he think he's the only person who knows how to *buy* an Earth Series Championship? Some of the newer owners have a few bucks too. They know how to buy floats as well."

"We'll see what happens. But this goes back to your original question. You know: Is it fair? On one hand if almost all of the players are juiced, then who's jerking whose chain? MBL baseball is then just one big juice-off." He paused to let this position set in and then offered up an opposing position. "On the other hand, if a smaller percentage of the players use PEDs then you could argue that it's cheating. And at a bare minimum, most of these drugs are illegal and that makes the juicers law breakers.

Flunking Chemistry Class

"Oh Lester, I think you are dramatically understating the problem. Kids look up to these floats. And these drugs are dangerous. The side effects of steroids are downright scary. They can impact your heart and liver big time. That's what killed that football player, Ly D'Lylayoh, in the nineties. Unless you are working under a prescription and direction of a physician it's real easy to overdue everything."

"You think it's stupid, Georgette. I know that. But some of these guys get some quack doctors involved in it as well so there's no telling what extremes they'll go to in order to hit a few more homers. And you left out some of the other side effects like getting your endocrine gland system all hosed up causing the crazy stuff like 'roid rage and other nonsense. And when they screw around with testosterone, the balls shrink, the dick withers and ... and ... and ... no wonder they go into a rage."

Postal almost seemed to be feeling a sort of visceral anger that occasionally overcame him whenever he felt needlessly challenged on a subject. He continued, "I can't think of anything that might piss a guy off more than a dysfunctional petered out pecker and shrunken nut syndrome."

The Postals resumed their slow stroll toward the Hyatt at the Embarcadero Center. They both lapsed into a quiet phase as they moved at a pace that slowed from gradual to glacial. When a cabbie driving a minivan slowed next to them and inquired, "Taxi?" they decided together that they would squeeze into the back seat of the taxi-van. The cab then quickly whisked them the rest of the way to the hotel. They walked inside and entered one of the glass elevators that lifted them toward their 38th floor hotel room.

As they rode up in the elevator, high above the dramatic open indoor lobby, Georgette reverted back to their earlier conversation. "You and I have both ignored one other constituent party that is significantly damaged by the steroid epidemic."

"Who's that?"

"The minor league ballplayers ... the ones who are clean and never make it to the majors. Their pathways are blocked by the steroid junkies who are breaking the law. They are also obstructed by MBL

The Juice-Off by the Bay

because of its lax attitude toward the problem. MBL is clearly negligent, at best."

Georgette thought for a second or two and then as the elevator arrived at their floor she added, "There's a significant difference in pay between the salary and endorsements of the 25th man on the roster and the guy who gets cut and has to play in a Triple A league. The difference is hundreds of thousands of dollars each year. Over a potential career, we're talking millions of dollars in compensation differential for the 25th man versus the 26th man. As a lawyer I'd have to say that there's a law suit in there someplace and no shortage of culprits to sue. Some day that has got to catch up with them."

They left the elevator on the 38th floor and the Postals made their way to their room near the rear of the floor. They were both a little tired but still in good spirits. Georgette went straight to the bathroom and began to take a long shower. Lester joined her briefly in the shower and then went back into the bedroom and donned a pair of undershorts. He lay down on the bed and then began clicking through the TV stations looking for a sports channel.

Georgette continued showering for more than twenty minutes and Lester knew that when she finally finished, she would be in an amorous mood. Lester Postal had a good deal more experience in the ways of the world than did his much younger bride. And although this was their honeymoon, Lester had mastered the intricacies of making love to such a large woman several months earlier. In fact he cherished the warm comfort of his new bride's gargantuan girth much more than he had appreciated the perfunctory sexual gambits of the four slender pole-spinning females who had been his previous partners. He vastly enjoyed satisfying his massive mate, whereas he regarded sexual encounters with his previous wives as simple urge fulfillment. And if the need wasn't there to scratch his itch, then Lester usually wasn't there either. Lester was happy that Georgette was not only a more suitable companion for him than any of his previous wives but she was also beginning to be much better at pole work.

When she came out of the bathroom, Georgette was wearing a two piece 4X hot pink night gown. The top piece angled out from her neck and shoulders and covered her body down to where her waist would have been had she enjoyed such a feature. It flared out like a large pink lampshade. Matching triple spandex pink pantaloons completed the two piece nightgown.

Georgette also wore an expansive smile and had taken the time to run a comb through her shoulder length brown hair. She noticed that Lester had a small pill box next to the bedside. She knew that Lester had been taking some medication for allergies and other minor maladies but had never inquired about these pharmacological remedies in the past. Lester was at least temporarily engrossed in the highlight replays on the TV and didn't seem to be immediately moved by her plentiful pinkness. So to move his interest away from the sports channel she inquired about his prescriptions.

"What sort of pills do you take, Lester?" It was intended to be an innocuous conversation re-starter.

Postal looked up from the bed and answered the inoffensive question with a steadfast response. "Not much ... I take Claritin for allergies; some kind of an anti-inflammatory drug that I can't pronounce to control my gout; and I also take Levitra as needed."

"Levitra? What's that?"

"You know, it's like Viagra and Cialis. It's for ... well it helps with ... you know... it's a PED ... a performance enhancing drug."

Georgette's smile flushed a full anticipatory pink that nearly matched her nightgown. She stared at her husband undershorts briefly and then flopped down on the bed next to him. She put her meaty right hand on his left upper thigh, and encouragingly intoned, "Okay Slugger; batter up."

X

CoJo and Jelly Settling Some Scores.

June 2004

Jelly Rogers and CoJo Janesco were meeting in a titty bar for jocks called the Score Book Club, in Miami. Rogers was in town because his current team the Houston Arrows was playing the Miami Minnows. Woody Lions was there also but the world's greatest golfer paid no attention to his fellow athletes. He was focused on moving his escort toward the privacy section of the VIP suites near the rear of the club.

There were several other recognizable athletes in the barroom area, adjacent to the center dance platform. The main dance stage had seven different stripper poles. At various different points in time these poles became limb support for the dancers in various stages of dishabille. There was another dance platform on either side of the main stage and each of these platforms embraced three more stripper poles. These dance platforms were elevated above the floor seating area that was being worked by the waitresses, who were strippers on break. The stripper-waitresses were scantily attired and would gladly serve more than cocktails if the proper financial incentives were produced. Continuous loud music permeated the main area of the club that contained the dance platforms and the seating area. Some of the seats were placed around small round tables and others lined the

Flunking Chemistry Class

perimeter of each of the dance platforms. Many of the male patrons sitting around the small tables were paying by the song to receive rhythmic private attention of varied musical duration from the stripper-waitresses. Occasionally when a patron wanted his waitress to hum a different tune they moved on to the VIP area for Valued Individualized Preferences.

The whole setup of the Score Book Club was laid out in such a way that the male patrons could adjust their interest level in the sexual offerings that were provided. The barroom area was the least intense. The visuals were still excellent with a number of attractive half naked barmaids mixing cocktails, but the only seating was about two dozen bar stools that lined the perimeter of the large oval bar. There was some standing room behind the bar stools but no other seating. This made the barroom area very impractical for the purpose of lap dances, although the next such performance would not be the first.

CoJo Janesco was very comfortable in every environment of the Score Book Club. He had always delighted in being surrounded by beautiful naked bodies. He was a frequent visitor to the Score Book Clubs in Tampa and New York as well as the one they were now sitting at in Miami. He was wearing tight denim shorts and a custom made open necked floral shirt, with shorter sleeves that allowed him to show off his massive arm muscles. His biceps and triceps were so perfectly formed that he delighted in reaching for things so that he could stretch and flex his muscles and flaunt his physique. He made a point of keeping his drink at least two feet away from him on the bar. Janesco found it hard to believe that he had now been retired from baseball for more than two years.

Jelly Rogers had also retired ... and then unretired from baseball. After going through a comedic charade of retirement antics in 2003 during his last year with the Bronx Bloomers, he made a u-turn decision on retirement and signed a contract with his hometown team, the Houston Arrows, thereby sending Larry "Bass" Sledgehammer into a tirade back in New York. The Jelly Man and fellow teammate and juicer, Randy Elfin, had deserted the Bloomers and signed on with the

CoJo and Jelly Settling Some Scores.

Arrows, in a manner that an irate Sledgehammer referred to as the departures of Judas and Benedict Arnold.

Sledgehammer, who had now endured three years in a row without an Earth Series Championship, had vowed to restock his 'float fleet' through free agency. However he was exasperated by the fact that most of the best floats in the game remained tethered to their own teams. He was only able to add one noteworthy free agent float and that was slugger Gorey Schlepfield, AKA "the Assassin." However Sledgehammer was not able to add a suitable free agent float to his starting rotation and he was growing concerned that the Bloomers' arch rivals, the Beantown Wallbangers, were beginning to come into their own. He was very worried. He didn't want to go another year without an Earth Series Championship because as everybody knew; there is nothing more important than the Earth Series.

Sledgehammer genuinely scared Jelly Rogers, and when Rogers went into a place like the Score Book Club, he acted as though he half expected to see a couple of Tony Soprano's men under contract to Sledgehammer and ready to rip his eyeballs out. So while CoJo Janesco languorously leaned back on his barstool, Jelly sat stiffly in his.

"You're not really going to rat out other ball players in this stupid little book of yours are you?"

"What difference does it make? Relax Jelly …you've already made about a guzzillion dollars. They can't take that back from you. You were about to retire anyway before you decided to do this gig with the Arrows. Besides, I'm only telling the truth."

"So why do you have to go and tell everyone. Everyone doesn't have to know about it. Why do you need to write a goddam book about it?

"Everyone *already* knows about it, Jelly. People realize that the game and most of its players are totally juiced. I'm just giving the insiders view. Hell, I started a lot of you guys on the stuff to begin with. I've been injecting myself for twenty years and have been helping the rest of you guys for most of that time as well. I think I deserve a lot of credit for turning the game of baseball around. I want to be known as the 'Emperor of Steroids.' Do you think for one minute that Popeye

Maloney would have smashed 70 dingers without my help? No way. I showed him the ropes, Jelly. Without my help Popeye would have been the 'Sultan of Squat.' I just want to get the credit I'm due that's all."

"Well I want to make it to the Corridor of Conceit. That has been a goal of mine since day one. I want to see my plaque on the wall. And that's the reason I wanted to talk to you … to tell you not to mention my name at all in this fucked up book of yours. Got it?"

"So you want a stupid plaque on the wall. How about a *PED-estal* in the hall? Wouldn't that be more appropriate?

"I don't see anything funny about this, CoJo. You're really fucking up a good thing for a lot of us."

"Relax Jelly. You look like you've got one of those stripper poles up your ass. If it makes you happy I'll leave you and Dolly out of it."

"What do you mean me *and Dolly?*

"Well if I'm going to tell the story the right way, I want to include all of the supporting actors and *actresses.* We both know that a lot of the ballplayers have encouraged their women to use steroids also. Look around you, man. You don't think these heavenly bodies just fell to earth the way they are, do you?" Janesco didn't wait for an answer from Rogers. He simply called over one of the girls that he had tipped well in the past. "Come here, Sugar and give CoJo a little feel." The waitress was working the floor outside the bar area and had to walk past several standing patrons to make her way over to Janesco and Rogers. She was wearing next to nothing at all, just some red lace panties and a sheer red lace halter. Her breasts stood out like two large melons. When she reached the spot where Janesco was seated, he handed her a twenty and then he reached inside her halter top and gave her left breast a slight squeeze. "Feels just like Dolly," Janesco laughed, but not in a mean spirited way. Jelly Rogers didn't laugh at all. In fact he was amazed that he was able to suppress the urge to belt Janesco in the mouth. Instead he just looked at the Cuban ex-ballplayer and said: "Fuck you CoJo."

XI

The Texan Does the Carolinas

July 2004

Sam Crockett was moving on up. He was gaining a certain degree of mastery of the strike zone that had eluded him in the past. He was still able to hit 97 on the radar gun with his four seamer but now he was able to hit 93 with his two seamer and cut it to either side of the plate. He still threw his curveball but it had become a minor part of his arsenal. He had only thrown four changeups all year and hadn't enticed a single hitter to swing at any of them, with three of the four off speed pitches harmlessly dropping out of the strike zone.

Two years after being traded to the Bloomers organization and his great debut in the Mexican fall league, Crockett was definitely on the radar of the Bronx Bloomers' brass. His first full year in the Bloomers establishment was interrupted by a knee operation after he had sustained a torn ACL shortly before spring training. The latter part of the season he spent with the Bloomers developmental team in Florida. After a second season in the Mexican Fall League, Crockett had pitched very well in the 2004 Minor League Spring Training camp of the Bronx Bloomers. This showing had earned him his very first full season Class A assignment. He was now pitching for the Beaufort Baby Bloomers of the Atlantic Coastal League and he was off to a great start with a 7 and 2 record and a 2.60 ERA in the first half of the season.

Flunking Chemistry Class

Most noticeable to the parent team back in New York was a combination of facts that were reported on a weekly wrap that was sent north from Beaufort: The fact that Crockett had struck out 82 batters in only 69 innings was a big plus even though he had also walked 32; The fact that he had hit six batters was considered a plus – meanness – rather than a minus; The fact that Sudden Sam Crockett was still only 20 years old meant that he was considered a "prospect," and that he had a shot at making it to The Show. The fact that Crockett had not yet embraced the STR, the *specialized training regimen*, was viewed both positively and negatively. From a positive standpoint the powers that be within the organization believed that Crockett's "easy cheese" was achieved without the benefit of PEDs. This meant that there was a much higher ceiling that might be achieved on the MPH of his heater. From a negative standpoint, according to his agent Brad Scott, Sam Crockett seemed to be one of the few young athletes in the system that was not open minded to the possibility of participating in an STR. This was disconcerting back in New York and might impact decisions later in the year.

The Crockett family had also made a decision. They were getting by financially – thanks to some of the Mexican League incentive payments and a couple of months working in the drilling bit business squeezed in between seasons. However they weren't thriving. Therefore Sam Crockett and his 19 year old wife, together with their 2 sons – two year old JR and one year old Rory – had decided to move into an apartment in Beaufort, South Carolina for the duration of the Baby Bloomers baseball season. While the organization certainly wasn't against family life, the Bloomers brass regarded this decision curiously. If Crockett continued to pitch well, they might think about promoting him from low Single A Beaufort to their high Single A affiliate in Tampa. The brass worried that the Crocketts weren't that ambitious. Had they already made the determination that they would be happy spending the entire season with the Baby Bloomers in Beaufort? That didn't seem logical. They obviously needed some extra money because Betsy Jo was occasionally getting paid a few bucks to baby sit some of the local children at the same time she was watching out for her own kids.

The Texan Does the Carolinas

Sledgehammer's minions in New York decided that they would keep a close eye on the developments in Beaufort.

Betsy Jo Crockett had never been out of the State of Texas until after she was a married mother of two young boys. Even after she was married she lived at home with her parents, Ben and Margie Boone, in the house that she had grown up in. She was a very pretty girl in a very Texas way. The men in her life ruled everything. Her father was the Lord of his castle and her husband was now the provider for her well being. Her mother set a subservient example by catering to her husband's every wish. She never disagreed with a single decision that he ever made. It wasn't that Betsy Jo's father was overtly mean in any way. It was simply a fact of his way of life that women were meant to serve and please their men and that the role of the male was to provide and protect the females of his family. So when Betsy Jo decided to take her children and follow her husband to South Carolina it represented a break with the past and a whole new life for Sam and Betsy Jo. They had finally grown up.

The first few home games for the Beaufort Baby Bloomers brought out very few fans. The kids were not yet out of school in South Carolina, so the fans were mostly family members of the team's players, a scattered couple of friends who happened to be in the area and a hard core of long term Baby Bloomers fans who seemed to have nothing better to do with their lives than watch the BB's, as they were known locally, attempt to compete against the prospects of seven other big league teams. These diehard fans frequently were disappointed by success. Whenever one of their players exceeded expectations he was moved up in the organization and the BB's were left holding the bag, so to speak. By the end of the second month of the season the fans in Beaufort had already fallen in love with Sudden Sam Crockett. Sam's beautiful wife Betsy Jo and their two young boys went to most games – whenever she wasn't babysitting for other children as well – and the people of Beaufort had embraced them also. But the good people of

Flunking Chemistry Class

Beaufort, South Carolina viewed Sam's success with a mixture of happiness and melancholy because they knew that Sam's success would soon lead to the departure of the Crockett family.

It was an early heat wave in Beaufort and Crockett was pitching a Sunday afternoon game. Sunday's games usually brought the biggest crowds and this was the biggest crowd of the year. There was already one out in the eighth inning and in spite of walking five batters, including two in the top of the eighth, Sam had only thrown 88 pitches. He had struck out seven and had yet to give up a hit. The Baby Bloomers were way ahead of the Savannah Mini Mutts, 11 – 0.

Coming up to the plate for the Mini Mutts was none other than Crocketts' former catcher and roommate Lance Leathermore. Leathermore had also been traded away from the Cheeseheads organization and was now the property of the *other* New York organization, the Metropolitan Mutts.

In the stands Betsy Jo was rooting hard for her husband. Betsy Jo was holding Rory on her lap while JR sat next to her in his stroller. There were less than a dozen maintenance and security people in the whole stadium and only two of them were younger than 50. One of these two younger men seemed to be assigned to Betsy Jo and her children exclusively, almost as though he was a private security guard. This made it a lot easier for the young woman to get her child's stroller in and out of the stadium and to maintain her seating just behind the home plate screening to the left of the home team dugout. To say that Betsy Jo enjoyed some special perks was to put it mildly. Not only did the young maintenance/security guard get food and snacks for Betsy Jo from the concession stand, he made sure that the park vendor provided these snacks gratis.

Only three of the other players on the Baby Bloomers were married and these players made their off season homes in the Dominican Republic, Panama and Venezuela respectively. These players' wives remained behind during the baseball season. This was all part of why

The Texan Does the Carolinas

Betsy Jo enjoyed some special treatment whenever she showed up at the ballpark. Another reason was Betsy Jo was a stunningly pretty young lady. Even after delivering two children, she maintained a tight shapely body to go with flawless features on a God-given beautiful face. It just seemed that everyone in Beaufort loved Betsy Jo. Beaufort was not a hotbed for baseball groupies but the few that chased after the single ballplayers were not at all put off by Betsy Jo because she posed no threat to their ambitions.

But on this particular Sunday afternoon, Betsy Jo was focused on the fact that her husband was pitching a no-hitter. What she didn't know was that Sledgehammer's boys back in the Bronx had imposed a strict pitch count on Crockett's starts. The manager of the Baby Bloomers was well aware of this limitation however and he knew he risked termination of his own contract if he allowed Crockett to throw pitch 101. Crockett was also aware of the restriction, but he believed that his manager would allow him a few extra pitches if he still had his no-no going. But Crockett also knew that he still had to get out of the eighth inning rapidly, so he was annoyed when Leathermore took the first two curveballs without the vaguest attempt to swing. Fortunately one of the pitches caught the corner for a strike. He was downright pissed off when Leathermore then proceeded to foul off four straight fastballs.

Crockett turned around on the mound and thought about Leathermore for a second and he realized that the swarthy catcher had never called for a change-up when they worked together as battery mates. It wasn't his best pitch and he hadn't thrown one the whole game, but this wasn't an ordinary game. He looked over at Betsy Jo and the boys and then got back on the rubber. He threw the change up and Leathermore blistered the pitch, but he hit it on one hop right at the shortstop for a 6-4-3 double play.

The Baby Bloomers added two more runs in the bottom of the eighth and when the Mini Mutts came to the plate in the top of the ninth, Crockett went to the mound with a 13 - 0 lead. He had thrown 95 pitches. As soon as he had completed the allotted eight warm up pitches, his manager, Chuck Doughty, himself a former MBL pitcher, walked out to the mound and spat.

Flunking Chemistry Class

"Hey Chuck, what are you doing here?" Crockett was already starting to come unglued about the prospect of Doughty enforcing the upcoming 100 pitch limitation, but he never expected to see him on the mound before he threw a single pitch in the ninth.

"Relax Sam. I've got an idea."

"You're not going to enforce the pitch limit. Are you?"

"Just shut up Sam and listen. He turned toward the catcher Luis Cedeno, and added; "You listen up too Cedeno." Once he knew he had their undivided attention, he began to unfold his plan. "You've given this next guy, Michael Walker, three free passes already. He'll be looking for another walk and will be taking all the way. I don't want you to waste any pitches on this jerk. Hit Walker in the ass with the first pitch, a fastball and don't miss."

"How's that going to ..."

"I told you once already, Sam. Just shut up and listen." He spat on the mound again for emphasis. "After Walker, you've got a free swinger, Pedro Patético. Patético likes to bitch about everything. So when he walks up to the plate he'll probably be bitching about the fact that you hit Walker in a 13 - 0 game."

Doughty was right up in his pitcher's face as he unveiled his plan. And their eyeballs interlocked beneath the bills of their caps less than two feet away from one another. After Doughty was certain that the plan had begun to register with Crockett he turned toward his catcher. "Now this is where you come in Cedeno. When Patético starts bitching, you agree with him. Tell him that Crockett here is *poto loco* and that you want to see the no hitter broken up. You tell him that a get-me-over fastball is coming right down the middle.

"Now Sam." He turned back to the pitcher. "This is when you use that crappy fucking changeup that you threw last inning. Patético will swing from the heels and he'll bang it into a double play and you'll have two outs with two pitches. Then you've got three more pitches to get out the third guy in the inning. Sound like a plan?"

Crockett glared at Doughty and realized that his manager had concocted this ridiculous plan to save his own ass rather than to help secure the no-hitter, but he thought that it might work. "Okay, Chuck,

The Texan Does the Carolinas

I'll try it. But let me tell you this. I'm not leaving the mound if the plan doesn't work and I still have a no-hitter going."

"Hey *mahn*, we *no* supposed to talk *'bout* this no-hit shit. Yes? It *be* a jinx. No?" Cedeno piped in his opinion in broken HispEnglish. He seemed genuinely concerned that they had just broken some long standing baseball covenant that now spelled doom for the no-no. He had never caught a no-hitter before and he realized that he might share slightly in the glory for calling the pitches. He muttered, "realmente mal estado," then shook his head and stared at the ground.

Doughty looked back and forth between the battery mates and simply spit on the ground two more times. Then he turned around and wordlessly walked back to the bench. Crockett decided it might be worth a try. He glanced over at his wife and two sons and was glad that they had made it to see the game, but he worried about how Betsy Jo would react if she had been in on the plan.

Michael Walker came up to the plate and took forever to get into the batter's box. In a certain way this helped build Crockett's resolve to plunk him. The pitcher went into his wind up and threw a tailing fastball at the Mini Mutts shortstop. Walker dropped to the ground as soon as he saw the seamed sphere hurtling towards his rear end. The ball missed him by a fraction of an inch and the umpire simply nonchalantly signaled ball one. Quite logically Walker argued that the ball had glanced off his ass. Quite illogically Cedeno jumped up and agreed with Walker.

The umpire had been plying his trade for nearly twenty years and he had never seen anything like that. He assumed that he had missed something but he wasn't going to lose any sleep over it. He simply said, "Okay take your base." Walker was mystified. And because he didn't want to give in to the hated Baby Bloomers on anything whatsoever, he jumped back in the umpire's face and changed his tune. "I didn't say he hit me. I said he was *trying* to hit me. You should throw his ass out of the game."

The flabbergasted umpire just said, "Take your damn base before I throw *you* out of the game."

Flunking Chemistry Class

Now with a runner on first base and four pitches left in the tank, Crockett started to think that Doughty's crazy plan might actually work. He watched the discussion between his catcher, Cedeno and the next hitter, Patético unfold. Everyone looked genuinely annoyed but it was difficult to determine what everyone was annoyed about. Cedeno and Patético were jabbering away heatedly in Spanish until the umpire finally made Patético get in the batter's box. All Crockett could do however was go with the original plan and see what happened. And so he wound up and threw his best change up. Sure enough Patético smacked into a double play, around the horn, 5-4-3 and Patético began screaming obscenities at Cedeno on his way back to the dugout.

The small crowd was now up and cheering loudly. They were hoping for one more out and Crockett would have his no-hitter. However the fans didn't know what Crockett knew that he would only have three more pitches to try and secure the final out. The final hitter was a big lumbering first basemen Frank Christian, who had a habit of backing out of the batter's box and making a quick sign of the cross and glancing skyward at least twice in every at bat. Christian had who had already fanned twice earlier in the game, and had blessed himself a total of five times. He had also tugged at his crotch a half dozen times for good measure.

Crockett thought that it was time once again to rely on his upper nineties fastball. He'd take his chances with three heaters in the zone hoping that Christian would either hit something right at one of his fielders or strike out again on three pitches. When Crockett threw his first fastball near the middle of the plate and Christian didn't even take his bat off his shoulder, he realized that the three pitch strike out was no longer an option. The umpire simply said "ball one," in a loud voice that was immediately booed vociferously by the home town crowd. The umpire must have thought that they now wanted to play some kind of "bizarro baseball," where balls were strikes and strikes were balls as un-hit batsmen were deemed to have been plunked and then claimed they weren't hit. When ball two followed Crockett began to seethe. There was a pitcher warming up in the bull pen.

The Texan Does the Carolinas

Cedeno called, "Time," and jogged to the mound. "That's 99 pitches, *mahn*. *Hees no goin'* to swing. You must *heet 'eem* too."

"I can't hit this guy also Luis. That will be my 100th pitch. Doughty's going to yank me out before I throw pitch 101. You know it and I know it."

"But *hees no goin'* to swing. He not even bless *hisself* after *dee lass* pitch. He *not goin'* to swing, so you need to *heet da mudderfugger*. *Den* you can *peek* him off when he get to first and you *steel* not throw *peech* number 101."

"All right get the message to Doughty, because if he comes out to the mound a second time, they'll force him to remove me. Tell him I'll pick Christian off after I tattoo him with some inside heat."

As he left the mound, Cedeno loosed one of his shin guards and motioned to the impatient umpire that he was going to the dugout for a second to get his a new shin guard. In the ten seconds that he spent getting re-outfitted, he relayed the new plan to Doughty. The next pitch from Crockett clearly hit Frank Christian, but the umpire simply called, "ball three."

Frank Christian then used some very un-Christ-like language to address the visual acuity of the blue-vested arbiter of balls and strikes. Both managers went running out toward the plate to argue for the same result so the umpire made a rare reversal of his call and awarded, Frank Christian, first base.

Crockett went into his stretch and threw late to first base.

Crockett went into his stretch and again threw late to first base.

Crockett went into his stretch and threw late to first base for a third time.

Crockett went into his stretch and threw low and late to first base and the ball skipped away a short distance but Christian got back to the bag safely.

Crockett went into his stretch and threw high and late to first base and the crowd began to buzz about paying attention to the batter rather than the runner.

Crockett went into his stretch and threw to first base once again. Christian slid in safely, even though he didn't need to slide.

111

Flunking Chemistry Class

Crockett went into his stretch and looked at first base. *Uh oh*, he thought. Frank Christian was standing with his left foot planted six inches away from the first base bag. He wasn't going to budge an inch.

"Time," Cedeno trotted out to the mound and called the infielders into the mound as well. When the infield was fully assembled, Cedeno announced, "*Eets* time for *da heedin* ball trick." He surreptitiously took the ball from Crockett and handed it to the first baseman, whose first reaction was, "This stupid horseshit will never work." However he covertly accepted the seamed cowhide sphere and returned to his position at the first base sack.

When Frank Christian took another six inch lead, the first baseman tagged him; the umpire yelled, "you're out;" Cedeno ran to the mound to embrace Crockett; Christian kept blessing himself; the Mini Mutts manager was lambasting the umpire and Betsy Jo Crockett was jumping up and down in the stands while the young security guard watched every bounce.

Over near the Mini Mutts dugout Lance Leathermore was discussing night time activities with three baseball groupies. When the celebration died down a bit on the Baby Bloomers side of the field, Leathermore walked over to talk to his old batterymate.

"Great game, Sam. How've you've been?"

"Thanks Lance. I've been just fine."

"You've got some cut on your heater now. That's cool. You're looking better than ever. The Bloomers got you on a specialized program yet?"

"No. I'm just dealing the regular; No need to go to the high test. But Brad keeps pushing me. Is he still your agent?"

"Yeah we're cool. He's been taking care of me. I've been on one of his specialist programs for the last two years and I think it's helped a lot. He asks me about you once in a while. I told him I hadn't seen you in over a year. He said that if you had gone to see Carlos in Scottsdale when he first mentioned it to you that you'd probably be ready for The Show by now."

The Texan Does the Carolinas

"You know I'm not crazy about that stuff, Lance. I'm sure I can make it to The Show without it. By the way forget about my pitching; I'm happier about the two doubles I hit."

"Yeah, you really smoked that second one off the centerfield wall. When I saw you hit it, I thought that maybe the Bloomers got you on a program. But then I remembered how you felt about the juice."

"Are you still catching? Was the DH thing today, a day-off or is that more common for you now?"

"Just a few days off ... I've got a few minor problems with my oblique muscles ...makes it tough to catch and throw."

Just then Betsy Jo came up with her sons and Crockett made a quick introduction of his wife and children to Lance Leathermore. Leathermore immediately understood why Crockett had been relatively disinterested in going along on groupie gropes with him in the past. He might have been a bit of a goody two shoes type but he sure had a fine looking woman.

"Hello Betsy Jo. Sam was always talking about you and the boys. Glad to finally meet you."

Betsy Jo took one look at Lance Leathermore and she knew exactly what Sam had been telling her was right. She had always felt that Sam was in excellent shape and that he worked hard to be successful at his profession. But the difference in body types between Sam Crockett and Lance Leathermore was blatantly obvious. Sam Crockett was buffed up; Lance Leathermore was beefed up ... Crockett was strong; Leathermore was powerful ... Crockett was built; Leathermore was hewn ...Crockett was cut; Leathermore was chiseled ... Crockett was rippled; Leathermore was absolutely ripped. The final difference that she noticed was that Sam was manly while Lance Leathermore was just plain massive.

They're conversation was interrupted by the Baby Bloomers' manager, Chuck Doughty.

"Hey kid. The guys all want to get you a couple of beers to celebrate. That okay by you Betsy Jo?" Doughty was old school and so he ignored Leathermore. He didn't like his players fraternizing with the opposition, especially someone from the Mini Mutts.

Flunking Chemistry Class

"Sure that's fine, Chuck." Betsy Jo answered for herself and Sam. "Just don't keep him out too late."

Leathermore was getting ready to head out on the team bus shortly so he just reached out and shook Sam's hand. "Nice game Crockett. We'll get another shot at you in two weeks down in Savannah." Leathermore didn't get that shot however, because two days later Sam Crockett was promoted two levels to the New Brunswick Blossoms, the New Jersey based Double A affiliate of the Bronx Bloomers. He didn't even make a stop in Tampa at High Single A ball. Meanwhile Betsy Jo and her sons tagged along and moved up north of the Mason Dixon line. It was a big change for everyone.

XII

Expansion²

September 2004

Buzz Selout was beginning to catch more grief than he had ever anticipated from the MBLWA. The media was finally beginning to catch up with the reality that the commissioner and the ownership group as a whole were doing substantially nothing to deal with PEDs proliferation in baseball. Meanwhile there were a few other colossal power shifts that were going on within the game. As the valuation of baseball franchises continued to rise, some of the owners and ownership groups were seeing an opportunity/need to sell their clubs. The escalating salary demands of the free agent floats together with the owners' propensity to pay these ransom demands in the hopes of securing a winning team were beginning to cause the debt ratios of some of the ball clubs to get out of whack.

There were a few different strategies in place to deal with these financial changes. The two LA area teams the Hollywood Hedgers and the Anaheim Afterthoughts, had been owned by entertainment and media conglomerates. These clubs often tried to cross market their products with other entertainment products and services within their respective conglomerates. However the varying economics of the different businesses made this difficult to manage and both teams had recently been sold once again to business speculators. The Afterthoughts were purchased by billboard entrepreneur and the highly leveraged sale of the Hollywood Hedgers left the team in the hands of an east coast car wash maven.

Other clubs were owned by small market owners who often appeared more interested in the redistributed booty that came from the luxury tax and profit sharing participation than they were in building a winning home town team.

However ownership continued to evolve over the years and now only four teams' ownership predated Selout's tenure as The Commish. These four teams; the Philadelphia Philistines in the Native League and the Minneapolis Clones; the Chicago Pantyhose; and of course the Bronx Bloomers of Amerind League, had strong closely held family ownership. This had been the early model through the initial growth phases of the MBL. Now however the valuations of the teams was every bit as swollen as the floats who played for the teams, and family ownership seemed to be giving way to a new entrepreneurial business model where certain wealthy billionaires and their close knit colleagues were actually speculating in team ownership as though it were a commodity. And some of these owners weren't necessarily committed to the team or the fans that supported it for the long run.

An example of this latter type of ownership was the recently transitioned ownership of the Beantown Wallbangers. The principal owner Jonathan Hanks had in fact been a successful commodities dealer, who had been dabbling in sports team ownership for the past dozen years. The new boss in Beantown had purchased the team from the family who had owned the franchise for seventy years. However since the early 1990's Hanks had also made a small equity investment in the Bronx Bloomers and had full ownership of the Miami Minnows, before selling that team when he bought the Wallbangers for nearly three quarters of a billion dollars in 2002.

This was the new age of baseball ownership. Selout knew that he was not even close to being an *independent* commissioner who weighed and balanced the best interests of the owners, the players and the fans. He was merely running a commodities market place for billionaires and wannabe billionaires, who were all playing a high stakes game of franchise flipping. In the past dozen years since he had been installed

Expansion[2]

as commissioner, Selout had facilitated more franchise transactions than there were teams in the MBL. And while it wasn't clear whether or not the market for MBL teams would continue to rise, it was certainly apparent that the underlying product was experiencing significant decay. There was now so much unhealthy fat in the product that it had become impossible for Selout to continue to ignore it. He knew that he had to do something about the floats or at a bare minimum *appear* to be doing something about the floats.

Even President Shrub had mentioned the problem last January in his State of the Union Address. And this simply served to elevate the perils of PEDs to the same discussion as the threat of international terrorism. Selout was about to meet with Danny Fowl, the executive director of the players association. Although there were some people who believed that Fowl and Selout were co-conspirators in the destruction of the integrity of the game, the truth of the matter was that they didn't really trust each other very much at all. Fowl came alone to the meeting, which was about to take place in Selout's office. Selout asked Timmy Burr to come as a legal assistant and as a knowledgeable statistician. Selout was growing ever more confident in the capabilities of his young assistant. But Burr was unaware of Selout's growing trust. And for the most part Selout was unaware of Burr's advancing alcohol problem.

"I think we can make some progress on the testing thing, Buzz. However we're going to need to be mindful of the privacy rights of my clients. And I think that we're together already on the international expansion plan for the next ten years."

Danny Fowl was still in his mid fifties and as such was more than a decade younger than Commissioner Selout. He was a lawyer by training and an aggressive advocate for the interests of his clients. He generally got the better of Selout in almost every negotiation but he had the common sense not to gloat about it. Fowl didn't know exactly which of his player/clients were using drugs and who was clean, nor did he care to know. And although there was a smattering of outspoken criticism of steroid abuse within the union membership, to date, not a single player had come to him and pressed him for more stringent drug testing.

"We have a contract in place that protects your so-called privacy rights to the point where it could be hurting some of your clients more than helping them. Certainly this is true for the players who aren't doing steroids. Remember our survey testing a couple of years ago had only seven percent failures. The other players must be annoyed at those who failed the tests. Of course they don't know who failed the tests because we haven't released the names."

"A lot of the guys are worried that this paranoia about steroids is going to leak into other areas of their medical history and they don't want some random blood test to be able to disclose that they are taking certain other medications for things like allergies, or depression, or in some cases medications associated with sexually transmitted diseases. Those are private issues between the player and his doctor. We don't want the public to be peering into the players' private lives in this way."

"Alright we agree on the privacy issue in principle, but not when it comes to anabolic steroids and some other performance enhancing drugs. There are specific tests for these things. For the integrity of the game we ought to make sure that the players are appropriately disciplined if they break the rules."

"I agree. So here's the plan that I propose. Annual testing for all players…The first time a player fails a test, he is notified, warned and a letter goes in his file. The second failure would entail suggested counseling and a *mandatory* trip to the 15 day disabled list. The third test failure would result in a *non-paid mandatory* trip to the 15 day disabled list, *mandatory* counseling and a *severe* warning that future infractions will result in public disclosure of the test failure and an unspecified lengthier unpaid suspension, maybe as much as 25 days." He took a breath and then added, "That should quiet some of the critics. Of course we don't want this to take the focus away from performance on the field so we should just announce that the Players Association and

Expansion²

MBL have agreed to rigorous steroid testing and that we will be policing our sport judiciously. That ought to do it. Or as President Shrub might say it; *Mission Accomplished.*"

"The public is going to want to know more of the details, Danny. Ever since Cam Commitadoosey died in October, the interest has risen by a thousand percent. People believe that steroids are causing people to flip out. Anabolic steroids are now linked to several suicides of amateur athletes who were following the example set by some of our MBL players. Some of the MBLWA writers are asking very specific questions these days, and they're kicking up a pretty big fuss and saying that there are no teeth in the current testing program. In fact, Lester Postal at *The New York Roast* has taken to calling me 'Gumby.' He keeps reminding everyone that we allowed that cocaine-addicted left-handed reliever Little Stevie Howl to keep playing even after we suspended him seven times. At some point we have to get this steroids problem under control. I'm not sure this is going to do it. Maybe we should add a 50 game suspension after the fifth failed test and a lifetime ban after the sixth one. Then they'd really know we mean business."

"How about after the seventh suspension we give them a lifetime ban. That way we'll keep the threat of the lifetime ban in the agreement so that everyone knows we mean business and that would line up well with the number of chances we gave Little Stevie Howl on the cocaine issue."

As he usually did in this type of a meeting, Timmy Burr observed the negotiations, took mental notes and a few physical notes but didn't join the conversation unless and until he was asked to provide information that might be useful to the negotiations. Rarely was he ever asked for a personal opinion on issues that were being negotiated. He found it absolutely fascinating that these two baseball executives honestly believed that they were doing something positive for baseball and that the public would swallow it hook, line and sinker. It was absolutely incredible how they had convinced themselves that sporadic random testing would shed real light on the problem. It was even more insane that they were only testing players once or twice

Flunking Chemistry Class

a year and that they were only testing for a certain kind of PED. A player had the same chance of being caught repeatedly as he had of winning the lottery on multiple occasions. As he listened to the discussion he thought that he was watching a remake of the Jim Carrey movie, "Dumb and Dumber."

Danny Fowl took out a handkerchief and wiped the perspiration from his forehead and receding hairline. He saw that Selout was "steeling-up" about the sixth failure versus the seventh failure and he wanted to move on to the other big item on their agenda.

"Alright Buzz, let me talk to a few of the player reps and I'll see if we can nail this down. Let's move on to the expansion issue. The players are generally receptive to the global expansion and the fact that it will create more than 150 new jobs at the major league level, but they are worried that the global weather patterns and the expanded travel schedule might expand the season unnecessarily. We've already had an Earth Series that spilled over into November in 2001 and we've had a few teams actually start the season during the last days of March. The players want assurances that the season won't expand along with the number of teams. They also want a two day holiday after any intercontinental flights longer than ten hours. Shortening the season back to the original 154 game format could help us achieve these reasonable goals."

"We are already dealing with the weather issue for the games that the Chaplains play as the Kangaroos. Sydney is the only team south of the equator. And admittedly it has been tough scheduling all of their Australia-based home games in March, April and September. That's changing this year of course with the completion of the Kangaroo Dome. The good news is that the other expansion cities that we are looking at are all in the northern hemisphere, although we may consider putting a team in South Africa at a future date."

"You're not addressing my concerns, Buzz. What about the shortened season and the two off days after long travel?"

"Forget about eliminating games. Tell your constituents that those games pay their salaries. Besides we have a whole hell of a lot of other issues to deal with over the next ten years of expansion."

Expansion^2

"Let's come back to that. First tell me how you and the owners see the near term expansion plan unfolding. Is it the same as we talked about last month?"

"Sort of …for starters we'll work through the full spin off of the Sydney Kangaroos and the Tokyo Carp. Then the Chaplains and Seafarers will go back to playing for the San Diego and Seattle communities exclusively. That will take place in 2006. Then in 2008 we'll add franchises in Seoul, South Korea and in the San Pedro de Macoris, in the Dominican Republic. Finally in 2012 we'll begin playing in Caracas, Venezuela and in San Juan, Puerto Rico. At that point we will have 36 teams in seven different countries on four different continents. Then each October we will play a true Earth Series. And as you know; nothing's more important than the Earth Series."

Timmy Burr cringed as he heard Buzz Selout utter his favorite phrase. However this was the first time he had had heard the official planned roll out schedule for MBL expansion. It seemed like both parts of this meeting were about expansion, first expanded ballplayers and now expanded leagues. Burr thought of it numerically as Expansion^2. He was aware of discussions and negotiations with different groups of people from different countries and he knew that others in the commissioner's office had traveled to various locations around the world as part of these discussions. However he felt as though Selout treated him like a lap dog. He was there to console The Commish when things didn't go his way and to concur with Selout's opinion on just about everything he said and did. He didn't want to be a "yes man" but he had somehow tumbled into this role without really understanding how he got there. So as he listened and watched the discourse between Selout and Fowl, he felt a rising anger that he didn't quite know how to handle. But then Selout turned to him and asked him a question that he knew Burr could answer without even looking at his computer.

"Timmy, what percentage of the players in the league this year were born outside of the United States"

"Forty-two percent, Mr. Selout." Burr immediately wished he had called him Buzz like everyone else did.

Flunking Chemistry Class

Fowl looked curiously at Burr as if it was the first time he noticed that he was in the room. But then he looked back at Selout.

"So you see, Danny. We're already a global business."

"So Buzz, what about Cuba and what about getting a European country as well?" Fowl was genuinely curious. His question didn't seem to have an attendant agenda.

"The European countries are all just starting out with their baseball leagues and programs. I'm sure that soon after I'm out of this office, baseball will expand to that continent as well. As far as Cuba is concerned the difficulty is mostly political. As long as Castro is still in charge down there the United States will maintain its economic sanctions."

"Cuba may have some of the best players in the world. Every time one of them defects there is a whole lot of interest in the player."

"Yeah, but for all we know they could be nurturing all of them on PEDs. If you listen to CoJo Janesco, he would have you believe that all of the Cuban-Americans from the Miami area have been doing PEDs for twenty years. He already fingered I Dork and Daffy Palmgreed and those guys were his childhood friends. Plus he has admitted juicing up himself. And Janesco and others are now saying that there's a whole process involved with Cuban defectors who are ballplayers. They're saying that some of the player agents are involved as well. They get these guys so juiced up down in Havana that they could almost float off the island by themselves. So whether or not we ever get a team in Havana, you can expect that we will have plenty of Cuban ballplayers on a lot of the other teams."

"If PEDs are a lot easier to get outside of the United States, then you're going to have a hell of a time policing the problem."

"So that brings us back around to the original topic and why we need a better testing program."

For the next forty five minutes or so, Selout and Fowl went back and forth over ground they had already covered without any real significant agreement although Fowl did agree to have further discussions with his union members about a slightly stepped up testing

Expansion²

program. Once Fowl had left the office, Selout turned his attention towards Burr, with a different angle on the steroid issue.

"Hey Timmy, you seem to get along pretty well with that guy Lester Postal over at *The Roast*. Don't you?"

"Yeah, you know, Mr. Selout. He's a lot like all of the other reporters who are always snooping around here. I've seen him at some of the sports dinners and that sort of thing. Why do you ask?" Burr purposely understated his relationship with the sportswriter.

"He's a pain in the ass. He never lets go of this steroid thing. You just heard me working on this with Fowl and the players association. And trust me we're going to fix the problem. But Postal just won't let go of it. Here we are coming down the home stretch of another successful season and he's not writing about the great rivalry between the Wallbangers and the Bloomers. Neither is he writing much about Itchy Kazuti of the Seafarers. That guy's probably going to set the all time single season hit record and Postal hasn't mentioned it at all."

"Well, I can understand the Itchy thing. Postal has a New York beat and Itchy plays his games in Tokyo and Seattle. And I know that Lester has been covering the Bloomers pretty regularly. Remember he's been critical of Sledgehammer and the boys for getting A Dork from the Drillies. And I'm sure that if the Wallbangers beat out the Bloomers this year A Dork will be the culprit because he's so un-clutch."

"Well Postal seems more concerned with making sure that everyone knows that A Dork is a float than with what A Dork does on the field."

"The two things are related though. Duh," Adding the "duh" part was the most brazen thing that Burr had ever said to Selout and he felt good after he let it loose. However Selout ignored Burr's argument and just plowed ahead with his criticism of Postal's reporting.

For the last three weeks, Postal has been harping on the Bay Watch Lab Company thing, the mess they're calling B'WHALE'CO. It wasn't like Postal was the reporter who uncovered the story in the first place. But now he's got an interview with that woman they're calling the Bay

Watch Bitch. She's the broad who ratted out these guys. And now she's making the rounds of a lot of talk shows."

"I thought she only implicated Harry Bombs."

"Well she's still responsible for the others. You're a lawyer. You know how this works. She got a sample of that transparent cream textured steroid that Bombs was using, and turned it over to the state of California as evidence. Then based on the evidence that they got from the Bay Watch Bitch, they raided the B'WHALE'CO lab and seized all of the records that implicated Bombs, Jambino, and Gorey Schlepfield, as well as a bunch of other athletes including a couple of Olympians.

"But anyway getting back to Lester Postal. I've heard that you know him a lot better than you're letting on. Is it true that you were the best man at his wedding a few months back?"

Timmy Burr began to get very red faced very rapidly. He didn't think that there was anything wrong with his friendship with the Postals, but he had been reluctant to let Selout know about it because The Commish was his boss and he knew that Selout detested Lester Postal. So now Burr knew he was trapped and he was going to have to find a logical way to explain not only his friendship with Postal but also his reluctance to disclose the relationship.

"Well yeah that's true. Of course I've known him professionally for a while. But his wife Georgette was a good friend of mine from law school. When she started dating Postal, we got to know each other a little better. And then because it was Postal's fifth marriage and he didn't have any real friends to ask, he asked me to be his best man and I agreed."

Timmy Burr did his best to spin this tale to make it sound like he was a "rental best man," but Selout knew better. However rather than embarrass his assistant any further, he decided to make the specific request that he had in mind when he broached the topic of Lester Postal in the first place.

"Well as long as you have this rapport with Postal, can you ask him to back off the B'WHALE'CO story until after the Earth Series. Make him some kind of deal. Tell him that you'll give him a heads up when we make the announcement about the global expansion. That story

Expansion[2]

should break later this year but during the off season. So if he backs off the B'WHALE'CO story for about a month then we'll give him the scoop on expansion later in the year. But right now I want to focus on the playoff and the Earth Series, because as you know …"

"Right, I got it; "Nothing's more important than the Earth Series."

XIII
The Congressional Hearings

March 2005

It was a media circus in Washington DC. Everyone wanted to look good but no one did. In fact the Congressmen, the ballplayers, the agents, the attorneys, The Commish, and the Players Association Executive Director all looked as though they were auditioning for a remake of the movie "Ship of Fools." The electronic media that covered the event live also looked like a bunch of pretentiousness buffoons. There was no legitimate attempt to describe the event for what it was: a shameful exhibition of overinflated egos preening and posturing for the cameras in an attempt to attract the support of an invisible public. None of these people had any idea that the public saw this absurd farce for exactly what it was: a circus.

Prior to the televised portion of the supposedly open hearing on performance enhancing drugs, the Congressmen had implored the ballplayers to personalize a whole horde of athletic memorabilia that had mysteriously landed in the hearing room. When a reporter had asked who supplied the hats, jerseys, programs, baseball cards, and other paraphernalia, no one seemed to have an answer. However it was clear that at the end of the day the autographed souvenirs would all be going back to the offices of the Congressmen. This material also included 150 autographed copies of CoJo Janesco's new tell all book on steroids entitled "Jacked Up." These copies were for the congressional

The Congressional Hearings

staffers who helped in setting up this circus that was attempting to pass as a congressional hearing.

Congressional Committee Chairperson Hans Waxear banged down his gavel as though it was the first time he had ever used one. He looked like a kindergarten student with a wooden hammer hitting his play table and enjoying the noise it made. "This hearing on the reported steroid abuses in the Multinational Baseball League will now come to order."

Each of the half dozen ballplayers and ex-ballplayers who were empanelled across from the Congressmen had a personal attorney/advisor sitting behind him. Much pre-gavel whispering had been conducted between the individual ballplayers and their attorneys. However the ballplayers intriguingly refrained from discussing their testimony with each other. It was almost as if they were afraid of tipping their pitches ahead of time. There was less unanimity among the ballplayers on how to handle the steroids question than there would be for Riker's Island inmates trying to decide on a lunch menu. There was one area of agreement that united most of the players at the table. Other than CoJo Janesco none of them really wanted to be there.

Behind the row of ballplayers and their attorneys, Danny Fowl, the Executive Director of the MBLPA and Commissioner Buzz Selout were also seated with a couple members of their respective legal staffs. Both Selout and Fowl had testified earlier before the Committee and each man had independently made the ridiculous claim that they were doing everything they could to stop the proliferation of PEDs in the game. Just before the gavel announced the start of this session of the hearing, Selout's statistician/attorney, Timmy Burr, slipped back into his seat next to two other Selout attorneys. Burr had snuck out to a Capitol Hill bar for a couple of eye-opener Bloody Marys, before returning to his job of advising Selout.

As the hearing began it became quite obvious that each of the ballplayers had a separate approach. There were two floats currently

Flunking Chemistry Class

employed by the Maryland Blackbirds, who had made their bloated claims to fame with other teams. One of these players was Corky Samuels, who had become the only player in the history of the game to hit 60 or more home runs in three different seasons. He did this while playing for the Chicago Gumballs of the Native League. The other player currently employed by the Blackbirds was 40 year old Daffy Palmgreed, who was in his second tour of duty with the Blackbirds after spending the previous five years with the Drillies, during which time he drilled an average of 43 homeruns and 120 RBI's.

As he sat in Selout's row in the committee hearing room, Timmy Burr was shuffling all of these statistics in his mind. He had spent so much time pouring over these statistical details during the last five years that not even a couple of stiff early morning Bloody Marys could add the least bit of confusion. He saw all of the statistical evidence as clearly as an early morning sunrise.

Burr knew, for example, that during the first 100 years of the MBL there had been 2 occasions on which a player had hit more than 60 homeruns in a season. He also knew that during the four seasons 1998 through 2001, Corky Samuels, the Gumballs' so-so outfielder, *averaged* 61 homeruns. And that in an overlapping four year span during 1996 to 1999 seasons, Popeye Maloney, also *averaged* 61 homeruns. These two poster boys for PED abuse were now sitting side by side and facing Congress along with the aforementioned Daffy Palmgreed and CoJo Janesco.

The fifth player puzzled Burr somewhat. Kirk Shrillage's career numbers certainly fit the profile of a float. He came to the majors at the age of 21. Through age 29 Shrillage had amassed a total of 52 wins - a raw average of 4.5 wins per season - in his twenties. At age 30 through 34 Shrillage won 80 games, an average of 16 wins a season. Most recently in the 3 seasons that Shrillage was in his late thirties he had won 52 games or an average of 17.5 games per season. Shrillage had his first twenty win season at the age of 34 and had three 20 win seasons by the age of 37. Statistically Shrillage was simply another float poster boy. However Shrillage had made a number of challenging statements about steroid abuse, calling all users "cheaters" and

128

The Congressional Hearings

publicly stating that he wanted to see MBL institute daily tests for substance abuse. Burr didn't doubt that Shrillage was a steroid user. He simply wondered if all of the juice had gone to his brain. Burr remembered the comment on Shrillage made by the guy in the brawl at *The Morning After* a few years earlier: "The pitcher doth protest too much, methinks." He again thought of this as the definitive explanation on the pitcher's participation in the controversy but he was hard pressed to understand why Shrillage would be so dumb as to believe people couldn't see through this charade.

As the players were each asked to make an opening statement, one was more absurd than the next one. Popeye Maloney, now seven years removed from his record setting homerun year, cried like a baby as he tried to make a statement that said something like "Steroids are real bad. They even affect your memory. Therefore I can't tell you what I may or may not have done in the past. I'm only here to talk about the future. Boohoohoo." Then he simply cried every time he was asked a question and gave the same pathetic answer. "I'm not here to talk about the past. I'm only here to talk about the future. Boohoohoo."

The simpleminded congressmen who had subpoenaed Maloney to talk about the past weren't sure how they were allowing Maloney and his attorney attempt to set up these new rules. But they were dumb enough not to have pursued getting an immunity grant for the players through the Attorney General's office. That immunity grant would have allowed the committee to compel more complete testimony from Maloney and the others. But instead they simply sat there and watched the oafish Maloney ball his eyes out like a two year old who was caught with his hand in the cookie jar.

It wasn't readily apparent whether Maloney was crying out of fear, out or remorse or out of simple rage at the idiotic advice that he had gotten from his attorney that allowed the whole world to see just how guilty Maloney actually was. It was blatantly obvious that Maloney didn't want to lie under oath by repeating the same lies that he had repeatedly told to the press, so he opted for the crocodile tears strategy.

When it was time for Corky Samuels, the so-so outfielder of the Blackbirds to testify, he and his attorney orchestrated a completely different lying strategy that they chose to employ. As absurd as it might sound, the so-so outfielder simply claimed that Spanish was his native language and he didn't understand English. Thereupon Samuels' attorney read a statement wherein the Gumball denied ever using any substances that were illegal in the United States and Latin America. Amazingly no one questioned the fact that Samuels had given several interviews in English when he was in the process of chasing the home run record. Samuels' attorney didn't bring along a translator and no one in the room offered to provide translation although there were several bi-lingual individuals who could have performed the task. This became even more bizarre when the three congressmen who made up the committee began asking Samuels questions in English anyway. Corky Samuels simply proceeded to make weird faces and pointed to his ears as though he couldn't even *hear* the questions.

As Timmy Burr watched these proceedings he was fascinated. He figured that Samuels, like Shrillage, had allowed the juice to get to his brain. Now he was demonstrating that steroid usage had not only made him forget how to speak English but it had apparently left him *deaf* as well.

When it became Daffy Palmgreed's turn to testify he utilized a completely different strategy, one that not been this effectively utilized since it was employed by President Clint Blanton seven years earlier. Palmgreed simply leaned forward in his chair and wagged his index finger defiantly in the faces of the congressmen as he said, "I did not have any stimulating relationship with these steroids." He sneered as he uttered his denial and everyone in the room had a flashback to Blanton's 1998 denial that ultimately led to a proliferation of oral sex in the country because by executive fiat it was no longer considered an element of extramarital *sexual relations.*

Timmy Burr was in awe. There was no attempt to cross examine any of these characters. Instead Chairperson Hans Waxear and his congressional colleagues simply followed up each statement by a ball-player with an even longer statement of their own condemning the use of performance enhancing drugs and claiming that such usage could cause an extensive range of maladies including everything from

The Congressional Hearings

intumescence, insomnia, impotence and irritability to incontinence, incendiary behavior and insanity. Burr quickly scanned the room to see if anyone had dozed off, because he was certain that there was ample evidence of the other "*i*-issues." He even wondered if Popeye Maloney, the big blabbering baby was wearing diapers as he cowered in front of his questioners. Burr suspected that Maloney was a potential victim of incontinence that might as easily be induced by his panic as by his steroid use. Meanwhile the self promoting congressmen went on to add cancer, heart disease, liver decay, depression and sterility to the list of known side effects of steroid use.

While Corky Samuels, Daffy Palmgreed, Popeye Maloney and even Kirk Shrillage all wore a dour countenance that emanated either from fear or from anger or from both fear and anger, CoJo Janesco smiled in stark contrast to his fellow ballplayers. As a group, the other players totally despised Janesco for writing <u>Jacked Up</u>. In typical Shrillage fashion he also called Janesco a "liar and a whore" for writing the book. Janesco had mentioned all four of the other players in <u>Jacked Up</u> and went so far as to say that he personally injected Palmgreed and Maloney with steroids. This was particularly irksome to Palmgreed, who like Janesco was a Cuban-American and a childhood friend of the former outfielder.

While he sat at the far end of the conference table, Janesco through his attorney had begged to be granted immunity from prosecution so that he could spill out all sorts of sordid ideas about steroids. However that never occurred and Janesco's attorney ensured that his client stayed silent on his own participation in the mess while he was under oath. However that didn't stop CoJo Janesco from spouting his information from the courtroom steps the moment the hearing ended.

All in all the hearing was a total embarrassment to everyone involved. It was so gruesome that many who watched the hearing on TV in their own homes denied having done so when asked by friends and neighbors. It was becoming abundantly clear that PEDs were now making liars out of everyone. It made people wonder; *is that why they call them the wonder drugs?*

Flunking Chemistry Class

Immediately following the hearing Timmy Burr wanted to make tracks to the closest bar as fast as he could. During the last few years, the little lawyer had picked up something besides his law degree. His closet drinking had now become somewhat of an obsession. He had also begun to grow restless working in the commissioner's office. Although he was now an attorney, Buzz Selout still treated him like a statistician. Burr had his resume out on the street but he had not yet found the position that might lead him on a new path. He loved baseball and he wanted to stay close to the game but he also wanted to utilize his law degree to maximize its value to him personally.

When he left the hearing room and made his way to the local bar, he made sure his cell phone was turned off and he got a good buzz on before taking the Amtrak train back up to New York.

Jelly Rogers watched the hearings from his hotel room in Orlando Florida. He was taking a break from his light spring training routine as he prepared for another season with the Houston Arrows. Dolly Rogers was back in Texas with their children, and Jelly Rogers was trying to extricate himself from an embarrassing sexual tryst with Margie Melrose that included no sex. Rogers' impotence was made all the more exasperating by Margie's continued entreaties and invitations for physical attention.

"Come on rub my belly, Jelly. Just do it the way you always used to do it." Margie Melrose had a strange relationship with Jelly Rogers that had endured for more than eight and a half years. Amazingly Dolly Rogers didn't seem to know anything about it, although rumors about the affair appeared in the tabloids from time to time. Margie actually liked Dolly Rogers and she had resigned herself to the fact that Jelly Rogers was never going to leave his wife. Although she didn't like to think about it, Margie was not really jealous of Dolly. She didn't get upset when Rogers left her to return to his wife. However what really ticked off Margie Melrose was when Jelly Rogers was cheating with someone else, a third woman, if you will. That set Margie off big time.

The Congressional Hearings

And so whenever Jelly was unable to perform sexually, a maddeningly common recurrence of late, Margie wondered if Jelly was chasing after some cheap baseball bunny. And naturally, she never thought of herself as one of those cheap baseball bunnies.

While Rogers was sitting on the end of the bed in his undershorts, Melrose was lying back on the bed in a sexy black lace camisole that Rogers had given her. When Rogers didn't respond to her request for some physical attention that she hoped would turn into foreplay, she reached out and grabbed his hand and gently pulled it to the warm skin of her upper thigh. However her warm up pitch did not strike a chord with Jelly Rogers. He simply stared blankly at the TV as the riveting and embarrassing scenario played out. Every time the camera panned over at CoJo Janesco, Jelly Rogers quivered. He was glad that Janesco had not named him in his book as one of the people that he had personally injected with steroids, but he worried about Janesco as he watched the proceedings unfold in the court room. Janesco was definitely a loose cannon on the ship. He was capable of unleashing broadsides at any moment and Rogers was infinitely grateful for the ineptitude of Congress in not offering Janesco immunity. Everyone had already been exposed to the multiple allegations that Janesco had already published and for some bizarre reason, no one appeared desirous of getting those assertions down under oath.

The other crazy thing that had happened was that Janesco was backpedaling on his published claim that steroids were a good thing for the game of baseball. In his book he was not at all apologetic for juicing and in fact he had emphatically encouraged others to get on a steroid program if they wanted to excel in their athletic endeavors. Now he was agreeing with the others that steroid usage was a harmful thing and that players who took steroids were cheaters. The reason for his reversal was not apparent and the congressional committee members looked fearful of opening up that can of worms. When the hearing ended, Jelly sat up straight and rigid on the bed and took several deep breaths, inhaling and exhaling in a rhythmic disciplined manner.

"Jelly ... what is it Jelly? Are you okay?"

Flunking Chemistry Class

Rogers didn't answer Margie right away. Instead he maintained his rigid backbone and stood and walked into the bathroom and looked in the mirror. As he had so often over the last few years he searched for the mini-jowl that appeared on random occasions when he wasn't on guard against such a slovenly managed slant of facial skin. He was happy that he couldn't see it. The mini-jowl was gone ... at least for the moment and so was the threat of exposure through CoJo Janesco. Now if he could only do something to quiet that fool trainer, Ryan McGhee.

The next day Lester Postal's coverage of the congressional hearing was a blistering attack on the evasiveness of the ballplayers in general and specifically of the teary eyed Popeye Maloney. Postal ripped the former Scarlet's outfielder's manhood, even making veiled reference to physical shrinkage. When he submitted his piece to the sports editor Will Morehead, the sports editor ran it under the back page headline of **MALONEY'S BALONEY**.

XIV

The Texan as a Jersey Boy

August 2005

Betsy Jo Crockett and the boys were at the ball park once again. This was now Sam's fifth year in the Minor Leagues and the ball parks were all beginning to look the same. JR would soon be coming up on his fourth birthday and Rory was a very precocious two and half year old. What was different about this game, however, was that they weren't going to see Sam Crockett pitch. They were there simply for moral support and because it was an early game on a beautiful Sunday afternoon. Meanwhile, the head of the young Crockett family was sitting on the bench with some of his teammates because his elbow hurt like hell.

At first Sam had been determined to pitch through the pain. When he was actually pitching it hurt a lot less than it did the day after he pitched. Then he would go a day or two in pain while the swelling subsided and he would be ready to pitch again. In previous seasons Sam had occasionally experienced some pain or muscle fatigue in his right arm but nothing that lasted like it did this year. And this was a very important year for Crockett. He was still just 22 years old but he had not made it past Double A and he was worried that he might lose his prospect status if he didn't continue to progress through the Bloomers farm system. After the two step jump from the Beaufort Baby Bloomers to New Brunswick Blossoms the summer before, Crockett had finished

Flunking Chemistry Class

the season in the Blossoms bullpen because the brass in the Bronx was worried about the number of innings he had thrown. But now right from the outset of the 2005 season he was once again a starter.

After a slow start in April, Crockett had righted himself in May and June and had put together a scoreless streak of twenty nine innings over five games. At the mid-summer break he had compiled a record of 6 and 4 with an ERA of 3.48. His manager had told him that he had been considered for the Future Paraders' Game, but that Sledgehammer's minions had held him back from what they considered needless overexposure. Coming out of the break, he had begun to pitch like it was April all over again. He had one mediocre start and then he got rocked two starts in a row and his ERA now sat at an even 4.00 as the final month of the Blossoms season began.

Crockett had pitched three days earlier and wasn't due to take the mound for another two days. There was a designated hitter rule in place for the Mid-Atlantic League, so between starts there was very little to do once the game began. However, the manager of the Blossoms, Flint Embry, was a 55 year old party animal, who was considered to be a "player's manager." And so to humor his young hurler he let him take batting practice with the position players and he had given him five pinch hit at bats so far during the season. Crocket had a double and a walk in the five at bats and had struck out the other three times he had gone to the plate.

In spite of the fact that he was worried about making it through the season with a sore arm, Sam Crockett had enjoyed this season more than any of his other summers in the minors. In addition to his manager there were several other members of the organization who had made it to the big leagues including three players on the team. Sam felt like he was closer to big leagues than ever before and his determination to make it to The Show had never been greater. He truly enjoyed all of the stories of the guys who had played in the majors with guys like Jared Leader and Jelly Rogers. There was even one player who was originally drafted by the Kansas City Crowns and who had played for several different major league teams and had been on the diamond with the likes of Harry Bombs, Alan and Igor Dorquez (A Dork and

The Texan as a Jersey Boy

I Dork) as well as Popeye Maloney and the so-so outfielder for the Gumballs, Corky Samuels. These former major leaguers made Sam Crockett feel that he was so close to The Show that he could almost taste it. But he also viewed these players somewhat cynically. These players were now back in the minors. Sam resolved to never return to New Brunswick, once he made to The Show. He was going to stick. A dozen or so years in the majors and he would then be set for life.

Among the roughly 3200 fans in the stands there were 3 New Yorkers who had taken the hour ride down the New Jersey Turnpike to watch the New Brunswick Blossoms play. Timmy Burr had accompanied his friends, Lester and Georgette Postal, because they all wanted to get out of the summer heat in midtown Manhattan.

Lester Postal wanted to do a story on the diminished talent in the Bronx Bloomers farm system. Georgette wanted to treat herself to a hot dog and a beer after successfully achieving her post-marital weight loss goal. She had lost 68 pounds in a little over a year of marriage, and now was just under 250. And Timmy Burr saw the opportunity to consume a half case of beer out at the ball game with the luxury of a designated driver for the ride home. He knew that Georgette would fastidiously limit herself to one beer, while he fully expected Lester to drink with him beer for beer. Burr was originally from New Jersey and had done his undergraduate studies at Rutgers University that just happened to be located in New Brunswick so he knew that he would feel right at home the moment he sipped his first Budweiser.

As fate would have it, when the New York trio made it to their seats at Blossom Ball Park, they were seated directly across the aisle from Betsy Jo Crockett and her two sons.

"Getting them started early, huh? Cute kids." Lester was starting the afternoon in a very convivial mood. He even tipped the usher who showed them to their seats, something he did only on very rare occasions.

Flunking Chemistry Class

"Why thank you, sir." Betsy Jo's Texas accent made 'sir' sound like "suh," and Postal didn't miss it. Besides no one in New Jersey ever said "sir" no matter how it might be pronounced.

"Well great day for a ball game. Hope you and the boys enjoy it." However Lester wasn't looking at Betsy Jo's *boys* when he said it. Instead his eyes were fixated on Betsy Jo's *"girls"* that were riding high just below her Texas smile. *That's some set of knockers,* he thought. *I wonder if they're real. She's probably one of the ballplayer's wives. There's nothing real with those people anymore.*

Betsy Jo was used to people staring at her chest and hardly noticed Lester's leering. In fact she would have simply considered it a compliment if they were in San Antonio. *I guess the dirty old man likes my tatas,* she mused. *He seems harmless enough and that big ole babe by his side will certainly keep him honest.* Betsy Jo didn't realize that Georgette had once been a whole lot bigger. And sure enough once Georgette had squeezed her way into her seat, she prodded her husband to stop ogling Betsy Jo with a quick tug at his arm. Meanwhile Timmy Burr was flagging down the nearest beer man just as they announced the Star Spangled Banner over the PA system. A few minutes later the ump yelled "Play Ball" and the afternoon in the New Brunswick sun was under way.

One thing that was common place at minor league ball games was the need to provide additional entertainment besides the product on the field. This often consisted of local advertisers sponsoring gimmicky between innings diversions. These included a baseball long toss for 12 year olds; and the Wonder Run where kids below the age of 12 would run from home to second base wearing the game worn spikes of one of their favorite players. Sam Crockett's size 14 spikes were in very high demand for the Wonder Run, which took place after the eighth inning and the management made sure to have several pairs of size 14 spikes on hand, and even asked Sam to wear these newer spikes on the bench during games that he wasn't pitching. All of this simply pointed to the

The Texan as a Jersey Boy

fact that Crockett was a favorite among the Blossom's fan base. There were lots of different promotional interludes throughout the game but the Wonder Run was one of the most popular and so management saved it until after the bottom of the eighth to keep as many fans in the stands for as long as possible in case the game was a blowout. This particular game was still close but many of the fans were anticipating the upcoming Wonder Run more than they were awaiting the outcome of the game itself.

For a ball game in a Class AA league, the play was pretty sloppy. By the bottom of the eighth inning the Blossoms were leading the Worcester Wallies 6-4 and the game had seen 5 errors. There were runners on second and third with one out and Flint Embry decided to have Sam Crockett pinch hit for the Blossoms weak hitting second baseman. After a couple of foul balls the count went to 0 and 2 on Crockett.

In the stands Betsy Jo bounced up out of her seat and was cheering for Sam to get a hit. Across the aisle, an inebriated Timmy Burr was in danger of toppling over as he stood and tried to figure out whether he too should begin cheering loudly or if he should simply continue on his original mission, which was to make it to the men's room and back to the concession stand before they stopped selling beer. This conundrum was settled by a beer vendor who came down to their row with the "last call for alcohol." The game was nowhere near as interesting as the numerous young women who sat in the stands and basked in the New Jersey sunshine. Meanwhile Lester Postal was also throwing back the brewskis at an accelerated rate.

The 0-2 pitch to Crockett was high and tight and Sam fouled it off just trying to get out of the way of the pitch. The ball zoomed towards the stroller where little JR sat next to his mother. Meanwhile Betsy Jo was now holding her baby Rory in her arms and at the last minute the ball started to slice in her direction. Three feet away Timmy Burr was in the aisle paying the beer vendor for a couple of beers. When the batted ball came rocketing toward Betsy Jo, Burr valiantly attempted to jump in front of the ball so that it didn't hit the young mother. Lester Postal had also leapt to his feet in an effort to corral the

Flunking Chemistry Class

cowhide sphere. When the two men collided with one another, the two cups of beer that Timmy Burr was holding went flying all over Betsy Jo Crockett. However Burr managed to grab the baseball three inches in front of Rory Crockett's face thereby saving the baby from being struck in the head by the batted ball that came from his father's half swing. Betsy Jo quickly covered her baby's head and body but she was well aware that if it hadn't been for Timmy Burr, her protective embrace would not have come in time to save her youngest son. As Postal and Burr collapsed on the seat next to Betsy Jo, her children began to cry as they too were beer soaked.

The small crowd of people that surrounded Burr, the Postals and the Crocketts began to cheer as they recognized the great play that Burr had made. On the field Sam Crockett stared over at his wife and children as the crowd began to cheer louder. Betsy Jo tried to dry her children and herself with a small receiving blanket that she retrieved from the back of Rory's diaper bag. Because it was quite cumbersome for Betsy Jo to comfort her children and dry herself off at the same time, she handed the receiving blanket to Postal who began to hand dry the young woman's chest, shoulders and face with the blanket. This activity brought on an even louder cheer from the sparse but acutely attentive crowd.

"Here, let me handle that." By this time Georgette had squeezed back out of her seat and was standing in the aisle next to her husband Lester Postal. Betsy Jo was still clinging to Rory while, JR began sucking his fingers in the nearby stroller as he watched the events unfold. Georgette was now drying Betsy Jo's chest and some of the crowd began to chuckle and heckle as they watched.

"Hey when do I get my turn?" Another inebriated young fan yelled at the group attempting to desiccate Betsy Jo Crockett. He was wobbling in the aisle as though he too might spill his beer. He was three rows behind the Crocketts, the Postals and Timmy Burr.

Meanwhile standing near the batter's box with a 0 – 2 count, Sam Crockett became fixated on the scene in the stands. Finally he trotted over to where his family was gamely trying to dry off one way or another. He put one hand on the field's guard rail and scaled the barrier and then made his way up into the stands.

The Texan as a Jersey Boy

Postal quickly realized that he was fortunate that Georgette had taken over the effort of dehydrating the ball player's wife's clothing, because Sam Crocket seemed like an enormously large individual once he bounded up to the fourth row where they were all standing. At 6'4' tall with another inch and a half of metal spikes under his feet, Crockett looked larger than life. The heckler a couple of rows back had hurriedly sat down and kept his mouth shut once he saw Crockett heading toward the scene of the attempted desiccation.

On the field the umpires had called time out, but were uncertain what was going on. The home plate umpire had wandered over toward the stands and simply yelled up toward Crockett, "Play Ball."

Crockett at first paid no attention to the umpire. Although he peered around menacingly at the fans surrounding his family, his voice was soft when he spoke to Betsy Jo. "Are you all OK?"

Betsy Jo seemed suddenly embarrassed by all of the attention that she was receiving and simply said, "We're alright. These fine people are just helping us out." Intuitively she was quick to exonerate Burr and the Postals from any wrong doing. "I think you ought to go back on the field."

The home plate umpire began to get some heat from the visiting team dugout and when Crockett didn't immediately heed his call to resume play the official pointed up at Crockett and yanked his thumb into the air signaling that Crockett had been ejected from the ball game.

Instead of racing back to the field to argue the decision, Crockett waved his hand dismissively at the umpire as though he could care less what the umpire wanted to do. He also turned to Postal and Burr and said, "Thanks for helping my family." Meanwhile he glared at the other fans as though they better not say anything bad about his wife and kids. Standing on the cement flooring in his spikes he towered over the surrounding crowd. He paid no attention whatsoever to the umpire.

By now the Blossoms manager, Flint Embry was out of the dugout along with several of his players and they were watching the scene in the stands unfold. Embry reflexively reacted to the umpire's ejection

Flunking Chemistry Class

of his player by running over and getting in the ump's face. So now the crowd was being entertained by dual demonstrations.

A minute or two after his ejection Sam Crockett just sat down in the stands next to his wife. It was an incredibly incongruous spectacle. Not knowing what else to do, Georgette, Lester and Timmy moved back across the aisle and returned to their seats. Although there were a few other fans in the stands wearing authentic New Brunswick Blossoms hats and jerseys, Crockett's well worn uniform that was dog-eared with faded pine tar stains clearly differentiated him from the Blossoms wannabees. But in short order they were now all part of a crazed atmosphere. When the umpire finally ejected Embry along with his player, he told the manager that he couldn't remain in the dugout either and so Embry also climbed into the stands and went up and sat down with Burr, the Postals and the Crocketts as the small crowd roared its approval. It took fifteen minutes to get the game restarted and the new pinch-pinch hitter promptly blasted the first pitch he saw over the centerfield wall for a three run homer.

After the eighth inning drew to a close it was time for the Wonder Run. More than a dozen young boys and girls aged 10 through 12 raced over to the Blossoms dugout and were given the spikes of various Blossoms players. There was a little pushing and shoving between two twelve year old boys who wanted an extra pair of Sam Crockett's spikes. When he saw what was going on Sam removed his shoes in the stands and threw them down to one of the boys. The crowd cheered wildly at this gesture. This seemed to rile up the home plate umpire once again and the ump came over to the railing near where Crockett and Flint Embry were sitting with the fans.

"I threw you guys out of the game. You can't be sitting there in uniform. Out of the game means out of the game."

"The rule book just says we can't be in the dugout. It doesn't say we can't be in the ballpark." Flint Embry was standing now and yelling

The Texan as a Jersey Boy

back at the umpire from four rows back. The manager seemed to relish every moment of the debate.

"You're still in uniform. I sent you clowns to the showers. You can't just sit here in uniform unless you want to forfeit the game."

"What the hell are talking about? Are you just making up the rules as you go along?" Embry ripped off his uniform jersey and threw it down on the seat "There," he said to the ump, "I'm no longer in uniform. Does that make you happy?"

The umpire was trying to regain some control, to give some appearance that he was still in charge so he simply pointed at Crockett and said, "Him too."

Sam Crockett had already discarded his spikes. He watched his manager scream at the ump and he wanted to join in the fun. So he slowly unbuttoned his jersey then removed it and swung it over his head a couple of times before throwing it back into the enthusiastic crowd. His muscular arms and shoulders drew a few catcalls from the young college women in the stands.

The crowd continued to cheer wildly and the young college girls began chanting "Take it off; Take it off; Take it all off."

Betsy Jo was a bit horrified by all of this but she was determined to stand by her man. However she didn't expect Sam to react the way he did. The ballplayer smiled at his fans and then sat down and removed his uniform pants as well. He threw them to his female cheering section. Then he sat down wearing only his boxers a sleeveless t-shirt and his white athletic socks. The cheering section screamed for more but Sam knew when to stop.

"No more, Sam. That's far enough." Betsy Jo gave her husband a very direct order just in case he had any wilder ideas in mind.

Back on the field the umpire was now very sorry that he had reinitiated the fracas. To make matters worse the team's administrative staff had just completed the Wonder Run, and the young boy who had gotten Sam's spikes won the race and this sent the crowd into further delirium. The umpire couldn't get the game started any faster, and he didn't call a single ball in the top of the ninth. Soon enough the

Flunking Chemistry Class

Blossoms went on to wallop the Worcester Wallies by a final score of 9 to 4.

Flint Embry and Sam Crockett remained in the stands with their fans until the final out was recorded. Even the concessionaire made an exception on the ninth inning rule and allowed Lester Postal to buy a couple of beers for his newest rental friends, Crockett and Embry. Of course, he would later charge these beverages to his *New York Roast* expense account.

At game's end everyone seemed to be in a much better mood. The crowd began to disperse. Crockett and Embry signed a few autographs while they were still up in the stands and then they began to wander down the steps towards the field, so that they could access the locker room through the dugout. Postal followed them to the field while Burr and Georgette remained in the stands talking to Betsy Jo Crockett. When Lester Postal caught up with Sam Crockett he took advantage of the circumstances to interview the ballplayer. He knew that anyone willing to be interviewed in his underwear would not likely be the type of guy to cover up his thoughts on other topics. He wanted to query the pitcher on his favorite topic, PEDs, and given the circumstances he wasn't planning on being subtle.

"It's been a pleasure meeting you, Sam. Do you mind if I ask you a question or two?" By this time Lester Postal had already identified himself as a *Roast* reporter. He had also managed to move the ballplayer away from the rest of the crowd and they were standing alone near the first base coach's box as they spoke.

"Sure, why not?"

"Do you come across many guys that you're competing against who are using PEDs?" Discretion was not an available implement in Postal's reporter tool box.

"Are you serious? More than half of the guys are doing stuff. We talk about this all the time. Not everybody admits it. But most guys just don't care. Some guys are even selling the stuff to other guys, or trading steroids for pot. But we don't rat one another out. That's for sure. However if you want to know the truth, it all kind of pisses me off."

"Why is that?"

The Texan as a Jersey Boy

"That shit has consequences for your body, man. And it also weirds out some guys a bit. They get hostile and flaky. I *dunno*. I'm just *sayin'*. Ya *know?*"

"How about you? Do people ever approach you about taking steroids?"

"Not so much the ballplayers. Most of them know how I feel about it. But there are others who are always letting you know that the shit is available and a lot of them say that the stuff is undetectable by the piss tests."

"Who are these other guys?"

"They're just guys from the gyms …you know, trainers and body-builders and occasionally … yeah …sometimes another ballplayer."

"Can you give me any specific examples?"

"Hey look, I don't want to get into this crap. I know you helped my wife and kids out. But come on man, you're a *freakin'* reporter. I've already said too much and I'm standing here in my underwear. What else do you want from me? I told you that ballplayers don't rat out other ballplayers."

"Did you ever think that the juicers are hurting you and your family?"

"All the time man, all the time."

"Don't you ever want to do anything about it?"

"Like I said, I'm just a ballplayer. I can't police what everyone else does. I'm just *tryin'* to make it to The Show. Yea, it pisses me off every time someone who is *juicin'* gets called up and I'm still here. But the way I figure it, I'll make it anyway, sooner or later. And when I make it, I won't have tiny nuts and be half crazed all the time." Crockett's voice tailed off at the end of that statement as he realized how ironic that must sound given his current state of undress.

"These juicers are stealing money from you every day that you're here and they're there. That's got to piss you off."

"Look, Mr. Postal. You're right it ticks me off plenty. But some of the guys who are *juicin'* are guys I've been *playin'* with in the minors for years. They just got fed up with being passed over and began doing the stuff also. They've just made a different decision than I have. That's all.

Flunking Chemistry Class

That's it. OK? We're done on this topic. I've got to take a shower and get out of here with Betsy Jo and the boys."

"All right, one last thing ... on a different topic. I promise it won't take but a second or two. You've pitched a lot of innings this year. How does the wing feel?"

"Like you said, I've thrown a lot of innings. Flint told me that the guys in New York only want me to throw a few innings in relief for the rest of the season. But I might also get some time in the outfield."

"But you're arm's OK? Right?"

"Yea, it's fine." Sam Crockett could feel a little tweak around his elbow even as he spoke. He was worried but he hadn't said anything to anyone, except Betsy Jo. He certainly didn't want to say anything to a reporter. "I've really got to go. Thanks again for helping my wife and kids. Oh yeah, and thanks for the beer." He laughed and then turned around so that there would be no further questions.

As Sam Crockett made his way back through the dugout to the locker room, Lester Postal made his way back into the stands. He saw that Georgette and Timmy were still chatting with Betsy Jo Crockett and helping her move her two children back up the short flight of stairs to the main exit level landing. He climbed up after them and noticed that Burr was listing a bit from his afternoon of imbibing in the New Jersey sunshine.

When he reached the top of the stairs Betsy Jo was smiling. Another ballplayer's wife had joined in the conversation and was complaining because her husband was not coming home right away but was instead going out boozing with some of his teammates. After she left, Postal had made it up to the top of the stairs and immediately took over the conversation.

"I just had a nice chat with Sam. He's had a good summer. Maybe the Bloomers will call him up from the Blossoms in September."

"That would be awfully nice. Sam always talks about the day he'll go from being a Blossom to a full fledged Bloomer. He knows he's close. He's worried though. He hasn't pitched as well as he was pitching in May and June. But we've got our fingers crossed."

The Texan as a Jersey Boy

Lester Postal was just trying to be nice. He knew that Sam would never be called up this year. There were at least three other minor league pitchers that the Bloomers could bring up before they got to Sam, and he knew through some of his rental friends back in New York that the club suspected that Crockett had a sore arm and was resistant to their suggestion that he work with some of his teammates on one of their specialized training regimens. They were more likely to shut him down for the season than they were to call him up in September.

"It seems unfair sometimes that guys who are clean living ballplayers like your husband get passed over by some of these guys who are doing performance enhancing drugs." The comment came from an unexpected source, Georgette Postal, who moved past Lester to join the conversation. "I don't know why Timmy's boss can't clean up the sport, once and for all."

"Who's your boss, Timmy?" Betsy Jo smiled as she asked Burr the logical question.

"I work for Buzz Selout the MBL commissioner. I'm a lawyer and a statistician." Lester watched Burr make this pronouncement without sounding too smashed, but one look in his eyes would belie any sense of sobriety. Still Betsy Jo seemed impressed.

"I'm happy that you guys actually take the time to go to minor league games. Wait until I tell Sam who it was that saved JR, Rory and me from that foul ball. And as far as all of the steroid cheats are concerned, my husband and I think that they're very foolish. But what is the commissioner's office doing about it anyway?"

Burr now demonstrated his true level of intoxication by just answering with a mindless shrug. His buddy, Lester Postal answered for him, "Not much, I'd have to say."

Then Georgette Postal chimed in once again. "I keep telling Lester that I'm surprised that the clean players don't sue the Multinational Baseball League and some of the players who have been using steroids."

"Are you a lawyer too?"

"Yes, but I don't work for MBL. Only my friend, Timmy, here does."

Flunking Chemistry Class

"You know I'll have to ask Sam about that. I wonder if anyone has sued, or threatened to sue. I know that Sam has said a lot of the clean players are real mad at the guys that use the stuff. He calls them 'floats.' Sam says that all floats are cheaters and that's that." Betsy Jo's Texas accent accentuated the final statement on the topic. Meanwhile Lester Postal was proud of the fact that the term that he had coined, "floats," was now part of the baseball vernacular, whenever anyone broached the topic of PEDs.

"Well if your man ever wants to talk about the possibility here's my business card." Georgette handed Betsy Jo one of her cards and shortly thereafter the three New Yorkers left the park and went out on the town in New Brunswick looking for something to eat.

Betsy Jo waited patiently with her sons as her husband showered after the game. Normally the post game clean up only took about a half an hour, but when Sam didn't show up for almost fifty minutes, she began to worry. Rory had fallen asleep in her arms but JR was beginning to fidget in his stroller and wanted to get out of the seat harness that had him strapped in. Finally Sam Crockett appeared from the locker room. He was walking rather slowly and Betsy Jo immediately sensed something was very wrong. When he got up near her she asked him directly, "What's wrong, Sammy, what's wrong?"

"I've been traded to the Tokyo Carp."

XV

A Dork and the Three Stooges

October 2006

It wasn't as if Alan Dorquez had had an awful season. In fact, A Dork was once again an All-Star and he collected his 2,000th base hit in mid July. His other statistics – 35 dingers; 121 ribbies and a .290 batting average – approximated his career norms. In the entire history of the Multinational Baseball League only seven other players had collected 2000 base hits by the age of 30 and all seven of these players were enshrined in the Coopersville Corridor of Conceit. Still for whatever reason there was no love at the ballpark for A Dork. The home fans cheered politely whenever his batting prowess delivered a win for the Bronx Bloomers and booed him lustily whenever he failed to deliver in the clutch, which was often. One of those fans also happened to be the owner of the Bloomers, Larry "Bass" Sledgehammer. Sledgehammer's chief beef was that A Dork was now a $25 million a year bust because the Bloomers had once again failed to make it to the Earth Series. Sledgehammer had now been paying the superfloat's enormous salary for three years and had zero Earth Series appearances to show for it.

A Dork couldn't understand why he was getting all the blame. Even before he came to New York, the Bloomers hadn't won the Earth Series for two consecutive years and now they hadn't won it five years in a row. *Why wasn't Jared Leader getting some of the blame?* A Dork despised the shortstop whom he regarded as a nerdy little twerp. *He makes routine*

Flunking Chemistry Class

plays look difficult just so the stupid fans will think he's going all out. And he's never hit 30 dingers in a season and I do that every year. Dorquez was beside himself trying to understand why Leader got all of the adulation and he got all of the scorn. Some of it was the sportswriters. He knew that much. They definitely had a double standard when it came to Leader versus A Dork comparisons. This was true in their off field activities as well as their performances on the diamond. *The little squirt can be seen out on the town with some tawdry young tart of an actress and all of sudden the woman gets treated as though she is as pure as the driven snow. I have one date with a girl and she's treated like a porn star. Well all right there was a porn star or two in the mix – I have to admit that.*

And then there was Joe Trophy. He talked about the shortstop as though he was his own son. *Can't Trophy see Leader's obvious flaws – no power at the plate; no range in the field; subpar arm strength? And why did I have to change positions so that a lesser talent can play the more glamorous position?* These thoughts constantly occupied A Dork's mind. He just could never get over his jealousy when it came to his teammate, and he secretly harbored wishes that Leader would fail. His most fervent dream was that in the seventh game of the Earth Series, Leader would make three errors and strike out four times and that he – the great A Dork – would come up in the bottom of the ninth and hit a grand slam home run giving the Bloomers the championship. Unfortunately even this dream ended with sportswriters gathered around Jared Leader's locker asking him about team chemistry, esprit de corps or some other intangible nonsense. A Dork hated Leader; detested him; loathed him; reviled him. He wished he had never agreed to play beside Leader on the Bloomers.

Well one way or another, the Bloomers had failed again and both Leader and A Dork were forced to watch the St Louis Scarlets beat up on the Motown Marauders. A Dork was still vexed about never having played in an Earth Series and he was doing his brooding in his midtown Manhattan penthouse apartment. He was accompanied by three call girls who customarily took turns easing his pain while lightening his wallet. Against his better judgment A Dork decided to watch the Earth Series while his trio of hourly employees sat around in their lacy

A Dork and the Three Stooges

work clothes. A Dork didn't know their real names or for that matter their working names. He simply chose to name them after characters in one of his favorite rerun TV series: *The Three Stooges*. So with no apologies for the obvious gender reversal he referred to them as Mo, Lari and Curlie.

Both the Scarlets and the Marauders boasted a couple of superfloats each. The Marauders had signed free agent catcher Igor Dorquez to a four year contract before the 2004 season and he had produced prodigious numbers. I Dork was a fan favorite even though he had been exposed as a juicer in Janesco's book <u>Jacked Up.</u> He never actually admitted taking PEDs but when a local sportswriter asked him about being one of the players who had failed MBL's survey testing in 2003 he famously answered "Only God knows." He said this in a vampish way that reminded folks of the old Clairol hair coloring commercials that professed, "Only your hairdresser know for sure." The other superfloat was Venezuelan outfielder, Maximus Balognez, who was yet another former teammate of CoJo Janesco. Apparently Janesco had shown Balognez how to grease his skids when they were both with the Chicago Pantyhose.

Meanwhile the Scarlets were happy to exhibit their own home grown superfloats including first basemen Alvin Pewnose, a beastly young stud with inflated forearms, biceps and statistics. Pewnose was so beastly strong that he was enabling the Scarlets' fans to forget about their previous superfloat first baseman – and crybaby – Popeye Maloney.

A Dork watched the rather one sided game unfold as the Scarlets were trouncing the Marauders soundly in the opening game of the Earth Series. He knew that the Motown team was the same group that had bounced his Bloomers out of the opening round of the playoffs three games to one. And he was also keenly aware that Bass Sledgehammer had alluded to him as a "loser," after A Dork had managed just three puny hits in more than thirty at bats during the last two

Flunking Chemistry Class

years' playoffs. Lastly he knew that Lester Postal of *The New York Roast* had reported that one of Dorquez' teammates had referred to him as "a narcissistic nobody." It was at times like this that he wished that he had never left the Drillies. The fans, the press and even his teammates in Dallas were much more understanding than their New York City counterparts.

Dorquez' ladies-in-waiting began to get bored with the mere anticipation of A Dork's pending participation in their games while he watched the Earth Series opener on TV. They began paying some attention to one another simply to keep their skills sharp, almost like a pinch hitter hitting in the underground batting cages while preparing for his time in the batter's box.

When Maximus Balognez came to the plate. A Dork muttered, "This guy must be doing some fine stuff since he left the Pantyhose. He gets bigger and hits harder every year."

One of A Dork's lacy employees, Curlie, volunteered that "I'll bet that Maximus is not nearly as big and as hard as you, A Dork. She rubbed the back of his neck and his shoulders as she said this and A Dork turned partially away from the TV and got a glimpse of Mo and Lari amusing each other. Then he turned and answered Curlie.

"You can't even talk about Maximus Balognez – or for that matter any other MBL player – as being in the same league with me. There is A Dork and then there are all of the other ball players. It's not even close. The next best player in the game couldn't even shine my shoes. And what's more, they all know it and that's why they're all so jealous."

Brazenly the young woman decided to challenge Dorquez' audacious self appraisal. The woman had been paid in advance for her time, so she was a bit dicier in her assessment of A Dork's potential. "Then why do the fans all say that you never come through in the clutch? A lot of them say that Jared Leader is the best player on the Bloomers. How can you be the best player in the MBL if you're not even the best player on the Bloomers?"

A Dork and the Three Stooges

Her questions were asked in a soft teasing tone. She wanted to get a rise out of A Dork. However the self-centered ballplayer was more insecure and more easily provoked than she had thought. "Jared Leader is a fake. He acts like he's always hustling and busting his butt. However it's all a charade. He's just an average ball player. In the MBL today there are at least six or seven shortstops that are better than Leader. In fact he's not even the best shortstop on the Bloomers. I am."

Alan Dorquez was now turned around on the bed and glaring in the young woman's face. The other two had stepped out of the box and had stopped taking warm-up pitches; they simply began to watch the argument. Dorquez was getting disgusted with his coterie of concubines, but he had always managed to avoid roid rage. He attributed this to the good work of his personal chemist, Butch Botch, also known as the "Butcher." The Butcher was quite adept at creating chemical compounds that managed to add strength and dexterity without inducing enragement or fury. A Dork liked the fact that he was able to keep his cool no matter how challenging the circumstances were. He didn't care that these combinations of PEDs sometimes left him like an emotionless zombie. The Butcher was simply the best chemist that money could buy. And A Dork knew that his investment in Botch's concoctions was the main reason that he now possessed the most lucrative contract ever signed by an MBL player. The working girls in his room were an expense item. The money he paid the Butcher was an investment. The only reservation he had at all about Botch was that the chemist had recently talked about undergoing a possible gender change. In fact Butch Botch had already started calling himself Andrea Botch. Whatever Botch was taking for himself, A Dork wanted no part of it.

"I think that you girls can all leave now. I want to watch the rest of the game by myself." And just as he was about to dismiss the three stooges, the lobby bellman rang up to his apartment.

"Mr. Dorquez ... Myronda is on her way up." John Lackey, the doorman was also a beneficiary of A Dork's significant largesse. Dorquez may have a lot of faults but he certainly wasn't cheap. Lackey wanted to tip off the ballplayer because he wasn't sure whether or not Myronda

153

was part of the game that was being played up in the penthouse. Myronda was a celebrity singer whose character was every bit as seedy as A Dork's reputation. She was a *material girl,* who was used to getting whatever she wanted. She went through men the same way that A Dork went through women. And when the allure wore off she would discard her latest obsession like a worn out pair of loafers. When Myronda arrived in the lobby she left her body guards behind and made a bee-line for the elevator without checking in with the doorman. This then prompted Lackey to call up to A Dork.

"Oh shit. I don't need her right now. You know that I have some other women up here with me. Can't you stop her and tell her that I'm not home?"

"I'm sorry, Mr. Dorquez. She just bolted right by me. She just breezed by the *borderline.* She'll be there in like ... *4 minutes.* And also I wasn't sure that she hadn't been invited to join your party. Of course I know she's *crazy for you.*" Then he whispered so that he wouldn't be overheard by the bodyguards. "Maybe you could just lock the door and pretend no one's home." Then he quickly realized how stupid this sounded because Myronda's security had been listening all along. But in reality he didn't care. He knew that Myronda wasn't naïve ... *like a virgin* ...or something.

The three stooges knew that this was an even firmer exit cue. None of them wanted to be there when Myronda arrived because the pop singer was a bitch on wheels if she saw that someone else was moving in on her latest lover. Her emotional reactions were never about the lover that she was losing. They were always about the person or persons that she was losing her lover to. Her rivals realized that they could thank their *lucky stars* if Myronda didn't physically attack them. However her verbal attacks were known to contain such vitriol that one of her adversaries actually crafted a pop song known as *"Mama Don't Preach"* to point out the inherent hypocrisy of Myronda's vitriol, protesting that her negativism was much more than Myronda simply *expressing herself.*

Partially at the urging of A Dork and partially for self preservation the three stooges began to quickly redress as the pop diva's elevator rose to the top floor of the building. When Myronda rang the bell to

A Dork and the Three Stooges

the penthouse apartment they were all out of the bedroom and in the front hallway. Mo, Lari and Curlie were ready to bolt past Myronda as soon as A Dork opened the portal.

The scene that unfolded looked like something out of a low budget comedy. Out ran the stooges and in walked the strumpet. The passing glances did little to allay the animosity that was palpable among A Dork's women but Myronda managed to *hold her head up* and control her venom until the three stooges were on their way down in the elevator. However when the door closed to the penthouse, Myronda threw her handbag on a hall table and lit into A Dork with her hands on her hips.

"Who the fuck were those bimbos?"

"Do you really care? They were just a warm up act, like the singers who go onstage for you before your performances. Now it's time for the real show to go on."

"Nice try. I'm not buying it. Either I hit lead off or I don't play your stupid games. I don't want to see any two bit bitches hustling their stuff around you. I'll bet making it with those bitches is like making it with grizzle. I'll bet they handle more bats in a week than you do in a whole season."

"I didn't tap even one of those women, I swear. They were just here to watch the Earth Series with me. If I knew that you were in town I would never have let them come up here."

"Alright I'll let it slide this time." Myronda began pacing around the penthouse. She was wearing a short plain heavy shapeless khaki dress that did nothing at all to enhance her tight figure. She also wore no makeup. However for some reason, she was wearing stiletto heels. Meanwhile A Dork had never changed out of the gym shorts and sleeveless t-shirt that he had been wearing all day. In fact he had been wearing these same clothes for more than 24 hours and hadn't bothered to bathe since coming from his workout at the gym the night before. Although the penthouse was spacious the air quality within the place was a bit clammy. While Myronda roamed throughout the apartment, A Dork went over and flipped on another TV in the living room area. He noticed that she said nothing at all about the other TV in the bedroom which was still on, thereby flaunting the fact that this had been the venue for his ballgame viewing with the Three Stooges.

"Why do you want to watch that shit?" Myronda asked. Doesn't it just piss you off?" She could see that A Dork was engrossed in the ballgame, and she thought that his viewing was a masochistic activity. "Just let it go. Face it you weren't good enough this year. That's all there is to it."

A Dork's nostrils flared in contempt. "This has nothing to do with me. So I didn't hit .300. I still hit my homers and knocked in plenty of runs. I'm a fucking stud, Myronda. I'm a fucking stud."

"If you're such a fucking stud then why couldn't you get it up the last time I was here?" Myronda knew that she was baiting him. But she also knew what she herself wanted, some rough sex. A Dork jumped out of his seat and went over to the singer and grabbed both sides of the bottom seam of her dress and yanked it up over her head as she raised her arms to help facilitate the process. As he suspected, she wasn't wearing anything under the short sack dress. He admired her tight body with his hands as she pirouetted in her high heels, but when he realized that his anger was negating his potential arousal, he went back to the couch and sat down again in front of the TV. With that Myronda removed her last articles of clothing, her shoes, and threw them at A Dork. "What the hell is wrong with you? Are you some kind of eunuch?"

A Dork was quite peeved, but he knew that if he removed his pants the evidence would show that he was certainly not ready for any of the sexual gymnastics that he knew Myronda had in mind, so he just tried to maintain his cool and changed the topic.

"I've got a lot of crap on my mind. The ballgame is a way for me to relax. I'm a bit worried about this guy Mitch Witchell and his bimbo sidekick, Heidi Hunt. Selout hired these two clowns to study the use of steroids in the game. People are saying that when the Witchell Hunt Report finally comes out it will give the names of players who used the stuff. That's not going to be pretty. The only thing that they have on me is the tests that I failed when I was with the Drillies in 2003 and those results are supposed to have been confidential. Selout told me as much himself. But if they start outing all of us who failed the test, it could put some kind of cloud over all of my stats. I don't want this report to eventually hinder my election to the Corridor of Conceit when I finally retire."

Myronda looked at him with disgust and derision but didn't say a word. She simply retrieved her heels, and her handbag, slipped her khaki dress back over her body and walked out the door toward the elevator.

A Dork went back to watching the game alone. He still had his $250 Million to keep him company, but he wondered what Jared Leader was doing tonight.

XVI
The Witchell Hunt Report

December 2007

Timothy Burr, Esquire had grown tired of his position as Buzz Selout's gopher. Six months earlier he had left the commissioner's office and joined the private law practice of his friend Georgette Postal. Georgette had recently celebrated three and a half years of marriage to sportswriter Lester Postal. This was record marital longevity for Lester. And given Lester's previous track record Georgette had decided that they would celebrate their wedding anniversary every six months rather than annually. Georgette also used these intervals to demarcate her remarkable weight loss. Although she was still a big woman, Georgette had now lost more than 130 pounds since her wedding day and had recently tipped the scales at 175 pounds and had actually squeezed herself into a size 12 dress. She had a pretty face that grew evener prettier with the weight loss. During their three and half years of marriage Georgette had an astounding influence on her husband. Lester still hung out in the Manhattan sports bars but he was now more conscientious about his public demeanor. He hadn't been thrown out of a single bar since the ceremony for his fifth nuptials had been completed.

Lester Postal felt like he was watching his wife morph from an obese Cass Elliott body type to a zaftig figured Cleopatra sized woman. He knew that she would never be scrawny-skinny like the pole-dancing spouses he had previously divorced and discarded, and he liked the fact that everything about Georgette was natural and real. He even started referring to her as "Gorgeous Georgie." For the first time that he could ever remember he treated a woman like an equal.

So when Timmy Burr and Georgette Postal decided to practice law together in Manhattan, Lester Postal was quite supportive. Georgette had already established herself somewhat as a plaintiff's attorney. She had won a multimillion product liability case against a major brewing company and bottler. Her client was a young radio commentator that her husband had met in a bar. Georgette had been able to demonstrate that the bottler and the brewer had both been negligent in their beer bottling process. The processes allowed contaminated animal urine to coat the caps of thousands of bottles of beer. In the case of her client these faulty processes had caused leptospirosis, liver damage renal failure and cardiac issues. Georgette's husband made sure that the trial received detailed coverage in the pages of the *New York Roast* and she had immediately gained a modicum of fame from the trial. After the trial Georgette's practice had begun to attract a growing number of clients beyond the barroom beer guzzlers that hung out with her husband. That's when she took on Timmy Burr as a minority partner to help with the case load and their joint practice was doing well.

Another change in Timmy Burr's life style came with a slight name change. Although his name on the office door, his stationery and his business cards read: Timothy Burr, Esquire, everyone he knew had always just called him Timmy. Now that he was a 31 year old minority partner in the law firm of Postal and Burr, he wanted people to stop calling him by the childish moniker, "Timmy." From now on he was going to be known as "Tim," even if it meant he would have to put up with all of the falling tree jokes.

Tim Burr still harbored hopes of becoming a player agent even though the law practice of Postal and Burr was not taking him in that direction. However he kept up his love for baseball by hanging around with Georgette's husband and they frequently discussed the hot topics of the game.

Flunking Chemistry Class

Lester Postal and Tim Burr both had teams in *The Morning After's* fantasy baseball league and Tim Burr had won consecutive championships in the first two years that they were in the league together. Part of the problem for Lester and his team was that he refused to have any floats on his fantasy team and as soon as a player on Lester's team was implicated as a juicer, Lester would immediately trade him. This contributed mightily to Postal's ninth place finish in a ten team league. Burr's attitude was more accepting in the fantasy world than it was in real life and he took advantage of Postal's willingness to dump his juicers at the trade deadline and happily took home the champion's share of the fantasy prize money.

While Burr and the Postals kept their friendship and business relationships growing they were an odd group. Only occasionally did Tim Burr find a date of his own and most of the time the three of them went out socially as ... well ... simply as a threesome. They had little in common except for a passion for baseball. Even in the off season, Burr followed the sport zealously. He was always dreaming up trades that he hoped his favorite team, the Metropolitan Mutts, could make. Although he never saw any of these trades come to fruition, he followed every article written during the Hot Stove League portion of the offseason. His legal workload kept him at work more than 60 hours a week. Whatever spare time he possessed he spent following baseball in one way or another.

Georgette was about to leave the office to meet a client for lunch. She looked over at her partner in a motherly worried way, even though she was only two years older.

"You know Tim; you've got to get a life. I know it gets pretty busy around here, but you can't just spend all of your free time with baseball stuff. I was wondering if I could set you up with a friend of mine on a blind date. We could double date ...you know ... Lester and me and you and Evangeline."

"Evangeline? Who is Evangeline?"

"She is a woman who I met at Overweight Observers. She's very nice and she's also a baseball fan."

The Witchell Hunt Report

"Well maybe ..."

Lester Postal had stayed up late the night before watching Monday night football. He had gone to the office late but wanted to handle some routine administrative issues before heading out to lunch with one of his rental friends. While he was wolfing down a couple of booze-absorbing doughnuts and sipping his third cup of coffee, the senior sports editor of *The Roast*, Will Morehead, stopped by his desk.

"Morning Postal." His greeting was more like an alarm clock announcing the time of day than it was like a salutation. There was only about 15 minutes left to the morning so the editor's greeting was tinted with more than a little sarcasm.

"Morning Morehead." His response came quickly. It was as though he were expeditiously reaching to extinguish the ringing clock and face whatever the day brought on.

"We got a call in here about an hour ago from some young kid who says he wants to talk to you. The kid says that he played in the Japanese minors last year but was with the Bloomers farm team in 06. Does the name Sam Crockett ring a bell?"

"Yea of course it does. You remember this guy. I did a pump piece on him that summer. Remember when I went down to New Brunswick with the commissioner's guy, Tim Burr."

"That's right. I was sure I knew that name Crockett from somewhere. How could I forget? This was the kid that you claimed was going to be a future stud with the Bloomers and then that same day after we're out in print with your story, we find out he got traded to the Carp."

Postal knew that Morehead was busting his chops. Morehead knew full well who Crockett was. He just wanted to lure Postal into a sense of animation before he squashed it with a reminder of the reporter's gaff. Despite Morehead's baiting and obvious amusement at being able to remind him of his past blunder, Postal was glad to hear that the kid had called. He snatched the small note pad sheet that his boss was holding and noticed that there was a callback number on the memo.

"Thanks Will, I'll run it down." His use of Morehead's first name was a sign of weakness. However he didn't want to rehash his past article with his editor this early in the day. He hadn't even had his first boilermaker yet. He just wanted to get Morehead out of his face.

"Oh by the way Postal, one other thing," Morehead now was ready to demonstrate that he had had a little more information than he was letting on. "I assume you noticed that this guy Crockett was just taken this morning from the Carp in the Cruel 5 Draft."

Morehead and Postal both knew that the sportswriter hadn't gotten that far in his morning work and it was simply Morehead's way of prodding his subordinate to be more industrious.

"Like I said Morehead, I'll run it down." Postal had regained his swagger and both the writer and the editor liked it better that way.

Buzz Selout was being besieged by media inquiries about the players who had been implicated in the Witchell Hunt Report. He missed his lawyer-statistician, Tim Burr. He never realized how much he had relied on Burr as a sounding board. There were plenty of other attorneys, accountants and businessmen and financial wizards in the employ of the commissioner's office who were older and more experienced than Tim Burr. However Selout's relationship with these staff members was a bit more reserved than what he had experienced with Burr. Selout felt that sometimes these other "advisors" talked down to him even though he was their boss. Burr on the other hand respected him or so he thought. He was also a bit annoyed to learn that Burr had joined Lester Postal's wife's law firm. What was the world coming to?

Selout's spacious office contained several expensive paintings that might have seemed out of place among the other sports memorabilia that created his office décor. However the paintings themselves were sports themed also, including two Leroy Neiman originals and one by Opie Otterstad. The general décor of his office had begun to reflect the increased opulence that came with his fat eight figure salary from the MBL. But as Selout sat alone in his office reflectively reminiscing about his years as The Commish, he realized that the one thing that he still craved was the respect from baseball's constituent parties. He knew that the players thought that he was the enemy; the sportswriters found him oafish; the owners felt he was weak and indecisive; and the fans sometimes thought of him as a dim witted buffoon. But he knew in his heart he was none of these things. Although it was true that he sometimes played dumb when confronted with facts about the steroid era, he was certainly not a buffoon. And he was far from an enemy to the players who had gained unprecedented wealth through their collective agreements as well as their individual contracts. Neither did he think of himself as indecisive when it came to dealing with the owners. He thought of himself as deliberate and resolute rather than hesitant. And finally, the sportswriters ... oh the hell with the sportswriters ... they didn't matter and they were the only ones who weren't making the big bucks off the game anyway ...maybe they were just jealous ... yeah the hell with them.

The intercom buzzed and Marguerite woke the commissioner from his reverie.

"One of the Little Hammers is on Line 2," Marguerite gum snapped.

Over the past two years Larry "Bass" Sledgehammer had been in failing health and he had gradually turned over the day to day operations of the Bronx Bloomers to his son *Daryl* and to his other son *Darryl*. The two men were only an additional "r" removed from one another. Other than the added consonant no one could tell them apart as they tried to emulate their father.

The Commish took a deep breath and lowered his voice to a more masculine timbre as he hit the speaker button on his desktop phone. "Selout here."

"Good afternoon, Buzz. It's Darryl here." It was *Double R*, but Selout had no way of knowing that. The tone reversal was obvious to both men although neither acknowledged it to the other person. But Selout was immediately suspicious of the Little Hammer's congenial tone.

"What's up Darryl?"

"All the noise about The Witchell Hunt Report has got us worried. I hope we plan on standing tall on the idea that this stuff is behind us. We can't fold our tent and allow the guys mentioned in the report to get suspended after all. There's nothing to that stream of thought. Is there?"

"Come on Darryl. That's not fair. You know that I have been keeping you folks briefed on this topic at regular intervals via some of our conference calls. We're not going to do anything like that. We want to move on from here and increase our testing so that the players aren't using the stuff in the future."

"I'm glad to hear that because these newspaper guys are kicking up a pretty good froth about all of this."

"I could care less what the reporters are saying. Anyway I have bigger worries with the Players Association. The damn MBLPA has been particularly uncooperative with Mitch Witchell, Heidi Hunt and their team of investigators. They're telling me that they may hold up approval of the next collective bargaining agreement if we try to discipline any of the players named in the report. And they're still bitching about the fact that we gave the names from the 2003 anonymous testing to the government."

"Why did we do that?"

Selout was frustrated in dealing with the Little Hammers. At least their old man understood what had to be done.

"We had no choice. The government promised to maintain the privacy of the list but the B'WHALE'CO investigation of Bombs, Jambino, and Schlepfield was causing subpoenas to be issued and answered. Nothing we could do about the fact that the government somehow leaked the stuff we gave them."

"Well after Harry Bombs got indicted for perjury in the B'WHALE'CO case last month, you would think that some of these guys would smarten up. But the Bombs mess together with this Witchell Hunt Report has really got the sportswriters riled up. They're now going back over the whole gamut of incidents over the last decade and referring to it as the 'Steroid Era.' They're rehashing the claims against a lot of guys who played on the Bloomers during our championship years."

"What can I tell you, Darryl? That's hardly unexpected."

"Did you see Lester Postal's article in *The Roast* today?"

"Not yet. Besides he's not exactly one of my favorite press guys."

"Basically Postal takes a position that says the Bloomers championships are tainted. Here I'll read it to you:

> "Maybe the reason that the Bloomers recognized such unprecedented success during the late nineties was because the Bloomers also employed an unprecedented number of steroid floats. Pitchers Jelly Rogers and Randy Elfin, and outfielders David Lawless and CoJo Janesco have all now been exposed by the Witchell Hunt Report. They join super-juicer Mason Jambino, who was outed by the B'WHALE'CO investigation three years ago. In light of the fact that these cheaters made up the heart of the Bloomers' playoff run and Earth Series Championships, MBL and Commissioner Selout should do the right thing and strip the Bloomers of their Earth Series Championships."

"Well that's just Postal and *The New York Roast* trying to sell newspapers. I wouldn't pay too much attention to what he has to say." Buzz Selout now understood the reason for Darryl Sledgehammer's conciliatory greeting. He wanted to make sure that the commissioner had their back. But Selout was deliberately deliberate. He took his time confirming that he had no intention of stripping the championships. He wanted to hear the Little Hammer squirm a little longer.

"That punk Postal sometimes has more influence with the fans than you think. I'm thinking about issuing a rebuttal press statement."

Selout was amazed at such a crazy idea, but he decided to humor Sledgehammer before telling him outright that a rescinding of the championships would not occur. "So what would you say in such a statement, Darryl?"

"I'd say that Postal has his facts all screwed up. Other than Randy Elfin, none of those guys are home grown Bloomers. For that matter Mason Jambino wasn't on our team when we won any of the championships. And then on top of that we go out and get the biggest juicer of them all – now that Bombs has retired – and we haven't won a single championship since A Dork has been on the team. He has been a total bust for the Bloomers."

Darryl Sledgehammer paused for a second and then added, "And for that matter we haven't won one with Jambino either."

"That argument won't go very far, Darryl. You would just be feeding more material to Postal. His position is that the Bronx Bloomers have always actively pursued floats."

"We've added a free agent or two along the way but our core team is guys we drafted and brought up through the system. Apparently some of the free agents that we got along the way were juicing for the other teams before we got them. Randy Elfin is the only exception who is mentioned in the Witchell Hunt Report. He was one of the guys who came up through the Bloomers organization – one of our core guys."

Selout just stared at the speakerphone on his desk. Didn't Darryl Sledgehammer realize that he was just buttressing Postal's argument? He was tired of toying with the Little Hammers and wanted to put this conversation to rest. He had lots of other things to be concerned about.

"Look Darryl, there's no way I could void the Bloomers' championships even if I wanted to. Think what a mess that would be. We've already paid out all of those Earth Series bonuses. And there are hundreds of other financial implications to doing something like that."

"I'm glad to hear you say that but I was still a little worried. Postal pointed out that the Olympic committee did the right thing and stripped that lady sprinter. They made her fork over the five medals she won at the Olympics in Australia after they found out she was juicing. By the way not only is he saying that the Bloomers should be stripped but he is also saying that you are a wimp because you allowed Popeye Maloney and then Harry Bombs to claim the single season home run record."

"He says that in the article? He actually calls me a wimp?"

"Well at least he's not calling you *Gumby* anymore. Here I'll read you that part also."

The Witchell Hunt Report

"What the Bay Watch Lab Company or B'WHALE'CO case tells us quite clearly is that the Multinational Baseball League has no control over the rapid expansion of steroid and HGH abuse. When you couple this with the recent revelations provided by the Witchell Hunt Report, it becomes ever more apparent that Commissioner Selout is completely out of touch with reality. He has more than ample evidence to take action against numerous cheating players. However he has proved himself to be an absolute wimp when it comes to dealing with cheaters. He should start by making an example out of Popeye Maloney and Harry Bombs, two ridiculous floats who sequentially stold the single season homerun title. However the Commish apparently does not have the cojones to deal with these thieves the way the International Olympic Committee dealt with their cheaters."

"Postal can say whatever he wants. But we're going to deal with this problem in a methodical manner that will eventually lead to a cleanup of our game. And to do that I need to have the cooperation of the MBLPA. We have to get them to agree to more frequent testing and stiffer penalties." Both Sledgehammer and Selout knew that this was simply the party line: stay the course; appear to be strict; make incremental changes and when in doubt blame everything on the MBLPA. But strangely enough they didn't trust each other enough to share those perspectives conspiratorially.

Lester Postal had been working Ryan McGhee – one of his rental friends – for several years now. Once again they were meeting in *The Morning After,* Postal's favorite midtown watering hole. It was a Tuesday afternoon during football season, but while most of the other patrons were rehashing the Monday Night Football game, McGhee and Postal were discussing baseball and the recently released Witchell Hunt report. During the last month or so McGhee had become quite notorious in his own right.

Flunking Chemistry Class

McGhee was regarded by some as a self-serving villainous opportunist who wanted to make a name for himself by taking down Jelly Rogers and Randy Elfin with his testimony to the Witchell Hunt investigators. Others viewed McGhee as an honest whistleblower, who truthfully exposed some of the game's best known cheaters. The local fans were divided on this issue, and it made for lively debate in the thousands of bars in NYC. There were 18,000 liquor licenses issued to bars and restaurants in New York and an estimated 1.2 million drinks poured in these establishments daily. That generated a healthy *(unhealthy?)* number of alcohol induced sports debates on any given day. Lester Postal's recent columns attacking baseball cheats had fostered many of those debates.

The Morning After was one of those places that always seemed to have a bouquet of freshly spilled beer. Joey Dee, the proprietor made sure that the floors and tables were always immaculately cleaned each day, but the history of 75 years of beer guzzling patrons of all ages had permeated the aroma of the double roomed establishment. Photos of athletes and other celebrities – some autographed and some not – adorned the walls and dated back dozens of years. There were more than 150 such photos throughout the establishment – mostly in small inexpensive frames - including a dozen or so in the men's room alone. The place had a homey feel to it and it was one of the premiere places wherein Postal often collected material for his column. He always tried to resonate with the fans' point of view, and *The Morning After* was always filled with fans. He had been thrown out of this place at least twice in the past for causing disturbances, but had been behaving better since his marriage to Georgette.

"It's hard to believe how much of an uproar the Witchell Hunt report has caused. You've become famous over night, Ryan."

"That's not necessarily a good thing. Some people hate my guts for throwing Jelly Rogers under the bus."

"F*** that s***. Don't worry about it. You did the right thing. That's all that matters."

"I'm not so sure. Bloomers fans hate me, but suddenly I'm pretty popular with the Mutts fans.

The Witchell Hunt Report

"Well the Mutts haven't won anything in a dog's age, so you gave them something to cheer about."

Both Lester Postal and his rental friend Brian McGhee paused to take deep gulps of beer. They had been having lunch about once every couple of months for almost five years. McGhee had come to trust Postal and thought that Postal would protect him as a source for a lot of details that he wanted leaked for public consumption without having to stand up as the source. He had very little faith in the legal system's ability to bring out the truth through its own procedures.

For his part, Lester relied on McGhee for details about which athletes he had personally supplied with steroids, amphetamines and HGH. In the case of Jelly Rogers, the details were quite salacious. Not only did McGhee claim to have injected PEDs into Jelly Rogers but he claimed to also have injected Dolly Rogers as well.

McGhee also instructed Postal in all of the nuances of the latest trends in PED compounding and how these various controlled substances affected the body. In the past Postal was careful never to expose his source. However now that McGhee was a household name, Postal wanted to be more direct in his reporting and he wanted to quote McGhee directly from his interviews when writing his column for *The New York Roast*. He believed that he could help stem the tide of negative publicity that McGhee was getting from other reporters.

Finally McGhee broke the silence and looked up from his beer first. "You know my lawyer is telling me that Congress is considering holding another hearing on the PEDs stuff because of the stir that the Witchell Report has caused. Do you know anything about that?"

"My sources tell me that if it happens, it will deal with very specific issues – not like the wide ranging circus that they conducted a couple of years ago. But with all of the denials that Jelly Rogers has issued so far and all of the names that he has called you, I wouldn't be surprised if your allegations are one of those very specific issues that Congress might want to explore."

Before McGhee could respond his cell phone rang and he picked it up and listened to what was obviously a one way conversation. He hung up the phone and turned back to Postal. "That was my attorney.

Flunking Chemistry Class

Things are heating up. The House Oversight Committee wants to take testimony under oath from me and from Jelly Rogers in January."

"I know that you think this is an ongoing nightmare. But think of it this way. Jelly Rogers will have to think twice before he lies under oath before Congress. That would be a felony and he could do some time in the can if he said that he didn't take any PEDs and you could prove differently."

"Well I actually do have some evidence. I kept some of the needles that I used to inject Rogers with HGH. They would have his DNA on them and they would also probably still show traces of HGH. I wanted to be able to prove my statements just in case Jelly denied the truth. I know this guy pretty well. He's capable of lying even when everyone knows he's being dishonest. It's incredible. So I kept the needles just in case. I had to protect myself. And now I'm awfully glad I did."

"Does Rogers know about this?"

"He probably does. Mitch Witchell's investigators know about it and this stuff leaks all of the time. But you have to understand Rogers' mentality. He's the most stubborn human being I have ever met. Even faced with irrefutable evidence he will just deny it. Once Dolly caught him red handed coming out of a hotel room with that young country singer who he's been doing for the last ten years. And you know what he tells Dolly. He tells her that she's a friend who was giving him singing lessons. Do you believe that?"

"The more important question seems to be does Dolly believe that."

"Yea, right. Fat chance. But she's not going to dump him when he's bringing home $25 Million a year." McGhee shook his head and sighed in frustration. He looked around at all of the pictures on the walls of the restaurant/bar and then added, "To tell you the truth I'm starting to hate baseball and all of these prima donnas. Most of them don't give a shit about anyone but themselves."

Postal listened intently and took another swig of beer and then wiped his lips before responding. "Don't be so hard on the game. There are still a lot of good guys out there. Things have just gotten out of hand lately. Maybe when *the fans* react negatively Gumby Selout will

The Witchell Hunt Report

finally come up with a plan with real teeth in it. The fans will have to be the ones that make a difference."

"The fans? The FANS?? Are you kidding me? Selout doesn't give a rat's ass about the fans! Come on Lester; I thought you were one of the few writers who understand what's going on here. Selout doesn't care about the fans. The owners don't care about the fans. The players don't care about the fans. It's all about the money and *only* about the money."

"All of these names that appear in the Witchell Hunt Report amaze me. There are ninety names. That's a hell of a lot of players. Sixty of these guys played in 2007. So you figure there are what ... maybe forty players per team over the course of the season? And now we have thirty two teams. That means that of the roughly 1200 players that played in 2007 – give or take a few – roughly five percent were caught doing steroids."

"That's only counts the guys that got named by me and by a couple of other trainers. That's just the tip of the iceberg. I'm sure the number is at least ten times that high. I'd bet the ranch – if I had a ranch – that more than sixty percent of MBL players are doing PEDs of one variety or another. I'll tell you this much though. Mitchell and Hunt wanted to get some big names in this report and they certainly did that."

"So I guess Jelly Rogers is the new PEDs poster child. Too bad they don't have an award for the most hated steroid user. Then in addition to an MVP we could also have the MVC Award, the Most Vile Cheater Award." Lester was proud of himself for coming up with this new recognition.

"There are plenty of candidates."

"Yea but at any given time there is only one MVC. First it was Popeye Maloney, who edged out Corky Samuels for the award. Then these guys were replaced by Harry Bombs who won the MVC several years in a row. Two years ago Daffy Palmgreed edged out the competition by lying to Congress and then failing a drug test two months later. And now it looks like Jelly Rogers has taken over the throne as the reigning MVC."

"What about A Dork? He has to be giving Jelly a run for his money."

Flunking Chemistry Class

"He wasn't named in the Witchell Hunt Report. So, at present, he doesn't have a platform to make a run at the current MVC. But I certainly wouldn't worry about that. Everyone despises A Dork any way. And it's just a matter of time before he gets caught. Then you can rest assured he'll displace Jelly Rogers as the MVC."

"Can't wait for that moment."

"Meanwhile I want to go live with the dirty needle stuff. You Ok with that?

"Yea, Lester. Go for it. Let's jiggle the Jelly man.

The day after Lester Postal met with Ryan McGhee, he wrote an expository column on some of the heretofore unknown details behind the Mitchell Hunt Report. In it he included the details that his rental friend had provided. Postal's boss, Will Morehead ran the article under the headline: **McGHEE NEEDLES JELLY & POKES DOLLY TOO.**

It was Christmas time in Texas but Jelly Rogers had just learned there was no Santa Claus. As a Christmas gift from his former trainer, he had been outed as a PED abusing float by the Witchell Hunt committee and specifically by Mitch Witchell and Heidi Hunt. To make matters worse he had just completed a rather unspectacular comeback with the Bloomers and now at the age of 45 it appeared that his career was finally over. And because of this one insignificant little twerp who somehow or other had saved needles with his DNA on it, his whole career was coming under scrutiny. In spite of seven Sly Jung Awards and two Earth Series Championships, people were now saying that his career didn't warrant enshrinement in the Corridor of Conceit. What a travesty.

But there was hope! Rogers recalled the decade old travails of then President Clint Blanton. He remembered that Blanton was challenged by the fact that Veronica Cummings-Dresser had saved her semen-stained

The Witchell Hunt Report

blue dress in the same way that Ryan McGhee had now saved the DNA stained syringe. Blanton somehow denied he had sex with Cummings-Dresser and beat the impeachment rap. He would do the same thing. He hated using a Democrat as a role model but in this case he believed Blanton provided the proper paradigm for action: *lawyer-up and deny, deny deny!* Rogers didn't realize that Blanton had the type of charisma that would make him appear like the little boy who got caught with his hand in the cookie jar. Unfortunately Jelly Rogers had the personality of the third grade bully who couldn't spell charisma.

While he brooded in the study of his Texas mansion, his wife Dolly Rogers scurried around in the kitchen, gossiping with the hired help and chasing after her teenage sons. Dolly still had the body of a teenager herself. Also she wasn't opposed to sampling the same kind of career extending substances as those that her husband used. In fact it was true that she had been injected with HGH by Ryan McGhee when the trainer was visiting Jelly and Holly at their Houston home. And of course Jelly Rogers didn't mind this at all. He was one of those males who obtained his trophy wife the first time around. He was quite proud of the fact that Dolly was physically attractive to other men. He treated her as part of his wealth. He cared little whether she could carry on a rational conversation. As long as she looked good the other things didn't matter. But there was no one else that Jelly Rogers could talk to at just this moment so he called his wife into his massive masculine wood paneled study.

"Dolly, Come here please."

Dutiful Dolly came dashing into the study. By now her husband was standing behind his desk holding on to the sports section of the local newspaper.

"Yes, Jelly?"

"Do you love me, Dolly?"

"Of course I do, Jelly. How can you ask such a question?"

"Well maybe because you're the only one who does."

Dolly smiled demurely, but privately she enjoyed the thought of having Jelly all to herself. She liked that he was feeling vulnerable. "Now why would you go and say something like that."

Flunking Chemistry Class

Jelly Rogers picked up the local newspaper and threw it across his desk.

"Look at this. No one believes me ... no one at all. This goddamn Witchell Hunt Report could seriously jeopardize everything I worked so hard to achieve."

"Well I ... I ... I believe you Jelly." Dolly couldn't believe she was actually saying this to her husband. "And *you* ... and *you* ... believe you ... don't you?" She wasn't at all sickened by troubling matters such as the truth. She only wanted to know what her husband wanted her to say.

"Don't be so dumb Dolly. Of course I believe me. But I'm worried that the writers might believe this other nonsense and that might have an impact on their Corridor of Conceit voting. I think that I should be the first unanimous selection to the C of C. No one else has as many Sly Jung Awards as I do. I'll just have to sue the bastards so the truth comes out."

"*The truth?*" Dolly wasn't so sure that that was what Jelly really wanted.

"Yes. The *truth* is that I'm the best pitcher ever to lace on a pair of spikes. That's the only truth that matters."

"Well then who are you going to sue to get that truth out?"

"I don't know Dolly. I don't know. On second thought, fuck the truth. I don't need anyone to tell me what the truth is."

XVII
The Last Cuts of Spring Training

March 2008

Sam Crockett was hoping that 2008 would not be his eighth year in the minors. He had pitched well in spring training and he had survived the first three rounds of cuts. Now at the end of March with opening day only five days away he had some serious hope of finally making it to The Show. The 2007 season had been so very frustrating. Because of the MBL expansion and the accompanying divestiture of the Tokyo Carp by the Seattle Seafarers, Crockett played the entire season in Japan. However he never made it up to the big leagues, instead playing for the Carp's minor league affiliate in Osaka. After multiple arguments with three different coaches about workout regimen and pitch counts, Crockett was demoted to a lower Japanese minor league team in Saitama where the living conditions were so subpar that his protests caused him to be left unprotected at the end of the season and he was available in the Cruel 5 draft. The Cruel 5 Draft was meant to protect players from cruel and unusual entrapment in the minor leagues.

Crockett got picked up by the Hollywood Hedgers and the Hedgers took him to camp as part of their 40 man roster. Now it appeared that his chances of making the team were the best they had ever been. The 40 man roster designation was superb news financially as well because Sam got to sign a split minor league/major league contract. This meant

Flunking Chemistry Class

that as long as he was on the forty man roster his pay would be governed by the contract that the MBLPA had negotiated with the MBL. By league rule, the Hedgers would have to keep him in the majors for the whole year or offer him back to the Carp at half price. The difference between a major league minimum salary and Triple A money was huge. The major league minimum was more than twelve times what he had made in his best year in the minors.

It looked like the Hedgers might keep 13 pitchers for opening day but even if they kept 12 he could make the squad. This was the year that two more franchises were being added, one in South Korea and one in the Dominican Republic and expansion was creating lots of new MBL jobs.

The Hedgers were due to open the season with an Asian swing with four games in Seoul against the Searchers; followed by four games in Tokyo against the Carp. Then they were going to Australia for four more games against the Sidney team in the Kangaroo Dome. If Sam made the team as the fifth starter, he would almost certainly work in the series against the Carp and nothing would give him more satisfaction than beating the team that had given up on him. This was also scheduled to be the Hedgers last Spring Training at their historic campsite called Hedger Town on Florida's east coast. The Hedgers new owner had decided to move the team to a different Spring Training facility in Arizona for the 2009 season.

The Hedgers had three stalwart starters coming back from good years in 2007. Veterans Bart Nickel and Darth Downy had posted double digit victory seasons in 2007 and the third starter, Bill Cardingsley was a budding young star that the Hedgers had moved from the bullpen to the starting rotation during the second half of the year. They had signed a journeyman free agent to compete for another one of the starting slots and the fifth spot in the rotation was up for grabs. In camp the Hedgers had a 20 year old fellow Texan, who was a left-handed flame thrower with an unbelievable curve. This kid, Clive Kerchief, was a first round draft choice and had the most complete talent that Crockett had ever seen. Crockett realized that Kerchief was a lock to make the team. That could mean that the starting rotation was set. However there were at least two bullpen spots up for grabs and

The Last Cuts of Spring Training

pending injury there was still an outside chance of a starting slot being open.

One wild card in the equation was that the ownership of the Hedgers had recently hired former Bloomers manager, Joe Trophy to take over the field management of the team. After the four years that Crockett had spent in the Bloomers organization, surely Trophy would know how talented the young right-hander could be. But then again the Bloomers were the team that had traded him to the Carp at the end of the 2006 season, so maybe the Trophy connection was overrated. By almost every calculation he went through Crockett understood that his chances of making the team hinged on three decisions: whether or not the Hedgers would keep two lefthanders in the bullpen – thereby *hurting* his chances; whether they would keep 13 pitchers instead of 12 – thereby *helping* his chances; and whether or not they would keep Tim Bartoni. Bartoni was a journeyman minor league right handed hurler who had seen brief call ups the previous two years, but who was also known to be a float who had flunked a minor league steroid test in 2003.

For the first time in his career, Sam Crockett's talent was being ballyhooed by some of the major sports outlets. Even though he was now 24 years old he had already pitched professional baseball for seven full years with four different organizations. Counting winter ball he had also pitched in four different countries. He would soon be celebrating his seventh wedding anniversary and had two young sons who were already in the beginning years of grade school. He still made his offseason home back in Texas and he and Betsy Jo had somehow scraped together enough money to combine with a loan from his parents to buy a small three bedroom ranch house on the outskirts of San Antonio five miles from his parents home and about two miles from Betsy Jo's parents place.

When he thought about it long enough, Sam Crockett knew that his life had already travelled down a very different road from that of his high school classmates, many of whom had completed college or were still plowing their way through that experience. He was beginning to realize just how different some of these experiences were as he began to reconnect with many of his old friends through the emerging phenomena of social media, particularly Facebook. He was also astounded to find out how many fans he had who wanted to *friend* him. At first he was reluctant to agree to be friends with people that he really didn't know. He knew Facebook had been a college thing for a couple of years. However when some of his high school friends began reconnecting with him he took a real interest. He accepted invitations from fans and he began seeing digital pictures of himself being posted by people who were at the ballparks where he had played. There were even 3 twenty second videos posted by a Rutgers coed showing him doing parts of his now infamous eighth inning strip at the Blossoms Park in New Brunswick.

Crockett had grown up in a computer friendly environment and had kept a laptop computer with him whenever he traveled. He found this new Facebook diversion to be a fascinating method of finding out what his friends – both new and old – were up to. He wondered if all of the other ballplayers were experiencing the same kind of Facebook following that he was suddenly enjoying. It was a bit of a buzz topic around the spring training camp but not all of the players had caught on just yet.

Crockett had been communicating with some of his ex-teammates through email over the last seven years but the interactions were somewhat sporadic. The same could be said for his email communication with his high school friends. But Facebook was allowing him to set up groups that others could join, and so he began a private group called *Heading to The Show* and invited some of his ex-teammates to join. He was amazed at some of the pictures his ex-teammates posted, including muscle flexing poses that accompanied blatant admissions of taking "super supplements" – code for PEDs – that were assisting some of them in their body building and career construction. Simply for his personal edification Crockett began to put together a spreadsheet of all of his ex-teammates as well as guys he had played against in the minors. He categorized the players as floats, non-floats and "uncertain," to the best of his knowledge of such classification. He had no real purpose in doing this but it kept him busy.

The Last Cuts of Spring Training

There was one more game to be played before the Hedgers headed out to Korea to open the season against Seoul Searchers. Sam Crockett was getting only his third start of spring training although he had also appeared in relief four times. In order to break camp with the parent club, Crockett figured he would have to go at least three innings and maybe more depending upon his pitch count. It was a time of great anxiety. In the final few days of camp Crockett's fate would be decided. But this was different from spring trainings of the past. The probability of making a major league roster had never been higher for the pitcher. But would he make it with the Hedgers or would there be a last minute deal? The latter scenario had been the story of his career. His Cruel 5 status played a role but it was far from a guarantee.

The game that day was being played against the Metropolitan Mutts in the Mutts Jupiter Florida ball park. In the top of the first inning the Hedgers staked Crockett to a seven run lead before he ever threw a pitch. Even Crockett got a hit, a two-run double into the left center field power gap. But by the time Crockett got out on the mound it had been a full thirty-five minutes since he had completed his warm up pitches.

Sam Crockett started the most important game of his career by throwing twelve of his first fourteen pitches out of the strike zone. The plate looked as small as a postage stamp to him as he stood on the mound with the bases loaded and nobody out. The pitching coach made a visit and the catcher went out to the mound twice but none of that was going to help him. The cleanup hitter for the Mutts was a muscular 33 year old switch hitting float who was now with his fourth big league team and was trying to justify his multi-million dollar contract.

Crockett aimed for the dead center of the plate with his best fastball and managed to split the base down the middle but the Mutts left fielder ripped the ball directly at the second baseman who doubled off the runner at first. The next batter lined the second pitch right at Crockett who snared the ball before it screamed into center field. He was out of the inning with the seven zip lead still intact but he certainly looked shaky in the process.

Crockett pitched three more innings and gave up only one hit, a long two run homer to the Mutts first baseman. However Crockett walked

Flunking Chemistry Class

four more batters making a total of seven free passes in four innings. He struck out four batters and threw a total of 90 pitches. He was nervous about how his performance would be perceived. He was also concerned because his teammate Tim Bartoni followed him to the mound with two perfect innings including four punch outs of Mutts batters.

When the game ended Crockett drove north along Route 95 to the apartment he was renting in Vero Beach. Along the way he was talking on his cell phone to Betsy Jo back in Texas. He gave her the details of the game and his performance and then tried to assess what his chances looked like.

"I wouldn't be surprised to hear something later today. I hung around a bit but no one told me anything one way or the other."

"That's crazy Sam. They have to know what their decision is. You guys are all set to fly out tomorrow for Opening Day in Seoul. The management has to know who is flying out and who isn't. What's the schedule like for tomorrow?"

"The first leg of the trip leaves from Orlando tomorrow night at 7 PM. Technically, we're all supposed to be at a team meeting back at Hedger Town at 11 AM. For most of the guys it's just a chance to clean the lockers and get ready to fly out. But for a few of us the wait for the final cuts is simply excruciating and we'll know how it shakes out by the time that meeting is over – if not sooner."

"Do you think it's coming down to you or Bartoni?"

"I think so."

"So the Hedgers need to make a decision between my husband – who has never done any steroids or any HGH or any of that other crap – and a float who failed a PEDs test. Have I got that right?"

"Not exactly. If they keep 13 pitchers we both make it and a utility infielder – probably Fred Nickerson gets cut."

"Wasn't Nickerson mentioned in the Witchell Hunt Report? Is he a juicer also?"

"Yes and yes."

"So if you don't make it, it's because a couple of steroid cheaters will be drawing major league baseball salary checks. Have I got that right now?"

The Last Cuts of Spring Training

"Yes, now I'd say that you have it nailed precisely."

Crockett was driving his four year old Chevy pickup and he was almost back to Vero Beach. He couldn't help but notice the silence on the other end of the phone. Betsy Jo was not a fan of dead air. She would always fill any moment of silence longer than three seconds with commentary of some kind, however inane. She was not the type to let thought interrupt discussion or allow conjecture and contemplation to disrupt discourse, so her silence was deafening.

Finally Crockett spoke again to Betsy Jo. "I'll call you tomorrow when I find out."

The Congressional Hearing the previous month had not gone well. Jelly was in a jam. Jelly Rogers stood in the men's room outside of his Texas attorney's office and stared into the mirror. The man in the mirror sneered back at him as though the image was saying, "Liar, liar, pants on fire." The only good thing was that when he gritted his teeth in anger his half jowl dissipated somewhat. All the rest of the news was bad. Now there was talk about Rogers being indicted on perjury charges.

The February hearing had boiled down to the veracity of two directly conflicting testimonies. Jelly Rogers claimed he never used anabolic steroids and Ryan McGhee asserted that he personally injected *both* Jelly Rogers *and* Dolly Rogers.

The Congressional Committee was once again chaired by Hans Waxear, a Democrat from California. This bothered Republican Rogers almost as much as the steroid allegations themselves. Amazingly Rogers had already convinced himself that he was not guilty. He managed this by borrowing a verb from the lexicon of the former first lady, Pilfery Blanton. Blanton, who was now running for president herself, notoriously *misremembered* things when she was caught in blatant Blanton lies. Rogers simply decided that he and Dolly and Randy Elfin simply *misremembered* all of the steroid stuff and therefore it was like it never happened.

Flunking Chemistry Class

However Waxear and his colleagues were about to demonstrate that the plea of *misremembering* was something that was only acceptable for Democrats. While Pilfery Blanton could misremember being *shot at* on the tarmac in Bosnia, Jelly Rogers was not going to be allowed to *misremember* being *shot up* in his bedroom. He stuck his tongue out at the man in the mirror and mumbled something like: "You didn't do shit, slugger." At about that moment, his avaricious and opportunistic attorney Reed Hurling happened to be entering the loo. He looked at his client and saw a massive moronic mess of a man, who now was in danger of trading in his Bronx Bloomer pinstripes for black and white striped pajamas at the federal prison.

"That's it Jelly! We'll use an insanity defense! We'll just tell them that the steroids affected your brain and that you actually believed that none of this really happened. We'll simply beat the perjury charge by copping a plea of nutso. And we won't even have to use the Democratic excuse. We'll invent our own new word. We'll tell them that because of your steroid use, you *dis-remembered* everything and therefore you are not responsible for anything at all. Bingo we beat the perjury rap!"

"There's only one problem with that logic, Reed. I don't want the sportswriters to *misremember* or *disremember* me when it comes to the Corridor of Conceit voting in a few years."

Reed Hurling said nothing at all. He too kept looking at Rogers' reflection in the mirror and he realized that Rogers had dismembered any chance of election to the C of C several years earlier. But Hurling got paid to represent his client in criminal proceedings and he was determined to get him acquitted of the charges that were being filed. Hurling didn't have a C of C vote.

XVIII

Double Dating at the Ballpark

April 2008

Lester Postal and Georgette Postal were out on a double date with Tim Burr and Evangeline Prim. They had gone for an early dinner at the Stadium Club before the game and Burr and the two women had now nestled into their seats right in front of the press box. Lester took his seat with the other scribes but he spent several innings seated with his guests as well. It was now the sixth inning and he was back in the press box, scribbling up a postscript for what appeared to be a Bloomer blowout win.

When Burr met Evangeline Prim she was more than he had expected. In fact in one important way she was actually *less* than he expected. Georgette had met Evangeline at her Overweight Observers class so Tim Burr anticipated meeting someone who was about Georgette's size. He never expected his blind date to be someone as trim as Prim. She was actually quite attractive with the exception of her high pitched squeaky voice. However Evangeline didn't seem to be the brightest bulb in the chandelier. And because she was self-conscious about her squeaky voice she didn't say much. She also had a habit of using single word responses to a lot of questions whenever she did speak. She said "wow," to express interest. She used the word "really?" as an interrogatory response. And her favorite word seemed to be the annoyingly agreeable retort, "whatever." She also maintained a frozen faced smile that was appealing at first but was tediously insipid when it didn't vary much with the conversation. In short she was the perfect match for Tim.

"This will be the last season that you will be able to see a game in Bloomers Stadium. They're tearing it down and next year the Bloomers will start playing in the building that they are constructing next door." Burr attempted to add a little magnitude to an insignificant early April ballgame. The game was pretty boring as the Bloomers had led throughout and were now leading 8 to 2.

"Really?" Prim answered with her single word interrogatory response but that topic ended right there and she just smiled demurely. Burr realized that his date had already had dinner and a few glasses of wine, but he offered up more refreshments as a way to slice through the tedium. "I'm going to the concession stand. Can I get anything for you ladies?"

"I'll take a beer," Georgette responded

"How about you, Evangeline? Can I get you a beer or a soda or maybe a glass of wine? Yeah, I think they serve wine there also. What would you like?"

"Whatever."

"How about a beer, then?"

"Sure, whatever."

"Is that a 'yes whatever' or a 'no whatever'?"

"A 'yes,' I guess. Oh, whatever." An insecure shoulder shrug accompanied her response. She also reissued her shy smile that made it beneficial for Burr to put up with her diffidence.

Burr moved out to the aisle and up toward the concession stand and Georgette turned to her friend and asked her about her feelings toward her law partner.

"Remember I didn't promise you George Clooney. But Tim is really a nice guy. What do you think?"

"Yea, he's nice."

"I think he likes you. I can tell by the way he's acting."

"Whatever."

"What? You don't think he likes you?"

"No. I do. I guess. It's just … well it's just … well nothing."

Double Dating at the Ballpark

"No tell me. What is it? It can't be nothing?"

"Whatever."

"No. Come on tell me. What is it that's bothering you?"

"I think he thinks I'm fat."

"Evangeline, that's crazy. You're a size four for Christ's sake. And you never have been fat ... not ever. When I first met you at Overweight Observers, I was pissed off that you thought you were fat. It's all in your mind. And for that matter I can tell you what it means to be fat. Trust me. You're not fat and you've never been fat."

"Then maybe he thinks I'm stupid."

This caused Georgette to pause a little bit. Her friend Evangeline Prim was not a rocket scientist. However she was amiable and pretty. There was no reason for her to be devoid of self confidence. She looked like she was searching for reasons for Burr to dislike her.

"No way. You're plenty smart enough for Tim." She knew she was stretching the truth a little bit. "Don't let the lawyer stuff fool you. Tim is a regular guy. He's not the kind of person who thinks he's better than you. I've known him since we were in law school together. He's a good lawyer and a good guy too. He's a bit inexperienced when it comes to dating and all that goes with it, but he'll treat you well enough. You'll see."

"Whatever."

The women kibitzed a bit longer while they waited for Burr to return to his seat. When he got back he was juggling three beers in a tray on his right hand while he held his cell phone to his left ear with his other hand.

Seeing him approaching, Evangeline jumped up to relieve him of the tray, while he continued with his phone conversation. Finally Burr sat back down with the women and Evangeline promptly passed him one of the beers.

"That was Sam Crockett on the phone," Burr said softly. He didn't want to say it so loud that fans seated near them could hear him talk. Crockett was not exactly a household name yet but people who followed the game closely knew who he was. Evangeline was not in that category.

"Who is Sam Crockett?"

"He's a professional baseball player and our client." Tim Burr replied while leaning in toward both Evangeline and Georgette.

"Wow." Evangeline was dutifully impressed.

"Tim once saved his wife and children from a batted ball at a minor league stadium." Georgette added the anecdote while she allowed her law partner to explain the nature of their relationship.

"Really? Wow." Evangeline squeaked her curt reply and was obviously becoming more awed by the moment.

"Crockett's a great guy and a very good ballplayer, but he has had a rough go off it trying to break into the big leagues. Last month was a typical example."

Evangeline was now leaning toward Burr and hanging on every word he said. Burr continued his tale.

"Sam Crockett has been playing in the minor leagues for seven years … in fact he's now in his eighth season. When he became the final cut from the Hedgers last month, he was offered back to the Carp at half the price that the Hedgers paid to draft him. But the Carp didn't want to put him on their 40 man roster either. So they released him and he became an unrestricted minor league free agent and signed back on with the Bloomers Triple A team, the New Brunswick Blossoms. That's the same team that he was playing for when we first met him."

"Really?" Evangeline's frozen smile feigned advanced interest.

"Yea, it's a bit complicated but the bottom line is that our client still hasn't even had a cup of coffee in the bigs. And what really ticks him off is that there are several players who have made it to The Show who are there only because they juiced up in order to get there."

"That's amazing." Evangeline beamed for no particular reason.

At this point Georgette was getting a bit nervous about people around them. She gave Burr a sidelong glance that said, *"Not here, not now."*

However, Tim Burr was trying to impress his light headed date. He was less interested in appeasing his heavy bodied partner. And so he plodded along cautiously with his story about Sam Crockett.

Double Dating at the Ballpark

"I've stayed in touch with Crockett via email and now Facebook ever since we met. Georgette's husband, Lester has talked to him several times about what goes on in the minor league training rooms. He's been a good source for Lester and a good friend for Georgette and me. So when he decided that he needed a lawyer, he came to us for legal assistance."

"So then are you ... like his agent?"

"Sort of." Now it was Burr who was offering up the truncated responses.

Georgette reluctantly jumped back into the conversation. "He has fired Brad Scott who had been his long time agent. We're just advising him a bit in the interim. Our law practice doesn't currently include contract negotiations for professional athletes."

"So if you're only ...sort of ...his interim agent or something ... then what is it he really needs a lawyer for?"

Evangeline's innocent sounding question just hung out there unanswered.

XIX

The State of the Sport Address

July 2009

Commissioner Buzz Selout was holding his annual *State of the Sport* press conference at the mid-summer Parade of the Stars Game break. He wanted to use this opportunity to announce the timeframe for the next wave of expansion for the Multinational Baseball League. However he knew that the press corps would probably have as many questions for him about PEDs as they did about expansion. It seemed like he could never get away from the issue. Every year there was a new steroid scandal or a new PED wrinkle. This year in 2009 four of the game's biggest stars had been implicated in illegal steroid use.

Before the season even got started it was revealed that the Bronx Bloomers third baseman, A Dork and the Beantown Wallbangers designated hitter, Peppy Orbits – sometimes called "Big Popout," because of his recent propensity to crush infield flies – had both tested positive for PEDs back in 2003. This was supposed to have been *anonymous survey testing* with no associated penalty for failed tests. Although there now were penalties in place for such failed tests, A Dork and Big Popout's transgressions went unsanctioned.

The third violation came at the end of Spring Training when Goren Outback the first baseman for the Sydney Kangaroos was caught all hopped up on testosterone right before the opening day in April.

The State of the Sport Address

The season was barely one month old when the news about Outback was quickly supplanted by the scandalous bulletin that Manboy Ramendez of the Hollywood Hedgers would be suspended for fifty games starting in May after his urine sample yielded evidence of synthetic testosterone usage.

The news about Ramendez was particularly irksome for the owners of the Hollywood Hedgers, Hymie Courtley and his wife Fran. After bringing Ramendez to the Hedgers in a blockbuster trade with the Wallbangers at the end of 2008, the Courtleys had spent most of the offseason deadlocked with the dreadlocked superfloat over a new contract. All of this made the Courtleys look like fools for spending almost $50 million on a new contract for the buffoon from Boston, without realizing he was just another float.

In his prepared remarks prior to taking questions about the *State of the Sport* Selout laid out the ground work for the upcoming 2012 expansion:

> "The Multinational Baseball League is proud to announce that our expansion plans are on schedule and we are now entertaining bids for two additional franchises that will begin play on the major league level in 2012. As you know prior to our expansion last year when we added franchises in Korea and in the Dominican Republic, we awarded franchises to the winning bid ownership groups, with enough time to develop minor league systems prior to beginning play at the MBL level. So also we will award franchises to the successful bidders for teams to be located in Caracas, Venezuela and in San Juan, Puerto Rico for the 2012 season. When the 2012 season begins we will have 36 teams on four different continents. We are proud of that progress as we look to continue the significant worldwide growth of our international pastime. While we have accomplished much by way of growth within our industry and its constituent businesses, I am proud to say that we have

always maintained the best interests of our customers, our fan base, and our players. I might add that, in these tough economic times our industry continues to create jobs and drive additional income on a global basis. Now I'll open the floor to any questions you might have."

Selout had gone over his opening statement multiple times before delivering his message. He was convinced that an aggressive message about the benefits of the strong growth in the industry was important. The worldwide economy was in a slump and Americans were still embracing their new president. The new Commander-in-Chief was the country's first minority president. He was half Native American Indian and half Asian Indian. His mother was born on a North Dakota reservation and his father was born in a South Delhi slum. He sometimes referred to himself as Slumdog Running Bear. However President Baroque O. Brahman was nobody's fool. He had managed to galvanize public opinion around an agenda for hope and change while getting the voters to ignore the ever inflating debt that these changes might well incur.

Similarly Buzz Selout hoped that he could get his fans to ignore the over inflated statistics (and players) in his game by embracing the changes that he was suggesting. Selout had hoped to enlist the charismatic new president in support of his sport but Baroque O. Brahman was more a fan of basketball, golf and tomahawk tossing. Nonetheless Selout did manage to score a political victory in this regard when he convinced Brahman to throw out the first ball at the Parade of Stars Game. The Indian/Indian President was a southpaw and Selout hoped that he would throw a strike that would be regarded as a good omen for things to come. All of these displaced thoughts were running through Commissioner Selout's mind as he looked out across the assembled media members and waited for their questions.

The first inquiry came from a reporter from a Southern California newspaper. It was a softball question and it allowed the commissioner to put the focus where he wanted it to be – on the light stuff.

"Buzz, how do you feel about getting Baroque O. Brahman to throw out the first pitch in tomorrow night's Parade of Stars Game?"

The State of the Sport Address

"Well we're certainly glad that the president could take the time to be here with us. The word on Baroque is that he's 'one hell of a lefty.' As you know his predecessor President Shrub was a baseball man before becoming president, and in fact I've heard a few of you suggest that he might be next in line to serve as commissioner should I ever decide to retire."

Selout loved his own answer to this question. It made him feel important. He subconsciously pawed at his toupee as he spoke but he was clearly enjoying the spotlight regardless. He stood up straight and waited for another inquiry.

The next question came from a pretty blonde female sportswriter from Brisbane in Queensland, Australia. "When the game is played in Sydney in 2012 will you get the Prime Minister to be a hurler?"

"We haven't gotten that far ahead in our planning yet, but we're certainly looking forward to the first ever Midsummer Masterpiece to be played outside of North America, and I can't think of a better venue to make that happen than the Kangaroo Dome." Selout loved that question also but he lingered too long on the face of the attractive Australian reporter who seized the opportunity for a follow up question.

"So what do you think about Goren Outback? He's our first Kangaroo cheater, but he certainly isn't alone. How about Manboy Raminez? Do you think a fifty game suspension is enough punishment?"

"Whoa, young lady. That's several questions at once. However to answer your question directly, I will tell you that we will continue to deal swiftly and strictly with those who violate the rules of our game. These rules and the sanctions that go along with them are governed by the collective bargaining agreement between the players union, and Multinational League Baseball."

The tide had turned. In rapid fire several questions were fired at Selout about steroids, and suspensions and the integrity of the game. In every direction he looked there was someone shouting a similar inquiry. Finally the voice of Lester Postal from the *New York Roast* was heard above the others.

"Buzz, is it true that some of the franchise owners don't want stricter enforcement of the PEDs rules because they have made vast fortunes during the Steroid Era? You know, why ruin a good thing?"

"That's a very unfair question, Lester. The team owners as well as the office of MBL have been unanimous in our condemnation of the use of illegal substances. We have done everything in our power to ensure that effective sanctions are in place to deter abuse of PEDs by our players and we will continue to do so."

Postal followed up quickly, "Come on Buzz. Get real. Effective sanctions? You and the owners have known about steroid abuse for more than a decade and have done nothing about it. Do you think allowing Manboy Raminez to collect $40 million of his $50 million contract is a realistic deterrent? How about A Dork? He's been cheating for years and will be getting paid a quarter of a billion dollars during his contract, without ever being suspended for a single game? And what about some of the retired floats like Jelly Rogers, Popeye Maloney and Harry Bombs? They made a mess of the MBL record books and have never missed a game or paid a single dollar in penalties. Is that your idea of a deterrent?"

XX

Playing the Outfield

August 2009

Sam Crockett was now an outfielder. He was in his ninth year in the minors and his second year as a full time position player. Where had all of the time gone?

After coming within a single player of making The Show out of spring training in 2008, Crockett had ended up back with the New Brunswick Blossoms. Three very good starts were followed by another sore armed set back. This time he knew that he would never pitch in the bigs. He got released by the Blossoms and any hopes of pitching for the parent club, the Bronx Bloomers were severed at the same time.

However with the support of Betsy Jo he determined that he would find another way to make it to the top. He had always had some pop with the bat, even though he hadn't taken much minor league instruction as a hitter. Going into the 2008 season Crockett had a career .285 batting average in a little over 550 plate appearances spread over his first seven years. He had also hit 16 minor league homeruns during that time span.

Crockett got an unusual helping hand in finding a team that might sign him to a contract in the minors as a hitter. *New York Roast* reporter, Lester Postal, wrote a column about the tough competition in the minor leagues and how difficult it is for a player to make it to the

Flunking Chemistry Class

Multinational Baseball League. He stressed how some people – without naming specific players – took illegal short cuts along the way. But Postal made the point that there was still a group of fledgling young athletes who were striving to make a living in the game without cheating. He then proceeded to give a synopsis of Sam Crockett's baseball odyssey including his latest tragic arm injury and his aspiration of continuing his quest as an outfielder. Ironically the baseball commissioner, Buzz Selout read Postal's column and was touched by the section on Crockett's travails. He was intrigued by the fact that Crockett was originally drafted by the Wisconsin Cheeseheads, the team that he had at one time owned. Without ever having met Crockett, Selout forwarded *The Roast* article to the current ownership of the Cheeseheads. Shortly thereafter the Cheeseheads did some homework and then signed their former farmhand to a new contract as a Single A outfielder with the Wausau Wedgies.

In 2008 Sam Crockett played the entire season with the Wedgies. After a slow start he put together a solid July and August and finished the season with 14 homeruns and a .289 average. The good news was that he hit eleven of those fourteen homers in July and August. And his average for the final two months of the season was .323.

Crockett earned a call as a non-roster invitee to the Cheeseheads Spring Training camp as a major leaguer but was once again slashed as one of the final spring training cuts. Nevertheless the Cheeseheads were intrigued by Crockett's potential and hoped that they might once again catch lightning in a bottle as they had with another young outfielder by the name of Brawny Glaun. Glaun had won the MBL Native League Newbie of the Year Award two years earlier. So this time rather than returning him to the Wedgies, Crockett was assigned to Cheeseheads Triple A club in Tennessee, the Memphis **Munsters.**

Crockett got off to a strong start with the Munsters in 2009. Through mid July he had clouted seventeen homeruns and was hitting .292. The rumor mill was indicating that Crockett might very well be the next call up by the Cheeseheads. But somewhere along the line the minor league scouting reports caught up with Crockett.

Playing the Outfield

The scouts all knew that Crockett had no problem getting the bat head out in front of a good heater. They also knew that he managed to track most of the Triple A curveballs that he had seen. The scouts were also impressed that Crockett was sharp enough to lay off the hard sliders that fell out of the strike zone. However the advance men finally discovered that Crockett had serious difficulty with his timing of off speed pitches. He was far out in front of most of these offerings even when the off speed pitches were thrown back to back. From mid July through the second week of August, Crockett hit a mere .181 with only one additional homerun – and that came on an inside fastball.

After a particularly dismal game in which he went 0 for 5 including a golden sombrero, Crockett began to realize that the call to the majors might not be coming that soon after all. But the bad news at the ballpark was overshadowed by some much sadder news that he had heard over the TV two nights earlier. Apparently his old catcher, Lance Leathermore, had somehow killed himself in a single car accident just outside his home in Las Vegas. During the last year or so Leathermore had made news off the baseball diamond by voluntarily coming forward as a steroid abuser and informing the media that steroids had caused him to exhibit bipolar behavior.

Leathermore had played a total of 26 major league baseball games but now had been retired from the game for more than a full season. The former ballplayer was quite frank in stating that even though he had never failed a steroid test, he believed that anabolic steroids had caused his career to come crashing down to earth. He attributed some of his downfall to dramatic mood swings including manic moments when his paranoia caused him to question everything in life. He then began to have trouble sleeping which drove him to take sleeping pills. A supposedly accidental overdose of the sleeping sedatives had infamously put him in a rehab hospital shortly after being cut by the Cincinnati Crazy Legs, his one and only major league employer. During the last year or so, without implicating specific ballplayers, Leathermore had become a minor celebrity by chronicling his own PED usage on a couple of the national news networks. So when the story broke that he had hit a tree going 105 miles per hour the media was filled with speculation that the crash was a suicide. This probability was further underlined by the difficulty of finding a tree in the Nevada desert.

When Sam Crockett heard the news about Leathermore he was deeply troubled. Although he knew that Leathermore was a steroid user, he was one of the few players that Crockett forgave for this transgression. Leathermore was simply the kind of guy that everybody liked. He was a party animal and was well known among the players at various levels of the game. In some ways he reminded people of CoJo Janesco but with a lot less native talent.

Crockett and Leathermore had roomed together in Arizona and then again when they played together for the Moose Butt Little Cheesies in Montana seven years earlier. Their paths had crossed several times during their respective careers and they had kept in touch even though they had very different life styles. Sam Crockett also knew that his wife Betsy Jo didn't care much for Leathermore and had reminded Sam on several occasions that Leathermore was cut from a different cloth. Regardless of his wife's intuition Sam Crockett had always felt a special kinship with Leathermore because of their early career beginnings together, and his death was a shock to Sam that went beyond its newsworthiness.

With the 0 for 5 golden sombrero performance still on his mind and the loss of Leathermore an even weightier problem, Crockett drove back to his apartment in Memphis and decided to call Betsy Jo. But he paused before picking up the phone to reflect on the fact that for too many years now his relationship with Betsy Jo had involved cradling too many phone receivers and not enough in person cradling. He was now 25 years old, still a young man by most measurements but considered to be long in the tooth for a minor league ballplayer. He wondered if it was finally time to call it a career and return to Texas and get a full time job.

Playing the Outfield

"Hi Baby Doll. How are things on the home front?" Sam started with his usual greeting but his wife of nine years could tell right away that there wasn't a lot of enthusiasm in his voice.

"Things are fine here, Sam. What's wrong?"

"Nothing, Baby Doll ... nothing at all."

"Bad game?"

"Bad game; Bad week; Bad month; Baby Doll."

"But that's not all. Is it?"

"No." He paused for more than three seconds and then added "I just hate Memphis."

"You loved Memphis in April, May and June."

"I was hitting nearly .300 in June."

"Exactly."

"Well, it's more than just that Betsy Jo. Everybody has a slump every once in a while."

"Exactly."

"It's also the Lance Leathermore thing. I can't get him out of my mind. I know you didn't like Lance, but honestly I thought he was a good guy, Betsy Jo. Lance was really a good guy."

"I didn't *dislike* Lance, Sam. Good Lord, I only met the man one time in my life. And that was what ... five years ago? For what? Five minutes? In Beaufort, North Carolina? You were pitching for the Baby Bloomers and he was playing for the Savannah Mini Mutts. I remember him, right well enough. He had muscles on top of muscles from *doin'* all them steroids.

"Yeah, okay, Lance was a certifiable float alright. But he didn't try to hide it or *nuthin'*. He'd tell it like it was."

"He just started *tellin'* people about it lately after he was out of the game."

"No that ain't so, Betsy Jo. He told me *everythin'* he was *doin'* right up front. He might not have told the newspaper guys, but most of the players knew about it. He got some other guys on the juice also. It wasn't like he was *tryin'* to cheat or anything ... because he thought everybody should be *juicin'*. That would make it fair."

Flunking Chemistry Class

"Well then look at what happened. Will you, Sam? The man just killed himself."

"Christ, Betsy Jo. Don't go *sayin'* bad things about the dead. Lance just lived large that's all. He was always in the fast lane. I guess that was true even when he died. It was a terrible accident."

"We're all just lucky he didn't take anyone with him on his last ride. And don't tell me that it was an accident, Sam. We both know better than that."

"Please Betsy Jo. Don't go there."

By now Betsy Jo was growing angry with her husband. His career had not been easy on her either. She had spent a lot of time alone in Texas with the kids while her husband was off chasing his dream of making it to the MBL. She liked baseball but it wasn't all there was to life. She was a twenty-four year old mother of two young boys and she was yet to tell her husband that they were now expecting their third child seven years after the birth of Rory.

"Tell me you don't think Leathermore's death was steroid related. Just tell me you don't believe that Sam."

"I don't know that for sure Betsy Jo."

"Don't lie to me Sam. You know as well as I do that it was steroids that killed your friend Lance. He's in the same category as that football player, who killed himself on steroids in the nineties. You don't have to know for sure. I'm just asking you … What do you think? Do you think it was roid rage or not?"

"Well, when you put it that way, I guess I'd have to say that I think that there's a strong possibility that steroids had something to do with it."

Sam Crockett sounded like a little boy who had been chastised by his mother rather than someone who was having a discussion with his wife. He missed Betsy Jo and he missed JR and Rory.

"Good. Now that you admit that much, you must understand why it's so important to do things the right way."

"But I'm not doing very well here with the Munsters. The team is in last place and the fans all make fun of us. They call us "The Munsters: the Cheeseheads stinky little farm team." One guy had a sign that

Playing the Outfield

said: 'Cheeseheads come from curd but the Munsters are just turd.' Basically they are saying we're shit. And to tell you the truth lately I can't hit for shit."

"You need to change your attitude, Sam. You can't listen to every little heckler that comes along. If you want to make it to The Show, you've got to take the bad days with the good ones."

"I haven't had many good days lately, Baby Doll. I've had it. I'm going to go to the manager tomorrow and tell him I quit. I'm coming home to Texas. I think I'm going to go work full time in the drill bit business."

On the other end of the phone Betsy Jo Crockett was livid. She exploded and the phone began literally crackling in the ballplayers hand up in Memphis as his wife's tirade came through the lines.

"Sam Crockett, you listen up and you listen up good. Stop *feelin'* so goddamn sorry for yourself. You aren't the only one who's been *makin'* a sacrifice. Do you think it's been easy *raisin'* two young boys every summer while you're *playin'* ball? We're in this together and we're in it as a family. You can't just quit because you've had a little slump."

"But Baby Doll ..."

"Don't Baby Doll me this, or Baby Doll me that. Get back out there tomorrow night and do your damn job. They're still *payin'* you through the end of the season. You've only got three more weeks. If you still want to quit after the season we'll talk about it then. Right now you go back out there and give it your all. If you still feel the way you do at the end of the season then we'll talk about things. Right now I don't want to hear about my boys' father *bein'* a quitter."

Sam listened intently. His wife had never before talked to him just that way. However he knew that she was right. He had put too much effort into trying to make it to the MBL to quit in the middle of the season. He was determined to do the best he could over the next few weeks and if things didn't go well, he would at least realize that he had given it his best effort. In an odd way he was energized by Betsy Jo's outburst.

"Alright Betsy Jo. I'm *goin'* to give it my best over the last few weeks. You're right. I owe us both that much."

199

"And you owe it to the boys too." She knew that this was not the time to bring up the pregnancy but it did cross her mind. "Your family is behind you one hundred percent, no matter what your *battin'* average is."

"Thanks Baby Doll."

There was a moment of silence but it wasn't an awkward silence merely a moment of mutual reflection and then Betsy Jo said. "And Sam …?"

"Yes, Baby Doll."

"I truly am sorry about Lance. I know he was your friend."

"Thanks."

Over the last three weeks of the season, Crockett hit .365 with four more homeruns, but he didn't get a September call up to the Cheeseheads.

Although two of the most infamous floats, A Dork and Jelly Rogers had gained a good deal of their career notoriety while playing for the Bronx Bloomers they had only been teammates for a half of one season. In 2007 during Rogers' final season as a pro, A Dork had his best season as a Bloomer. But neither performer was able to nail down an Earth Series victory for the ball club. And because the Sledgehammer family always insisted that "nothing was more important than the Earth Series," the two floats had been regarded as a failure during their one year together as teammates. In addition they had very little respect for each other and rarely talked to one another during that season or any time thereafter. Now two years later the two athletes were at different stages of their careers.

Jelly Rogers was not playing anything but golf while he awaited word from a federal grand jury that was convened in January to hear evidence of Rogers' potential perjury before Congress. The bipartisan Congressional committee had turned a report over to the Attorney General for investigation of more than a half dozen inconsistencies in Rogers' testimony. The AG's office had then convened the grand jury.

Playing the Outfield

Rogers was still in the deny mode and refused to budge from his stance that he never did any PEDs. Meanwhile he was losing the battle in the court of public opinion as he was asked to step down from positions on various charity boards.

A Dork had a different approach. He freely admitted that he had used PEDs. He had nothing to lose or so he thought. He acknowledged using steroids in 2003 while playing with the Dallas Drillies but he denied using PEDs since he began playing with the Bronx Bloomers. No one really believed him but A Dork didn't care. He thought that as long as he was making his money he didn't care what anyone else thought. He knew that Jelly Rogers was all caught up in the Corridor of Conceit controversy. However as far as he was concerned, A Dork reveled in the fact that he still had nine years remaining on his newly renegotiated contract. He also had Harry Bombs career homerun record to run after. A Dork also believed that the outcome of the C of C controversy would be determined long before his career was over.

Evangeline Prim became Evangeline Burr in late September of 2009. Lester and Georgette Postal served as witnesses to the small intimate nuptials that took place in Evangeline's parents' home town in Hatteras, North Carolina, along the Outer Banks of the Tar Heel State. Georgette had lost another 20 pounds and wore a size 10 dress to her friend's wedding. The law firm of Postal and Burr had its best year ever and was in the midst of representing several clients of one family who were suing a tobacco company in the same state of North Carolina. They also were now discussing the potential representation of a group of baseball players in a legal matter. The players were Sam Crockett and a number of his Facebook friends but these weren't names familiar to the average baseball fan.

XXI

Flunking Chemistry Class

January 2010

"Some people just don't get it? Do they?"

"You've got this clown Popeye Maloney finally admitting that he took steroids in 1998 when he broke the homerun record. Then he has the utter gall or unbelievable stupidity – I can't decide which it is – to insist that the *PEDs didn't help* him hit homeruns and that they had nothing to do with him breaking the homerun record."

"Obviously the juice got to his brain. He has to be totally fried to make that kind of a statement."

"Well the guy is kind of a moronic oaf to begin with. And some of these people couldn't do anything else with their lives if it weren't for the game of baseball. Popeye is a good example. The only reason he is coming clean is that he wants to get a coaching job with his old team the St. Louis Scarlets."

The conversation was a three way dialog between three baseball fans who had just left the Sheraton Hotel in midtown Manhattan after the annual MBLWA dinner honoring the post season award winners from the previous season. Lester Postal was the only one of the three fans who was a sportswriter. The other two Tim Burr and Will Morehead were listed as Postal's guests. And that that wasn't exactly accurate because Morehead was actually Postal's boss and would be picking up the tab for dinner for the three of them once Postal submitted his

Flunking Chemistry Class

expense account charges. They had reconvened at *The Morning After* and they were due to be joined shortly by trainer and steroid snitch, Ryan McGhee.

"Do you think that Popeye is fessing up now that he sees that his chances of getting into the Corridor of Conceit haven't budged much?" Morehead seemed generally interested in Postal's opinion on the matter.

"I think that that's certainly part of it. He has been out of the limelight for the past few years but baseball fans and sportswriters in particular have long memories. This was now the fourth ballot on which he was eligible and he still hasn't even received more than twenty-five per cent of the vote. He's a long way from seventy-five per cent and I guess he's hoping that if he comes clean on the PEDs stuff he'll do better in next year's ballot."

"Not with asinine statements like the one he made about getting no lift out of steroids. To my mind he's just another cheater anyway."

The waitress brought over their round of drinks just as the group was joined by the aforementioned Ryan McGhee. This put a bit of a pallor over the conversation because no one particularly liked McGhee. He was a classic parasite personality that was capable of sucking the life out of any friendship, any conversation or any business relationship. However he was the type of contact that Lester Postal had nurtured throughout his career as one of his "rental friends." Some such personalities were informants and as such were a necessary part of his job. And while other men might have been repulsed by these characters, Postal actually enjoyed nurturing these relationships. And occasionally – as was the case with Tim Burr – one of these *rental* friends actually became a *real* friend.

"How was the awards dinner?" McGhee inquired as he pulled up a chair. It went without saying that it would have been in truly bad taste for Postal to have invited McGhee to the MBLWA dinner along with his other guests. McGhee was reviled by almost everyone these days. Most of the players in particular detested the trainer.

The ironic part of the equation when it came to McGhee is that at one time he was everyone's best friend. Although he was always a bit

Flunking Chemistry Class

of a sycophant when it came to his relationship with players like Jelly Rogers and Randy Elfin, he was generally accepted around clubhouses as someone who could help a player's career. But over the last several years he had been kicked to the curb by the athletes he once mingled with and he had to be satisfied with friendships with folks like Lester Postal.

"The dinner was the usual spectacle. They gave out the post season awards for Most Venerated Player, The Sly Jung Awards, Field Supervisor and the Newbie of the Year Awards. The players stumbled through a few awkward words of thanks and everyone drank more than a little bit of booze. But all of the buzz was still about the size of some of the players. They all looked larger than life."

"The chemicals keep getting better every year. What do you expect?"

Postal, Burr, Morehead and others were scathing in their criticism of those that cheated and those that condoned the cheating. However what they all feared most was that the cheating was becoming more rampant than ever. They didn't need McGhee to remind them of this fact. Morehead stared at McGhee and suddenly had a better appreciation for the kind of work that his subordinate, Lester Postal, was called upon to do. Consorting with low life characters like McGhee was not pleasant work.

Meanwhile McGhee was also sizing up Morehead. He had only met the senior sports editor for *The Roast* once before and he wasn't sure that he could trust him in the same way that he had trusted Postal over the last several years. He did have a new bit of information to share but he wasn't sure that this was the appropriate time to do so. However Postal was the best at extracting new juicy details from his informants.

"You say that the chemicals keep getting better every year, Ryan. Do you have anything to support that?"

"It's pretty obvious, Lester. The PEDs police can't stay up with the PEDs peddlers."

"And I guess you include yourself in the latter group?" Tim Burr had been quiet up until now. He had already consumed more than his fair share of booze and was starting to get wobbly even while he was

Flunking Chemistry Class

seated. McGhee just glared at him in a dismissive manner and readdressed his dialogue to Postal

"As you are well aware, Lester, from our many discussions on this topic over the last however many years ... Selout and his cohorts at MBL ..." He stopped and glanced once again at Burr remembering that it was not that long ago that Burr had been part of Selout's staff. "Ahem," He nodded at Burr whose eyes were now fluttering shut. "Selout and his cohorts at MBL have been playing footsy with the players union for almost a decade. They claim that they're cracking down on steroids, but everyone is doing HGH. These are the days of designer drugs and MBL is still testing for the generic stuff."

"But aren't they doing whatever they can do. MBL is complaining that there are no effective tests or testing procedures for some of these new designer PEDs." Once again Will Morehead overstepped his role but this time McGhee just blasted away at his objection.

"That's horse shit. Will. MBL can develop whatever tests they want to detect this stuff. Don't let them feed you that line of crap."

"That's not what they're saying."

"You heard the man. It's horse shit. The league doesn't want to have pervasive testing. They're making too much money." Now Postal was disagreeing with his boss and Will Morehead wasn't sure whether Postal was just cultivating his source or being an argumentative subordinate.

"Think of it this way." Postal continued. "The compounds that are being developed for the players are being done by semi-amateur druggists who are experimenting with different substances so that they can get by the testing. They are compounding drugs and stacking steroids that allow them to do lots of things with their bodies, way beyond pure muscle build up. They also mix in a number of masking drugs to try to hide their usage. If the players can afford to get these compounds created by amateurs ...then surely the MBL with all of its resources can pay the big drug companies to develop tests to detect them."

"Part of the deal is that Selout and his crowd ...," Again McGhee glanced at Burr who now had his eyes closed and his chin resting on his chest. "...they think that they understand what is going on and they

Flunking Chemistry Class

don't. In the clubhouses the discussions are no longer about who's the better ballplayer, Mickey or the Duke; they're about whether anavar or winstrol is better for fast twitch muscle fibers."

Postal's view was even more cynical than McGhee's position. "F*** that s***. Believe me they know all that. Their attitude toward the media is like the high school bully who wants the smart kid in the class to purposely fail his chemistry exam so that the teacher will curve the grades. These guys know all about PEDs. They just want us to back off on the issue of testing the players for chemicals. The MBL is doing it on purpose."

"Doing what on purpose?" Morehead asked.

"Flunking chemistry class." Postal answered. They are flunking chemistry class on purpose.

XXII

"Yeaoww!"

March 2010

The decision was not really a tough one to make. Betsy Jo and Sam Crockett had made some adjustments in the way they approached life in general but neither of them found it practical to give up on their dream of making it to the Multinational Baseball League. There was too much upside and the downside was no worse than what they had already endured. Sam did pass up the winter league baseball however and stayed at home with his expectant wife and worked with his father-in-law in the drill bit business.

In early February 2010 Betsy Jo delivered seven pound seven ounce Sally Ann, who became the first daughter to bless the Crockett home in San Antonio. Sam Crockett was thrilled and he hated leaving his young family to head off to spring training again three weeks later. But because he had been protected by the Cheeseheads on their forty man roster Crockett felt that he would once again have a good shot at making it to The Show. And now that he was officially in his second year on the forty man roster, he would be assured of making no less than the minor league minimum for second year roster players of $65,000. However he was yet to play a single game in the MBL and there the minimum was a little over $400,000.

Once spring training got started down in Arizona, Sam began getting lots of playing time. He was also seeing lots of change ups. During

Flunking Chemistry Class

the third week in March he had a game during which he hit two homeruns, giving him four so far for the month. His batting average was an even .250 a little on the low side but he also had two doubles and was slugging at a robust .583 over 36 at bats.

The next morning when Sam Crockett appeared at the club house he was asked to step into the men's room in the company of a male drug tester who administered a controlled urine sample collection in accordance with the random drug testing provision of the current joint agreement.

Seven other members of the Cheeseheads roster were also asked to submit to the test, including Brawny Glaun, the Cheeseheads emerging young athletic icon. Glaun had shattered several franchise performance records by hitting more than one hundred homeruns and had more than 300 RBI's in his first three seasons in the bigs. Glaun was already a certified superstar.

After the urine samples had been collected another of the young players was heard complaining, "It's amazing how they just spring this test on you from out of nowhere."

Glaun responded to his teammate by saying, "If you're clean, you have nothing to worry about. I think that it's disgraceful that guys who are using performance enhancing drugs are allowed to compete against the rest of us."

When Sam Crockett heard Glaun's statement his respect for his star teammate grew even further. Glaun was twenty six years old, the same age as Crockett, but Glaun had only spent two seasons in the minors and was about to enter his fourth season in the Multinational Baseball League. Sam was envious but not jealous. He was glad to hear that Glaun had gone about his business the right way. He was living proof that you didn't need PEDs to become a superstar. Sam wanted to model his career after that of his teammate. However he was still a bit in awe over how much Glaun had accomplished. In addition, Glaun wasn't the most accommodating player when it came to associating with rookie players and Crockett was careful about approaching the franchise player and asking for any kind of professional advice.

"Yeaoww!"

Once again Crockett was fighting for a position on the twenty-five man squad as spring training was drawing to a close. He had had a good camp but the Cheeseheads had several good corner outfielders in addition to Glaun. It appeared as though the Cheeseheads would keep a total of four outfielders. Crockett never had the foot speed to be considered a centerfield prospect. Crockett had been given a chance to play a few innings as a backup first basemen during the spring but he knew that that position was firmly anchored by the Cheeseheads other superstar, the prodigious producer, Vince Wielder.

In addition to his hitting prowess Brawny Glaun was also a Mighty Mitt winning left fielder, so barring injury the only starting position that Crockett had a shot at was right field. Of course he could also make the team as the fourth outfielder and as a power hitter coming off the bench. Being that the Cheeseheads played in the Native League, there would be no DH option. Despite his injury as a pitcher a couple of years earlier Crockett still had an excellent throwing arm so that was a big plus. However because of his limited tenure on the forty man roster, Crockett still had minor league options left and his competition for the last job on the team was an effective veteran utility outfielder Victor Spleen. Spleen was out of options. Oddly that was an advantage for Spleen. However the Cheeseheads loved power hitters and Crockett had displayed ample oomph throughout March. The competition for the final outfield spot was the lead sports story in the Cheeseheads camp as well as back in Wisconsin.

Before the final game of spring training in Arizona, Sam Crockett was thrilled to see his name penciled into the lineup as the right fielder, batting fifth right behind Glaun and Wielder. They were playing the Chicago Pantyhose and the Cheeseheads' manager had put together what appeared to be his potential opening day lineup. Crockett could feel it in every bone in his body. He was going to The Show! And he was going to be the Cheeseheads starting right fielder!

Sam felt light as a feather when he came to the plate in the bottom of the first with runners on second and third and two out. After letting two off speed pitches drop outside of the strike zone, Crockett lashed an outside fastball into left center field heading toward the gap. Two more ribbies, he thought. That would give him the team lead for the Spring! He rounded first and headed for second as the Pantyhose left-fielder backhanded the ball in the gap. The Chicago player had a hose for an arm and he gunned the ball toward the keystone as Crockett headed into second. But Sam Crockett began his slide way too late and he abruptly slammed his ankle into the bag.

"Yeaoww!"

It wasn't a good yeaoww.

XXIII

Dreaming on the Outer Banks

July, 2010

It had been a hot and busy summer for the law firm of Postal and Burr, which now had six associate attorneys to help with the work load. But it had been a very successful summer also. Their clients had settled their lawsuit against the tobacco company for $13.5 Million and Georgette Postal had been featured on several television shows excoriating the evils of tobacco use on people's health and berating the companies who produced tobacco products. The young attorney had gotten her own health completely under control as she had her weight down to a svelte 135 pounds and a size 6 dress. She looked like a completely different lady from the obese woman who had graduated in Tim Burr's law school class with him in 2004. And she was a lot less than half the size of the woman who married Lester Postal the same year. Georgette was now quite an attractive young woman professional who had reinvented herself while still in her early thirties. She was definitely the driving force behind the firm's success but she loyally shared some of the limelight with her partner, Tim Burr.

To celebrate the successful conclusion of their tobacco case, the Burrs and the Postals decided to vacation together on the Outer Banks of North Carolina. They left their law practice for a week in the hands of their associates and rented a two bedroom house on the ocean front in the beach town of Avon on Hatteras Island. Tim Burr's wife

Flunking Chemistry Class

Evangeline had grown up on the island and they had been married the previous summer in a nearby Catholic Church. Both Tim and Lester had grown up on Long Island in New York State as had Georgette so they all loved the calm of the ocean tides. They all also knew how to balance that calm by drinking and carousing on the ocean beach.

Lester Postal was a good bit older than the other three members of the group but recently he was feeling more and more like he was back in his thirties himself. The night before the two couples had finished off a dozen beers and two and a half bottles of wine while also putting a serious dent in a bottle of 21 year old Glenlivet single malt scotch. They had begun drinking and playing cards right after coming back out of the ocean, while still sandy and salty from the beach. Somewhere in the midst of all of the drinking they had managed to go to a seafood shanty by the name of *The Mad Crabber* and had devoured several platters of king crab legs. By the time they returned to the beachfront house to play cards Lester practically carried his little buddy through the sand covered parking area and up the wooden deck stairs to the top floor breezeway deck. Like almost all of the houses in the beachfront row their rental was built on stilts that allowed majestic views past the expansive sand dunes and out over the shoreline. While Tim Burr was leglessly re-seating himself at the table where they all had been playing card games for most of the early evening, Lester grabbed the deck of swollen well worn cards and began dealing again. They all enjoyed the fact that the card games were a social throw back to the days before video games became the far more common diversion. The two women were also looking a bit cross-eyed at that point and so everyone went to bed after just a few more hands of hearts.

Lester was the last person to make it to bed. He opened the bedroom doorway before he got under the sheets so that he could listen to the ocean tide lap at the shoreline and breathe the salty air that curled along the wooden stairs and deck to the upper reaches of the house.

Dreaming on the Outer Banks

He curled up next to Georgette and within three minutes he was snoring away. Within five minutes his mind had entered the zone wherein the bizarre dreams of Lester Postal were formulated:

Nearly forty years of writing a sports column and this was Lester's first book. He was winning an award at the MBLWA dinner in New York. His body was much younger. His mind retained all of his experience. He was surrounded by many beautiful women – women who had never before appeared at one of these dinners. These women were laying roses at his feet as he went up to the dais to receive his plaque for having penned his parody of the Multinational Baseball League, entitled what else but: <u>Flunking Chemistry Class</u>.

Just before he began his acceptance remarks, an emaciated pole dancer who resembled his demonic first wife handed him a glass of water and a piece of chocolate the size of a chunky bar. He took a large bite out of the chocolate bar and offered the other half back to the pole dancer. He was relieved to see that she ate the other half of the candy but he noticed that the candy had turned red like an apple. As she smiled in a deceptively devilish way, Lester could see her hair parting slightly to reveal two reddish horns that appeared to be slowly growing out of the top of her skull. He also noticed that her breasts were beginning to swell. Then her thin face and lips took on a botox-ian manifestation. Her appearance went from frail and flat to curvaceously chiseled but didn't stop there. Her body continued to swell going all the way past the cute but corpulent stage and on to prodigiously plump plateau. But then she continued to swell, finally settling in as round, rotund and revolting.

Standing at the dais Lester began to notice his own body swelling also. He held the award plaque in his hands and he began to notice a slight puffiness in his fingers. When he went to lick the slight remnants of the chocolate bar from his rapidly dilating digits the chocolate had turned red and tasted like a Macintosh. He could feel his shoes tightening around his swelling feet and his collar choking his now bulging neck.

Below the dais on the main floor of the ballroom he noticed a group of pole dancers who resembled some of his other wives and comfort companions from an earlier era of his life. They were wearing skimpy negligees and were performing as waitresses, distributing ten cubic chocolate bars to each of the tables of ten around the room. As patrons bit into the chocolate bars the candy all turned into apples. Everyone began to swell up. A few of the men began to burst through

Flunking Chemistry Class

their business suits in an Incredible Hulk fashion. However their rippled musculature continued to swell.

The other people on the dais were award winning baseball players who already had swollen bodies. Each of them in turn shook their head when the scantily clad pole dancer-waitresses offered them candy. Below the dais, Georgette and Evangeline were among the few women guests at the male dominated dinner festivities. They both stared back at him vacuously from their front row table.

"I want to thank the members of the MBLWA for this award." As Lester Postal began to make his acceptance remarks, he unbuttoned his shirt and removed his tie to allow room for the body ballooning which continued unfettered by his dialogue. He felt his head begin to expand and his puffy ears begin to extend from his head so that his visage looked like a taxi going down Broadway with both doors open. He looked down helplessly at his table where he saw Tim, Evangeline and Georgette huddling their chairs together in rapt attention waiting for Lester to continue his acceptance speech.

"I am honored that you enjoyed my satirical parody of the Multinational Baseball League. As you know the MBL ... " Then as Lester was continuing his remarks he began to feel still another bodily change that caused him to drop his plaque on the table and drop both hands to his crotch. His thoughts went from the adventures of the Incredible Hulk to another movie by the name of the Incredible Shrinking Man. His puffy hands began searching for his dwindling nuts and he became petrified that his pecker would proceed down the same path. As he manually explored his nether region, in the background he suddenly heard the music from the 1960's hit song Searchin' by the Coasters and he simply repeatedly muttered to himself, "Gunna find 'em."

As the music grew louder the guests in the audience began to rise out of their seats and then they began to rise from their respective tables. The audience began bursting through their clothing and their ballooning bodies began floating to the ceiling like so many bloated corpses in a Grade B lakeside horror movie. Before long there were two hundred or so floats who had risen to the 30 foot ceiling of the Sheraton's ballroom. The bodies were bobbing to and fro, gently banging into one another as they hovered around the crystal chandeliers. However three people remained down at their table. Tim Burr had quickly warned Evangeline and Georgette not to eat the candy as soon as he saw Lester begin to blow up. Several of the older floats were wearing emergency button necklaces around their

Dreaming on the Outer Banks

neck and began pushing the buttons and calling 911. They all said pretty much the same thing.

"HELP, I'M FLOATING AND I CAN'T GET DOWN!"

Meanwhile back on the ballroom floor, Tim Burr was running around collecting the seating cards from each table setting. "Evidence, lots of evidence," was all he could say.

Georgette then pointed up at the dais. "Let's help him, quickly."

Evangeline simply responded, "Whatever."

Tim Burr commented, "Holy Shit!"

Lester now had both of his puffy hands frenetically grabbing the slanted top to the podium, which had been screwed into place earlier in the day. However Lester's inflated body was now totally inverted with his feet pointing toward the ceiling and his head hovering upside down as he tried to hold on. As his wife and friends rushed the dais platform, Lester looked around his upside down world. The sportswriters and their guests had floated to the ceiling, but the ballplayers remained in their seats. That's when he noticed that all of the highly paid floats had been tethered to their seats by barely discernible transparent ropes. They had eaten their candy earlier and had avoided the need to take a bite out of transformative forbidden candy/fruit.

Just before Georgette and the Burrs reached his table Lester took one hand off the podium and pointed with his index finger at the secretly tethered but still seated armada of superfloats.

"You fuckers are ruining the game. You...oh...oH...OH!" Postal couldn't hold on to the podium but as he let go he changed his index finger to the neighboring phalanx and was saluting the seated cheaters with the bird even as his own body took flight.

Postal woke up as the waves continued to lap at the North Carolina shoreline. He was shaking all over. But he simply glanced at his gonads and then, reassured, he went back to sleep.

Lester was the first one up in the morning and he had already forgotten his dream, although it hovered in his subconscious mind. He dragged out his laptop to see what trades might be going down during the last forty-eight hours before the non-waiver trade deadline of July 31st. There was an inconsequential deal between the Pittsburgh Pillagers and the Anaheim Afterthoughts and he noticed that the Wisconsin Cheeseheads had picked up a utility outfielder. There was one other item that was much more significant.

Lester began reading the comments by Congressman Hans Waxear after the announcement that Jelly Rogers had been indicted by a federal grand jury for perjury nearly two years after his testimony before a congressional committee. Waxear seemed to be indicating that if Rogers went to jail, Congress would have provided a significant deterrent to steroid use. Meanwhile Rogers issued still another statement denying everything and promising a rigorous defense. After reading the article, Postal just shook his head in disgust. He couldn't decide which person was the more self-absorbed imbecile, Rogers or Waxear.

He was still clicking through the news postings when he saw Tim Burr approaching. Burr had grown a full beard in the last few months in an attempt to look more mature but it hadn't helped. The beard was now long but much too sparse to effectuate the desired appearance. The hair on top of his head also needed to be cut. It was thicker than his beard and was now matted up in the rear in a sleep clump of a cowlick that further accentuated the young lawyer's hung-over expression. He was wearing only his boxer shorts and an undershirt that was two sizes too small to cover his newly emerging beltline bulge.

"What's new in the world outside of the Outer Banks?"

"Big news ... they indicted Jelly Rogers."

Burr twisted his face back in a distasteful grimace. "I don't want to hear about that asshole. What else is new?"

"Just checking on the sports news," Postal paused as if to indicate that if Burr wanted news on nuclear disarmament he would have to get a different source. "Looks like our friend Sam Crockett would have made the Cheeseheads if he didn't get hurt, They just traded for another outfielder. That's the third one they've added since April."

Before Burr could respond Georgette and Evangeline appeared in shorts and tank tops and declared that they were going for a walk up to the Food Lion and would bring back some breakfast snacks. Before they left Evangeline started a pot of coffee.

"Yeah it's too bad about Sam. Did I tell you that we got an email from him last week about his Facebook page?"

"You might have ... or Georgette might have said something. What is the latest with all of that?"

"He certainly has been cooperative but frankly he's hoping that he'll never need our help. In some ways it all comes down to timing ... if we sue and when we sue. A lot depends upon which way his career goes. However, to tell you the truth it might not even matter if he eventually makes The Show. He has already suffered damages by the years he already fallen short."

"It's a shame what happens to these ball players who want to play it straight. They don't have much of a chance. The deck is stacked against them. It seems like the floats have taken over the sport. So what does Crockett want you to do?"

"We already have more than enough information to initiate litigation on Crockett's behalf, but he wants to give it one final chance. He won't be playing at all this year. But he says that 2011 will be the 'make or break' season for him. We're willing to wait. We already have plenty of work and as you know Georgette and I are talking about taking on several additional associates and maybe even a limited partner or two."

"I'm aware of that but back to the baseball suit. If Crockett doesn't sue, will you sue on behalf of one of the other players?"

"That's up to the players themselves. We don't want to be chasing after these things. Believe me they'll find us sooner or later. But right now we're simply working for Sam Crockett ...and we're doing it pro bono."

"So then what's your opinion? Will you eventually file suit on behalf of one of these players? I really hope you do. I'd like to see all of these cheaters hung by the balls and that includes the floats, their agents, the Commissioner and the corrupt owners. Screw 'em all."

"Let's put it this way Lester. Crockett has given us a list of names of talented minor league players that he thinks are honest athletes. He has also given us a list of players that have made it to the MBL and

Flunking Chemistry Class

that he knows are PED users because they have told him so directly. In a couple of cases he has even witnessed this use. One such example is that guy, Leathermore who died last year. With the information we have gathered I have no doubt whatsoever that if we file suit, we will have no trouble certifying a group of players as a class for a class action suit.

"How does that work?"

"The principle is referred to as CANT which is an acronym for Commonality, Adequacy, Numerosity and Typicality. Basically the court checks to see that the plaintiffs have all suffered common injuries … in this case …the restricted ability to earn a major league salary … and that the firm …in this case Postal and Burr … is adequately resourced to prosecute the claim for the entire class of plaintiffs. They will also look at things such as whether the named plaintiffs … in this case probably Crockett and some of his pals …are truly representative of the class. And they'll evaluate whether or not this would better be handled by individual lawsuits. We'll have to demonstrate that defendants treated all of the members of our class in a 'typical manner.' There are several other issues as well. But I'm sure we could certify."

"That sounds like a lot of work, and could cost a lot of money if you're only working on a contingency." Postal looked up from his laptop at the young lawyer, as Burr began trying to shake his hangover. Postal thought that somewhere amidst Burr's bedraggled hair, bloodshot eyes and the too-small-T, there was a brilliant mind.

"That's the risk we'll take. But we've only begun to scratch the surface. We're laying the groundwork. This will take years to work through. There are a lot of defendants to go after but we'll definitely want to go after all of those folks because the final verdict will almost certainly be a very big dollar amount … probably an unprecedented dollar figure, in fact."

"Wow. You and Georgette could be awfully busy."

"That's another reason why we're expanding the firm now. We want to be able to handle the case without a whole raft of other plaintiff partner firms. And like I said there's a lot of grunt work to do in setting up call centers and such to corral all of the potential plaintiffs,

Dreaming on the Outer Banks

and then sorting out who fits the class criteria. We will probably want to focus on the so called 26th man, the final cuts of each team, each season, over a number of years."

"You can't always tell who that is. Sometimes several guys are cut on the final day."

"That's fine. We still want to focus on people like Sam Crockett, who almost get there but never make it. The concept of the 26th man is simply a clever convenience. The media will eat it up."

"You actually believe that it will be worth it all?"

"I think that there will be minor leaguers coming out of the woodwork to get a piece of the pie."

"How big do you think this law suit could be?"

The accountant/lawyer loved doing the mathematical part of the summation. "Think of it this way, if the average 26th man makes the Triple A maximum of $65,000.00 ...a generous assumption I might add ... he is still being paid $335,000 less than the major league *minimum*.

"If instead you use the *average* salary of a major league player, which is more than $4 Million, the differential grows astronomically. So let's say we use something in the middle and say the player loses an average of $2 Million a year over a projected 12 year career. That means that the player would lose out on about $24,000,000 during the course of his career. Multiply that by about 250 eligible minor league players and we're suddenly talking about $6 billion dollars. Then consider treble damages for the anti-trust violations that are inherent in the conspiracy. We now tally $18,000,000,000, not exactly chump change. And of course none of these calculations consider lost endorsement opportunities."

The waves kept lapping at the Carolina coastline.

XXIV

Jelly's Travail

Spring 2011

After breaking his ankle and severely straining his Achilles tendon both in the same slide, Sam Crockett had missed the entire 2010 season and he also missed his closest chance ever at collecting a MBL paycheck. The only good news was that the Cheeseheads had been so impressed with his potential that they kept him in their organization and also kept him on their forty man roster. He was put on the minor league disabled list but he collected his full minor league salary for the year. Now after 10 years of baseball without a day in the MBL Sam Crockett was certain that 2011 would be his last year in the minors. It was MBL or bust.

When he analyzed his career to date, Crockett recognized that he had spent a full four years in the Bronx Bloomers organization. He also had some split time with the Wisconsin Cheeseheads that also totaled four years. In between he had dabbled with short sojourns in the Carp organization as well as with the Hedgers. He had spent the first seven years of his career as a pitcher and the last three years as an outfielder. He was going to give it one last chance. He was going to make a MBL roster in 2011 or he was going to call it a career.

But there were problems. Sam Crockett's resolve didn't match up well with his behavior. The healing process had gone slowly. He couldn't really begin his rehab in earnest until almost seven months

Jelly's Travail

after his injury. In the interim he had returned to San Antonio, but because of his cast he was very limited in working with his father-in-law in the drilling tool business. Betsy Jo worked part time and her mother watched their three children whenever both Crocketts were out of the house. Sam only worked sporadically throughout the winter months of 2010/2011. As a result he spent an inordinate amount of time just sitting on the couch watching football and basketball games on TV and sipping an exorbitant quantity of Lone Star Beer while occasionally chasing after the kids. By the time he was due to report for Spring Training in February he was fifteen pounds over his playing weight.

By the end of March Sam's slash stats were not what he had hoped and .245/.319/.389 earned him a return trip to Memphis.

Jelly Rogers couldn't believe it. He had been indicted and was going to trial! And now he was being lumped together with some of the most infamous steroid cheats. What about his 300 plus big league victories? What about his record setting strikeout marks? Was he now going to get squat for his whiffs? Was he going to be sent to jail? Even before he was convicted of anything he had already been ousted from two charity boards who no longer wanted to be associated with him. Was this justice? Rogers had convinced himself that he had done nothing wrong and yet ironically he detested other steroid users. He was a tree about to fall in the forest but no matter how much he screamed he couldn't hear himself.

However Jelly had a new plan. Or at least it was an old plan with a few new wrinkles. "Deny! Deny! Deny!" was now being augmented with "Attack! Attack! Attack!" He filed a law suit against his primary accuser Ryan McGhee. He was determined to punish anyone who would attempt to impugn his integrity. Dolly Rogers was doing everything she could to console her husband but Jelly simply didn't like being smeared.

"It will all be over soon, Jelly. The trial is only a month away. Then we can go back to leading our normal lives."

Flunking Chemistry Class

"*We don't lead normal lives, you idiot.*" He thought it but he didn't say it. Instead he massaged his mini-jowl and then said "What if something goes wrong?"

"What could possibly go wrong, dear?" Her attempt at a soothing smile met with a bit of a Botox block but she managed to curl up her mouth in an attempt at encouragement. "You have a terrific attorney and he says that you won't have to take the stand because this is a criminal case."

"Would you stop saying that please?"

"Stop what?"

"Stop calling it a criminal case?"

"But that's what it is. Isn't it dear?"

"Yes but you don't have to keep reminding me. I'm not a criminal."

"Of course not, dear. You're a good man. And when you're acquitted in this stupid trial, everyone will know that you're not a criminal."

"They'd better know that. This case is costing me a fortune. Reed Hurling may be one of the best attorneys in Texas but he doesn't come cheap."

"Like I said. It will all be over soon."

"I certainly hope you're right about that. I haven't thrown a pitch in the MBL in almost four years but I'll bet I could still win 20 games. And I'll bet there are a dozen teams out there that would pay me an eight figure salary to do it. You know what Dolly? I'm so wholesome and spectacular that I'm surprised they haven't put my picture on a goddamn Wheaties box yet!"

"I thought we agreed that you were finally retired. We'll just get this trial over and move on with our lives. And don't worry, Jelly, maybe they'll put you on the Wheaties box some day. After all they once put Harry Bombs on the box."

"Don't remind me."

"Why are you so upset? I've told you over and over again. It will be over real soon."

"Well I'm worried that it might somehow get delayed. You know, speaking of Bombs, they also indicted him for perjury. They said he

Jelly's Travail

lied in connection with the B'WHALE'CO investigation. Bombs was indicted in 2007 and he just went to trial a few months ago."

"I understand Jelly. But he didn't have to go to jail and neither will you."

"You're missing the point, Dolly. He got convicted of a crime. It may only have been obstruction of justice, but he still is a *convict*. He got house arrest and community service time, but people forget what it's for. They just consider him a criminal. Period."

"Well they're not going to do that to my Jelly."

"They better not drag this out like they did with Bombs. I'll be eligible for the Corridor of Conceit when they vote at the end of this year. I want to be clear of any doubt when that election takes place."

The following month the trial of Jelly Rogers was delayed indefinitely due to a prosecutorial misstep. Jelly Rogers was so worried about the delay that he considered another comeback. He figured that a comeback would reset the clock on his retirement period all over again. Maybe in another five years the steroid era would be looked at differently. There were sportswriters like Lester Postal who thought such a notion was preposterous. "Liars are liars and cheaters are cheaters, forever and ever." Postal had recently begun inscribing this bit of wisdom as the last few words of every column that he wrote on the topic of steroids.

XXV

The MVP and the Botch Job

Fall 2011

CoJo Janesco was still a celebrity in the Cuban community in and around Miami, Florida nearly a decade after his MBL career had ended. He was regarded as one of the few ballplayers who didn't try to obfuscate the steroid crisis. In fact he *celebrated* the steroid issue and didn't consider it a crisis at all. For the past several years Janesco and his twin brother had been the owners of a health, fitness and longevity center in Miami called *Beautiful & Bodacious Bodies by CoJo*. It was also called CoJo's Triple B's.

Membership prices at *Beautiful & Bodacious Bodies* were steep, but the clientele was well heeled. More than two thirds of Triple B's clients were women but the male clientele tended to be younger and more affluent than the cougar crowd. Although Janesco had freely admitted personal use of both legal and illegal drugs in the past, he was careful to stay on the right side of the law when it came to the dispensing of steroids and nutritional supplements at Triple B's.

Janesco had now been divorced from his wife Chiquita for five years. She had grown tired of all of his womanizing. That particular vice had gotten out of hand after CoJo had used his fitness center as a launching pad to produce his highly successful cable TV celebrity dance contest "Dancing with the Bars" which featured pole dancing

The MVP and the Botch Job

by B and C list celebrities along with some of the local Miami T and A talent.

Although Janesco went through his money like rain water down a sewage drain, his funds never seemed to dry up. Everything he touched seemed to turn to gold. He even had a winning Florida State Lottery ticket that netted him $900 thousand in second place money in the state's Mega Millions Game. He sold his second book on the baseball steroid era entitled: <u>Validated</u> and he was a frequent guest on talk shows. His one failure was his attempt to make a comeback as a player when MBL expansion took root in the middle of the decade. He couldn't even hop on with the lowly Kangaroos. So he contented himself with his celebrity in the Cuban community and a keen eye for new ventures.

So while the ever evolving saga of steroid use in MBL continued to unfold, CoJo Janesco was living out his post MBL career as a fitness and nutrition guru. He didn't make any false claims about having a medical degree like a certain one of his competitors, because Janesco's own background was well known. Nevertheless it was amazing how people could attribute medical knowledge to someone merely because he was in the four hundred homer club. His clientele trusted his views on steroids and other PEDs because he told them what he used personally. There were plenty of legal drugs on the market that had anti-aging properties. Some of these supplements were available over-the-counter and some required prescriptions. To satisfy these needs Janesco had several licensed physicians on his payroll at *Beautiful & Bodacious Bodies*.

Of course CoJo's Triple B's was not the only health and fitness center in Miami. And oddly enough it wasn't even the one with the most famous clientele. That distinction belonged to an entity called *Myo-Nemesis*. However *Myo-Nemesis* ran under the radar. Andrea Botch was the transgender proprietor of *Myo-Nemesis* and the purveyor of a vast array of mail order steroids and other performance enhancing drugs.

Flunking Chemistry Class

Myo-Nemesis derived its name from its tag line which was: *"Don't be your own worst enemy. Shape up; whatever it takes."* More cynical names for the place included *"My own menaces"* and *"Buy-own medalists."* However the clinic was often just called *Myo* by most of its clients.

Botch didn't run a mail order drug business only. *Myo-Nemesis* actually had a health care facility. However it was not a luxurious facility like Janesco's *Beautiful & Bodacious Bodies*. In fact it was not even on a par with the local YMCA. Botch ran her facility as a front for the much more lucrative business of providing professional athletes with whatever body-enhancing chemicals they wanted. Baseball players were her sweet spot and her clientele included some of the sports largest luminaries.

After Manboy Ramendez of the Hollywood Hedgers was caught using synthetic testosterone in 2009, MBL got a whiff of the fact that Manboy's supplier was Andrea Botch and her Miami based *Myo-Nemesis*. At the time Buzz Selout was widely criticized for not doing a better job of policing the drug usage in the MBL. Selout had never been a big fan of Manboy because he perceived the outfielder as being disrespectful of the game. On several occasions in the past, Manboy Ramendez had been accused of deliberately delivering less than optimal effort on the field. In fact his lackadaisical attitude was one of the primary motivating factors underlying his trade from the Wallbangers to the Hedgers in 2008. So when Manboy failed his test, Selout decided to start digging into his background. He realized that he needed a poster boy or two to demonstrate that he was getting serious about controlling PEDs. And he had a plan to do just that.

Because he was trying to live within the law for a change, CoJo Janesco was a bit surprised when he got a visit from Heidi Hunt, one of the co-authors of the celebrated Witchell- Hunt Report.

The MVP and the Botch Job

"So to what do I owe the honor of your visit, Ms. Hunt?"

"Just call me Heidi, please."

"Heinie?" He purposely mispronounced her name while surveying her booty.

"No, Heidi." She smiled crookedly and Janesco began to get worried. She would not normally endure an insult, even a slight one, unless she had something she wanted. Now he was concerned.

"Alright then Heidi, what can I do for you? We haven't seen each other in few years." Their conversation was taking place in the front lobby of Triple B's because Hunt had shown up unexpectedly without an appointment. Janesco just happened to be in the lobby at the time.

"Yes, well after our report was published in 2007, Mitch Witchell went on to other things However I was recently re-commissioned by Buzz Selout to explore some of the same turf."

"That's interesting. I thought the steroid report thing was a one and done kind of deal."

"That wouldn't make much sense if you think about it."

"No I guess it wouldn't." He was still nervous but he wasn't sure why. Heidi Hunt was actually a dreadfully homely looking woman. She had a great body but a face that could stop London's Big Ben. Her dog-face included oversized nostrils, fleshy cheeks and runny-looking eyes which she constantly squinted. However Janesco couldn't help himself. He always thought about bedding every woman he ever met. He remembered that he had once heard Jelly Roger's refer to Heidi Hunt as a two bagger – the kind of woman that a guy could take to bed if he put a bag over her head – and also put one over his own head in case hers slipped off.

"This is a beautiful facility you have here CoJo. It looks like business is going well."

"I have nothing to complain about." As they continued talking Janesco grew slightly less apprehensive. However he didn't want to continue the discussion in the lobby. Even as they were speaking two or three shapely young female customers came through the front door and each of them greeted Janesco with a big smile and an extra cordial, "Hi CoJo."

Flunking Chemistry Class

"Why don't we continue our discussion in my office?" Janesco held out his mega muscled arm and pointed with his palm in a direction that led down the hallway He walked behind Hunt partly to assess her curves from a rear perspective and partly to avoid looking at her hook nose, beady eyes and sagging cheekbones. He liked the rear view and thought that he could do her as long as he went with the two bag strategy or did her doggy style. Her body was her redeeming quality. She had an interesting intellect but CoJo didn't really care about that. He was simply prequalifying her as another notch on his gun. He figured that he was now getting into the range of some of the most prolific porkers of all time, and he wondered if he was approaching the record setting pace of the former basketball player Stilts Wonderland, who had claimed to have scored more points in his bed chamber than he did on the hard court.

When they made it to his office, CoJo shut the door with a bang and then repeated his earlier inquiry, "So how can I help you?"

"I guess you'd like me to get right to the point, so let's not beat around the bush. How well do you know your competitor, Andrea Botch, over at *Myo-Nemesis*?"

"I don't really know him ... or her ... or whatever Botch is ... very well. She ... yea let's give her the benefit of the doubt and go with 'she' ...has tried to engage me and Triple B's in some kind of non-financial partnership ... or whatever ... in the past. I'm not too sure what she wanted other than to be friends."

"So she was coming on to you?"

"Hell no. Not in that way. Yuck. There aren't enough brown bags in all of Mia ... oh never mind. Why do you ask? What's your interest in Botch and *Myo*?"

"We have some reason to believe that she may be supplying some of our players with PEDs. We know for sure she supplied Manboy Ramendez. We're almost certain that there are others."

"So then what does that have to do with me? Everything I do here is perfectly legal."

"Well, Botch doesn't want to talk to me. We thought that you might convince her to change her mind."

The MVP and the Botch Job

"That's crazy. To begin with, we are competitors ... at least on a certain level."

"Botch's business is selling steroids in the mail. Is that what you do also?

"No, of course not ... but she has a healthcare facility here in Miami. And that *is* similar to what I do here."

"Come on CoJo, we're both smarter than that. Her facility is just a front for her mail order business. You, on the other hand, appear to have a legitimate healthcare business."

"I see no reason why I should get in the middle of your investigation. What's in it for me?"

"You have been quite vocal in your belief that a professionally administered regimen of steroids and other prescription drugs can not only enhance a person's performance in all different walks of life but may also extend a person's longevity.

"That's correct."

"But I should also tell you that it has come to our attention that your own recent prosperity might have a lot to do with businesses that extend beyond *Beautiful & Bodacious Bodies.*"

"I'm a celebrity. What can I tell you? I have dabbled in a lot of businesses."

"What about the business of illegally assisting the immigration of Cuban nationals into the US? Is it true that you are using your Cuban roots to facilitate the migration of ballplayers from the island? And by the way, it seems that many of these players have come to the US as well developed floats as soon as they arrive. Their body building regimens may not have been subject to the same scrutiny as others during their wonder years. There may be some people who believe that you may have been instrumental in helping some of your fellow countrymen develop their protocols."

"Hey, what's this fellow countryman stuff? I'm an American citizen and have been for years. I haven't been to Cuba since my family left there when I was a child."

"But that wouldn't stop you from helping some folks with the same ancestral background. Now would it?"

Flunking Chemistry Class

"Hey I don't know anything about any of that? Sure there's a lot more people leaving the island than there was in the past ..."

"A lot more ballplayers, anyway."

"You've read the stories. A lot of these guys come over on rafts. They want their freedom just like you and me."

"They're certainly appears to be a whole raft of these raft stories ... I'm not so sure. These guys are doing so many PEDs I wouldn't be surprised if these floats just dove in the water and swam the 90 miles."

"Like I said, I don't know anything about it." CoJo was a bit flustered. He didn't like the pooch-faced investigator and he had already rethought his double bagger desires. He also had little to no interest in getting involved in this Botch mess, in any way, shape or form. But he also didn't want to get on the wrong side of Selout when he appeared to have a bug up his ass, so he simply said, "I guess I could talk to Botch."

"Good."

"But before we go any further I just have one other question."

"Okay and what might that be?"

"Why, all of a sudden, is Selout getting so hard-nosed about everything? He never did much about this for more than fifteen years."

"It's about his legacy. He doesn't want to be remembered as the *Steroid Commissioner*. He's going to retire soon and he wants to have a plaque in the Corridor of Conceit along with some of the other long term commissioners."

XXVI

Is It Over?

December 2011

Another baseball season had come and gone. Sudden Sam Crockett never did make it to the MBL. Shortly after rejoining the Memphis Munsters he was afflicted with a series of minor injuries that had him on and off the minor league seven day disabled list three different times. By the Parade of Stars break he had been dropped from the Cheeseheads' 40 man roster and he was given his unconditional release in mid August. He tried to hook on with another club, but the word on the street was that he had never quite recovered from his injuries. When he returned home in August, he was dejected but not bitter. He had given it his best shot and now it was time to get on with his life. He began looking for a full time job and he and Betsy Jo discussed the possibility of his taking some college courses at night. When he finally had put baseball behind him, he took his first couple of night courses starting in September.

Things changed one night in December when Crockett was listening to the sports news on TV with his wife at his side. The kids had already gone to bed. Sam Crockett had a hard time believing his ears. His onetime teammate on the Cheeseheads, Brawny Glaun, was now being accused of being a PEDs user! This was the same Brawny Glaun who had just edged out Mitt Kipp of the Hedgers for the Native League MVP. It was the same Brawny Glaun who had been so outspoken in his condemnation of other PEDs users. And it was the same Brawny Glaun who occupied a position in the Cheeseheads outfield while Sam struggled unsuccessfully to make the roster. Sam Crockett was seething mad.

"Do you believe this Betsy Jo?"

"I thought you liked Brawny Glaun."

"I thought I liked him too. This can't be true. He's one of the few guys that I didn't doubt. He told everyone that he was clean. And we all believed him. He was the guy we looked to and said it was still possible to excel without PEDs.

"Well so much for that theory."

"He's saying that it's all a mistake. He still claims that he didn't do it. He said that the test was a 'real botch-job' and that when all of the facts come out he will be cleared."

"Come on, Sam. Do you really believe that?"

"No, I guess I don't."

"Doesn't it make you even angrier that Glaun has the unmitigated gall to call it a botch job rather than fess up to being a good-for-nothing-lying-cheating-scum-of-the-earth-shithead?

Crockett had never heard his wife string together such a hyphenated phrase before, but he knew that it was warranted. He now despised Glaun with a passion.

"First thing tomorrow morning, I'm going to call the folks at Postal and Burr. I'm ready to go through with the law suit."

XXVII
The 26th Man Law Suit

April 2012

After more than twenty years as the acting commissioner and then the official commissioner of the Multinational Baseball League, Buzz Selout was finally contemplating retirement. Buzz Selout was burning out. He knew that he was getting too old to continue the daily grind of being the chief executive of the Multinational Baseball League. It was time to move on. But what would his legacy be? He had presided over a period of unprecedented prosperity for the owners and the players. He had expanded the business globally. In fact 2012 was now the first year that the final phase of expansion was taking root as teams were added in Caracas, Venezuela and in San Juan, Puerto Rico. He didn't have any more expansion plans after that. Let the next commissioner worry about further globalization of the game. Selout felt that he had certainly done his part.

The pluperfect example of how much capital creation had occurred during the Selout Regime was the valuation of the Hollywood Hedgers. The franchise was one of the oldest and most revered clubs in all of the MBL. Only the Bronx Bloomers had a panache equal to that of the Hedgers. However like all iconic institutions they were not without their period of trouble. The Hedgers had struggled for almost two decades as ownership passed from the O'Hara family ownership to a media conglomerate and then on to the litigious Courtley family.

Flunking Chemistry Class

The O'Hara's had brought the Hedgers west from Brooklyn in the 1950's and had rebranded the Long Island Duckers as the Hollywood Hedgers. The O'Hara's sold the Hedgers to the media group in 1998 for somewhere around $350 Million. After fumbling around with the franchise for six years and never even making the playoffs once, the media group sold the team to Hymie and Fran Courtley, two east coast opportunists from Boston.

The Courtleys made their original millions by owning a string of car wash franchises known as Courtley Car Wash. The car washes had a prominent clown logo and in the early stages of their business Hymie Courtley often dressed up in a clown suit to entertain the children who came to the car wash with their parents. But the Courtleys also knew a thing or two about property appreciation. Hymie Courtley paid around $430 Million for the Hedgers franchise in 2004.

Unfortunately for Hedgers fans, the Courtleys were actually fans of the Beantown Wallbangers. They set about trying to improve the Hedgers by importing ex-Wallbangers, including superfloat, Manboy Ramendez. The on-field success rate of the Hedgers during the Courtlys ownership was sparse. When the Courtleys began divorce proceedings the ownership of the team came under some question, but Hymie Courtley prevailed. He settled his financial dispute with his ex wife and then sold the Hedgers for an amazing total of $2.1 Billion!

Buzz Selout had never much cared for Hymie Courtley and he dismissed Fran Courtley as someone better suited for a reality TV show than as an MBL owner. He never realized what a favor he was doing for them when he coerced Hymie Courtley to sell the Hedgers at auction. Surely Courtley went crying all the way to the bank. Buzz Selout had turned a Car Wash Clown into a billionaire.

The sale of the Hedgers was good news for the fans as the new ownership group was headed up by a seven foot tall magician. And it looked as though the Hedgers were going to need all the magic they could get.

The 26th Man Law Suit

The ink was barely dry on the sale contract for the Hedgers when Buzz Selout and the rest of the MBL became part of an even bigger story. Sitting in his New York City Office Selout read the encapsulated version of the story in the New York Roast:

> *"Commissioner Buzz Selout and the 36 ownership groups who comprise the leadership of the Multinational Baseball League have been hit with a class action law suit filed for an unprecedented $13.5 Billion by the so called 26th Man. The law suit filed yesterday in Federal Court claims that MBL and its owners conspired against law abiding ball players by a systematic encouragement of the use of certain illegal performance enhancing drugs. The law suit also calls for the abolishment of the game's antitrust exemption. Sam Crockett and other plaintiffs (collectively the 26th Man) claim in part that MBL; its franchise owners; and the league's players association, the MBLPA, have all conspired to eradicate competition on a global basis and that their permissive behavior with respect to the control/or lack of control of performance enhancing substances is one their effective tools for doing so. Crockett and the other named plaintiffs have resigned from the MBLPA prior to the filing ... "*

Selout was at least gratified to see the *New York Roast* article acknowledged the fact that one of their sports reporters was married to the lead attorney for the plaintiff. He was far more annoyed that another member of the plaintiff's legal team was a former MBL employee. Timmy Burr had been his personal assistant and statistician and now he was turning on him. And another annoying part of the lawsuit was that the lead named plaintiff, Sam Crockett, was a player that he had personally tried to help by sending a newspaper article to the Cheeseheads a few years back and advocating that the Wisconsin team give him a shot.

One additional problem for Selout was that he had a much bigger issue with the Cheeseheads than their failure to promote Crockett. The Wisconsin team was also protecting Brawny Glaun, their MVP float, from the rigors of the investigation on the part of Selout's office. Glaun had failed a drug test in October of 2011 right before winning

Flunking Chemistry Class

his MVP, but he had escaped punitive action on the part of MBL. There had been a minor issue ... a collection process technicality ... and an arbiter ruled that Glaun could not be sanctioned in any way. The Cheeseheads had a heavy investment in Glaun and chose to allow the curdling process to unfold without intervention regardless of the stench. They then provided a mold of support around the player.

The general public had a hard time figuring out Selout's real position on steroids. If nothing else it had evolved very slowly over the years. For the longest time Selout had seemed to do little or nothing about the PEDs problem. Then gradually he took on the role of instigating minor agreements with respect to testing players. The purpose of these tests was widely regarded as an attempt to mollify the fans who wanted a clean and competitive sport. The tests were originally autonomous and without penalty.

Following several federal government actions including both the legislative and the judicial branches in DC, the commissioner had launched his own investigative probes to determine the extent of drug use in the sport. Again little or nothing was done with the results. In more recent years Selout had started to feel the tide of public disgust turn against him. He realized that he had lost the fans trust. Even the cheating floats had their own subset of fans that adored them and supported them and eventually forgave them for their transgressions. This forgiveness usually had two requisites. First they had to apologize and secondly they had to continue to perform well. Selout had no plausible way of meeting either of these conditions and so he felt that he was starting to become the scapegoat for the whole mess.

Then during the last couple of years the commissioner began to get very serious about pushing the blame elsewhere. He needed to grab a couple of trophy floats to punish. He needed to serve up a few fatted calves so that the fans wouldn't eat his legacy instead. And now in 2012 Selout believed he knew just where to find those fatted calves: at *Myo-Nemesis*.

XXVIII

Coopersville

June 2012

The annual Corridor of Conceit celebration took place in the upstate New York town of Coopersville. The festivities included speeches, photo ops, autograph signings and plaque presentations. The town took on an atmosphere of a state fair. Baseball memorabilia was being sold next to table vendors, hawking corndogs and cotton candy. Fans of all ages wandered through the streets of town before the ceremonies trying to catch a glimpse of a star or two from a bygone era. There were more than a half dozen bars lining Main Street that were within walking distance of the baseball museum. The red brick building, which housed the Corridor of Conceit, was catering to capacity challenging crowds. While the fans were wandering through the tables of the street vendors, or meandering through the hallowed halls of the C of C, the sportswriters were hovered together in the aforementioned bars.

Lester Postal had been to the Coopersville baseball shrine more than twenty-five different times. However this was the first time that he ever brought Georgette with him. It was also the first visit ever for Tim and Evangeline Burr. While his three companions were wandering through the museum, Lester Postal was bellying up to the bar in a place called *Toothless Ruthie's Dive Bar*. It was one of those places that seemed to have been there since the beginning of time. It was not nearly as grungy as the name might imply. But it had been around for nearly 100 years. Originally a subterranean basement tavern during prohibition – that's how dive bars originally garnered the moniker – Toothless Ruthie, added a ground level to her establishment shortly after the passage of the 21st Amendment in 1933. The popular legend was that it had never been closed a single day since. The establishment was filled with pictures of famous people who had wandered through the portals of *Toothless Ruthie's Dive Bar* over the years, and there was a long wall in the back of the bar that contained the autographs of many of these famous folks. The wall was covered by a thin glass casing so that mere mortal patrons would not take the opportunity to cast their own signatures amongst those of the celebrities.

No one seemed to *really* know much about Toothless Ruthie – the original proprietor – but enough contrived sagas and parables were spun by visitors to create a television miniseries. Throughout the years the many sportswriters who visited *Toothless Ruthie's Dive Bar* created their own little legend about the woman and the establishment. However amidst the many pictures of celebrities around the bar there was only one picture of Toothless Ruthie and that was taken in 1942 with none other than the Bambino by her side.

One of the unsubstantiated stories about Ruthie was that she had killed her husband, Tony, in 1929, simply because he was a Wallbangers fan, and then secretly buried him under the basement area of the bar. He was sometimes referred to in the bar legends as Ruthless Tony, for a combination of different reasons which made for good barroom debate.

Soon after Lester Postal settled in on a corner barstool, the give and take with his fellow sportswriters began to unfold.

"I think we got it right this year. Larry Barking was the only guy deserving of my vote and I'm glad he got in." Postal made his declaration about the long time shortstop of the Cincinnati Crazy Legs and then threw back a shot and sipped his beer chaser.

Coopersville

"The veteran's committee did the right thing by electing Rolly Bantor though. He was very deserving. Too bad they waited so long. Besides all of the dingers he hit he was one hell of a third baseman. He won five straight Might Mitt awards when he was playing for the Gumballs." The scribe from the *Chicago Tribute* piped in his opinion.

"Most importantly we continued to keep the floats out," offered Tim Veracity of *Games Thrillustrated*. Those clowns are never going to get my vote. I'm glad that Popeye Maloney slipped somewhat this year. He's done. He got less than twenty per cent of the vote."

"Yeah," Postal concurred. "He's buried deeper than Ruthless Tony. Same goes for CoJo Janesco's Cuban pal, Daffy Palmgreed."

"Palmgreed didn't get enough votes to stay on the ballot for next year. Same goes for his Drillies teammate, Lon John Zalez. He won't be on the ballot next year either. It looks like we're getting it done. We're keeping the floats out of the C of C." This time the comment came from the reporter from the *Dallas Herald*.

"Next year's ballot will be the real story. There will be some real big floats on the ballot for the first time"

"Yeah, Bombs, Rogers, Palazzo and Corky Samuels will all be on the ballot for the first time."

"Let's just hope it's the first and last time."

The rapid fire commentary was coming from a half dozen different reporters who were seated around the bar. Each chimed in their opinion but there seemed to be no support whatsoever for the class of floats that was now coming before the MBLWA electorate.

After several rounds of beers were consumed along with a few Ruthie Burgers, Lester Postal posed a question that had been on his mind. "What about Selout?"

"What about him?"

"What about Selout and the Corridor of Conceit? He's planning on retiring soon. Do you think he should get in?"

"That's an interesting question. Every other commissioner who has served as long as he has is already in The Corridor. And he has made unprecedented strides in expansion of baseball on a global basis."

Flunking Chemistry Class

"F*** that s***. What about the steroids stuff? He is also the 'Steroid Commissioner.' He's the guy who let the problem get out of hand. You could make a case for the fact that he's every bit as much to blame for the PEDs problem as the cheaters themselves."

"Yeah, you're right Lester. Selout has fucked over the fans. He has let the whole mess get out of hand." The comment came from Bruce Manley, a reporter from the Golden Gate Gazette. "Ticket prices are prohibitive for a reason. It's to pay the floats and their owners. You can't afford to take a kid to the ballpark anymore. And you can't even teach the kids the history of the game because Selout has let the stats become meaningless. Yeah. I'd have to say that Selout has certainly fucked over the fans.

"You're right, Bruce. And we're the only ones looking out for the fans," Postal responded. "So what do you say guys? Is he in or is he out?"

"I say fuck him," Manley responded, "like he's fucked over all of us."

Most of the writers at the bar nodded in agreement.

As they were leaving the museum, Georgette Postal and the Burrs were spotted by one of the few reporters who wasn't imbibing at one of the local pubs.

"Hello, Ms. Postal? Can I have a word with you?" Georgette had come a long way from her days as grossly overweight unrefined book wormy law student. She was now the svelte and sophisticated managing partner of Postal and Burr. Even her partner Tim Burr had managed to put on an appearance of an urbane and experienced legal plaintiff's advocate. And now reporters were actually calling her Ms. Postal instead of simply Georgette.

"How can I help you?"

"Are you up at induction ceremonies in conjunction with the pending law suit against MBL?"

Coopersville

"No, actually we are all here on holiday as guests of my husband, Lester Postal. Do you know Lester?" She was self indulgently proud of how she had stylishly morphed the word 'vacation' into the term 'holiday' right there on the spot. It was so continental sounding. But she didn't want to overdo it. After all *she* was certainly aware that she was still Georgette, even if everyone else wanted to treat her royally.

They began walking down Main Street in the direction of *Toothless Ruthie's Dive Bar* but the pace was a meandering one. Georgette was quite willing to talk to the young reporter. After all, that might have been Lester no so long ago … well all right … a long time ago.

"Will you be seeing any of your clients while you are up here? And will you be meeting with Buzz Selout while you're both here in Coopersville?"

'We get some new plaintiffs who want to join the class every week, so I can't say 'no' to your first question. With respect to Mr. Selout, we have no plans to meet with him or his counsel here or in New York any time soon. We will be meeting them in court as the appointed trial schedule unfolds. As I said, we are here on holiday." She still liked the way that sounded.

The reporter either didn't know who Tim Burr was or didn't care who he was because he directed all of his questions to Georgette "Do you believe that your clients' case will effectively end the anti-trust exemption for MBL?"

"It's a very complex issue in some regard but quite simple from another perspective. The business of MBL is very definitively a global business. MBL has definitely formed a global monopoly, a cartel of sorts. And yes I think that it's a gross violation of free trade. My clients were restrained in their efforts to make a living by the very structure of the Multinational Baseball League alone. On top of that they were barred from entering the MBL playing fields by teams and players who covertly sustained a clandestine covenant of support for the use of performance enhancing drugs."

The young reporter was trying to ensure that he had captured every word on his recorder. He struggled to keep abreast of the others

Flunking Chemistry Class

even though the pace was slow because he was juggling his note pad and his recorder and trying to snap a photo with his iPhone all at the same time. But Georgette remained gracious and smiled demurely when she realized that she was having her photo snapped.

They had almost reached *Toothless Ruthie's* when the reporter added one final question, without realizing that the same debate was raging just behind the doors of the *Dive Bar*. "Do you believe that one day Commissioner Selout will be voted into the Corridor of Conceit?"

It wasn't the first time that Georgette had thought about this question and she was well aware of her husband's position on the topic. But she truly believed that at some point in the still distant future others would look back on this period of baseball history from a different vantage point. They would look for some kind of acknowledgement of what actually occurred during the steroid era. So she had her own prognostication.

"I think that twenty-five years from now – if the next commissioner truly cleans up the game – they will excavate the basement of the museum and create a dark damp room that they'll call 'The Dungeon of Deceit' and then they can vote in the whole lot of them – Bombs, Samuels, Rogers, Maloney and yeah – Selout should be in there too."

The verdict was in. Jelly Rogers had been acquitted in federal court. The jury found that he had not lied to Congress after all. There were not any lesser charges of "misspeaking" so he was not found guilty of anything. He stood on the steps of the Federal Court and spoke to reporters tearfully saying that justice had been served by his acquittal. Rogers wisely had not testified in his own defense and the jury was left with the ambiguous testimony of Rogers' teammate Randy Elfin and the disputed testimony of Rogers' former trainer Ryan McGhee. They opted for acquittal. However Rogers was just beginning to realize that acquittal and vindication were two different things. There was only one thing that Jelly Rogers knew for sure; he was unlikely to speak to either Elfin or McGhee ever again.

When he came down from the courthouse steps and entered the back of his limousine, he was greeted by his wife who had scooted into the back seat just ahead of him. The car pulled away from the courthouse and Dolly Rogers turned to her husband and said, "There now was that so bad, Jelly?"

A Dork was livid. He walked around his Manhattan penthouse apartment and yelled at the speaker phone on the end table. On the other end of the phone were Daryl Sledgehammer and his brother Darryl Sledgehammer.

"My friends tell me that Selout is trying to connect me to the *Myo-Nemesis* place in Florida where Manboy got his juice. That's just nonsense. I wouldn't do that to you guys and the Bloomers. With all of the potential scapegoats out there, why is Selout choosing me to be the one to bear the brunt of the media criticism?"

"Because you're the man," said Daryl.

"You're the big fish." echoed Darryl.

"You make the most money," Daryl concluded

A Dork didn't mind hearing his bosses prop up his ego. But he should have stopped there rather than press for further affirmation of his indignation. But that was not his style.

"Is that it?

"No, of course not ... He's going after you because everyone hates you already anyway."

A Dork sniffled slightly on the other end of the line. In fact it was more of a snort than a sniffle. "I don't care what people think. I just want to hit homeruns and win ball games. And I'm not going to let that bastard Selout stop me. You guys are with me on that. Right?"

After a brief moment of silence, the Bloomers third baseman was peeved. He finally followed up his inquiry.

"Darryl?"

"Daryl?"

XXIX

Starting and Restarting

Summer and Fall of 2012

In some ways Sam Crockett felt like a very old athlete. In other ways he felt like a very young man. After spending parts of eleven different years playing minor league baseball, he hadn't laced on a pair of baseball spikes in a little bit over a year. By filing a law suit against MBL, Crockett had gained more fame than he ever would have had as a journeyman baseball player. But the fact of the matter is that he still missed the competition. He missed the challenge of turning around a mid 90's fastball. He had just about finally put those days behind him when he got the call from his attorney, Tim Burr.

"Hey Sam, I got a very interesting call today that you might find hard to believe."

"Don't tell me. They want to settle already?"

"No it's not about the law suit. As we have said on several occasions, the law suit is very likely to take years to resolve. There are motions upon motions from both sides. Remember we are in the early stages. The MBLPA wants to separate from the other defendants. We've filed against that motion because we believe they are part of the conspiracy. Then there's the issue of our ever growing class of …"

"Alright, Tim. I get it. I know it's going to take a while to get somewhere, but if you didn't call about the law suit, then what was this 'very interesting call' you got all about? And how does it involve me?"

Starting and Restarting

"I got a call from your former agent."

"From Brad Scott?"

"None other."

"I haven't talked to him in years."

"Scott acknowledged as much and he wanted to know if I represented you as a player agent as well being your attorney with respect to the pending civil litigation."

"What did you tell him?"

"I didn't really answer him, until he gave me a little more to go on. So he asked me what kind of shape you were in and whether or not you had played any baseball at all this year."

"And?"

"And so I asked him why he wanted to know all of this."

"Then what?" Crockett was actually very intrigued by all of this and he knew that Tim Burr wasn't just dragging out the story to get to a punch line of some sort. It was just the way Tim was. He always had to provide a context for everything he said. Crockett tried not to be impatient. He knew that Burr always tried to help him. Burr was one of the few people that Crockett trusted these days.

"Well Scott finally got around to saying that there was some ongoing interest in you as a ballplayer. He was quite explicit about it in fact. He said there was interest from three specific teams. The Dallas Drillies and the Houston Arrows have made some inquiries and the Metropolitan Mutts, for one reason or another have also expressed interest."

"Don't you think that's strange seeing that I haven't played all year?"

"According to Scott, these teams have taken an interest in you after examining your past record. They also realize that you have become somewhat of a fan favorite because of the law suit. He said that the two Texas teams might want to offer you a Triple A contract as a good will gesture to the fans. I don't know whether he's bullshitting or not but he said that there is a real chance that a solid month of August at a Triple A affiliate might warrant a September call-up, especially in the case of the Arrows who are going to lose more than 100 games this year anyway."

"And what was the story with the Mutts?"

"Again remember this is Brad Scott who is saying these things. And you know him better than I do. However he said that the Mutts are simply 'bottom feeders' – now don't take offense to that – and they would not be his first choice."

"How serious do you think I should take all of this?"

"Well let me put it this way. Brad Scott didn't call just to say hello. My guess is that there is some legitimate interest from the Arrows, and that the stuff about the Drillies and the Mutts was just window dressing. He seemed to be pushing the Arrows opportunity to the exclusion of the other two teams."

"This is crazy. I haven't played in a year and when I was playing I wasn't exactly knocking the ball out of the park. On top of that I'm now 28 years old. What is this all about? It's about the law suit. Isn't it?"

"Look I spoke with Georgette about this just before I called you. She says that even if you got a September call up it wouldn't hurt our case one bit. She said it might even help it. As far as being too old to get your career in gear, her response was that if she could lose more than 175 pounds after the age of 28 you should be able to hit a 175 homeruns after that age as well."

"Fat chance of that happening."

"Well Georgette says that if you want to do it, just go for it. Naturally you'll have to be a bit more positive in your approach. Whatever you decide, you'll have our support all the way."

"Thanks, Tim. I'll talk to Betsy Jo and let you know."

The Earth Series ended without much excitement as the Bay City Mammoths blew out the Motown Marauders in four straight games. The only real intrigue with this year's post season was that for the first time ever, an international expansion club had actually made the playoffs, and two of them had done so. However after the Dominican Sugarlanders defeated the Seoul Searchers in the opening round of the playoffs, they lost to DC's Capital City Congressmen, who in turn

Starting and Restarting

were bested by the St Louis Scarlets in the middle rounds of the newly expanded playoffs.

It was now nearly November but it was still 85 degrees in Miami. CoJo Janesco was having another meeting with Andrea Botch. The two had managed to work out an agreement whereby Janesco would relay information to Heidi Hunt from Botch in exchange for cash payments to cover the *Myo* proprietor's legal fees and some other outstanding financial difficulties. The cash outlay to MBL was a drop in the bucket. Even with legal fees that could get exorbitant the cost was not going to be a lot. However Hunt – and by extension Selout – were playing hardball about the amount of money that would change hands. They didn't like the image that might emerge if they paid a significant sum for the information. So the thorny negotiations using nefarious intermediaries continued.

This was the first time that Janesco had met Botch at her facility. The previous meetings had taken place at *Beautiful and Bodacious Bodies*. Janesco was gratified to see that the *Myo* facility wasn't anywhere near as plush and luxurious as Triple B's. In fact he felt as though the place was a little on the crude side. Yet there were plenty of local customers coming and going through the front door of the facility, so it was apparent that Andrea Botch did more than just cater to the mail order steroid crowd. Similar to their previous meetings Botch did a lot of complaining.

"I don't like it at all CoJo. I'm getting a lot of heat from the local authorities. I've already been fined for pleading no contest to the charge that I have represented myself as a physician, but I can't afford the kind of medical staff that you have. I'm losing clients left and right and I'm going broke."

"We obviously have very different business models."

"Alright I realize that and you already know that I have supplied some stuff for the baseball crowd. But I can only charge these guys so much. They can get the same stuff through other contacts in Mexico and Central and South America."

"We've discussed this before. The money is in the protocol not in the juice itself. That's where my staff comes in. And my clientele is different. I don't have a lot of ballplayers as clients these days. But the membership at Triple B's certainly does include a lot of ex ballplayers."

Flunking Chemistry Class

"My baseball clients are under siege from Selout and Hunt. A couple of guys have offered me cash and they have also threatened me if I turn over evidence about them. This is not the way I want to live ... in debt and in constant fear. I need more money. I could get more from some of the players but I don't want them to go to the authorities and claim extortion." She paused and then added, "There have been some unilateral offers, however.

"Oh yeah. Who is offering you a bigger check than MBL?"

"I really don't want to say."

"Why not? If you can prove they offered you the money, maybe MBL will loosen the purse strings also."

"I can't say for sure but I think the same people who have offered to buy me out are the ones that have friends that want to harm me."

"Well let me talk to Heidi Hunt to see what I can do. There might be a few more bucks in this after all. But next time we meet, we're going to have to have names and records and whatever other evidence you have. I don't think Selout and Hunt are going to sit on this forever."

A funny thing happened on the way to his retirement. Sam Crockett actually made it to The Show. After not playing for a year, Crockett signed a contract with the Houston Arrows AAA affiliate, the Tulsa Tomahawks in August of 2012. He proceeded to tear the cover off the ball, hitting seven homeruns in three weeks, slashing .343/.453/.565. His OPS of 1.018 earned him a call up to the parent franchise in September. The Arrows weren't going anywhere but Crockett was a story that drew great press coverage and put a few more fannies in seats around the Arrow Dome. With the big league club in September Sam Crockett slashed .310/.395/.471 with two more dingers and 15 RBI's in just 76 at bats. It made for a delightful Christmas for the Crocketts in San Antonio.

XXX
Spring Training in Miami

March 2013

Hope springs eternal for baseball fans during March each year as they get ready for each new season to begin. In Hollywood the 7 foot magician had continued the importation of players from the Wallbangers that had been started by his predecessor, the billionaire car wash clown. At the end of the previous season the magician had performed a dazzling trick by turning four Wallbangers into Hedgers. He also handed the Wallbangers a 'get out of jail free card.' But that wasn't the only trick the magician had up his sleeve as he managed to move ace pitcher Satch Cranky from one side of Los Angeles to the other while the Anaheim Afterthoughts weren't looking. Cranky would now team with Clive Kerchief to form the best one-two rotation punch in baseball. Meanwhile the Afterthoughts were wishing they had shown more forethought before signing free agent outfielder Judas Hambone.

On the east coast the Toronto Thunderbirds had revamped their lineup and pitching rotation and were regarded as the co-favorites along with the Bronx Bloomers and the Tampa Bay Groupers. The Wallbangers were thought to be using their get out of jail free card which they had received from the Hedgers to support a rebuilding year.

Flunking Chemistry Class

In the Native League East the co-favorites were two playoff teams from the previous year, the Capital City Congressmen and the Sugarlanders from the Dominican Republic. The latter team had signed a couple more floats who had defected from Cuba during the offseason and were now enjoying the spoils of freedom.

Lester Postal was in Florida covering the spring training sites of the Bloomers and the Mutts for the *New York Roast*. Over the years he had developed a rapport with some of the players and irritated many others. But Lester always had a good eye for a story. This year however almost all of the ballplayers would be very careful about what they said to Postal. The law firm of Postal and Burr was threatening the livelihood of their sport and the players had been advised by their agents and their union to avoid speaking with Postal. For the most part Lester understood all of this and the challenge just made him that much more outspoken and aggressive in his pursuit of a story. Besides he was personally living much more comfortably these days now that the Georgette and her law firm were so prosperous. He flew first class but he still drank boilermakers.

As long as he was not the most welcomed man on campus, Postal felt no qualms about bringing his wife along with him to the various spring training sites he was scheduled to visit. He knew that Georgette would be treated as even more of a pariah than Lester himself. But neither of them cared. The first stop on their trip was Miami. The team from the Dominican Republic did something unusual for their spring training – they travelled north. The Sugarlanders flew the 800 miles north to practice in a beautiful new spring camp in Miami. They were scheduled to play an exhibition game against the Metropolitan Mutts and so Postal and his wife started their Floridian training camp tour by taking an early morning flight into Miami. In addition to watching some baseball, Georgette had planned on tracking down Sam Crockett and giving him an update on the course of their litigation.

Spring Training in Miami

In spite of his terrific showing in September of 2012, there was no guarantee that Sam Crockett would make the Houston Arrows parent ball club out of Spring Training in 2013. In fact he never really got that chance. In a shift of attitude the Arrows no longer wanted the distraction of Crockett and his "26th man law suit" for the new season. They traded him to the Dominican Sugarlanders for three young prospects right before spring training began. Crockett found himself preparing in Miami with a team that made the playoffs in 2012 on the backs of several new floats. The influx of Caribbean floats was so numerous that the commissioner's office was looking into the possibility of still another steroid scandal; this one emanating out of Cuba.

Sam Crockett believed that it was more than just coincidence that he was now surrounded by the very floats and float supporters that he was suing in federal court. He didn't see the Dominican team as being much different from the other MBL teams in terms of overall ethnic makeup. However they did seem to have a disproportionate number of floats. Several of these bloated bodies were newly arrived from Cuba. They had not gone through the traditional minor league system in the United States. He recognized this was a sign of things to come. In the last few years as the MBL continued its global expansion, preparatory minor league systems were sprouting up in different parts of the free world as well as in dictatorships such as Cuba. But all of the money to be made was still vested in the MBL.

During the first two weeks of spring training, Sam Crockett was impressive at the plate. He picked right up where he left off in September. However off the field things were different. The other players were more cautious. No longer was there any joking around about PEDs abuse and who was using what. The players all wanted to avoid getting embroiled in the legal controversy that was growing more pernicious to the game on a daily basis. So Sam Crockett had become a bit of a loner, and he was becoming a bit paranoid. Sometimes he thought that some of the other players were cursing him out behind his back and sometimes even to his face in another language. It often seemed as though all of the players except him – even the Asian players – spoke Spanish. He wished that he had taken Brad Scott's advice and learned to speak Spanish when he first became a professional ballplayer. But he realized that the best way to thwart his critics was to simply keep hammering the ball.

Of the named plaintiffs in the 26th Man Law Suit only four were currently in major league camps still trying to make it to The Show. Of these four players, Crockett was the only one with MBL experience. He wondered if the other three ballplayers were also being shunned. At least the other three guys were all training in the Phoenix area, as the spring camps of the Hollywood Hedgers, the Chicago Pantyhose and Denver Doobies were all in close proximity. All of the other plaintiffs in the 26th Man Law Suit had already left the game.

The Sugarlanders' new training facility was a state of the art complex. However the management of the franchise preserved a relaxed casual atmosphere where the players could interact with the fans on their way to and from the clubhouse to the stadium. There was a rope lined passageway which was reserved for the players and they were free to stop along the way and converse with the fans or sign autographs. It was currently very hot and sunny in Miami and the Sugarlanders had just completed a thumping of the Metropolitan Mutts. Sam Crockett was the hitting star with two doubles and a walk.

"Well look who's here." Crockett smiled for the first time all day when he saw Georgette and Lester Postal sauntering over toward the rope autograph line. "Did you guys catch the game?"

"Sure did. Looks like things are going well for you."

"Well I'm hitting the ball well and there's an opening in right field now that there's been a few injuries. The manager here is a bit of a whack job but he knows his baseball. He's one of the only people around here who talks to me"

"I'm glad you're getting along with Gilliam. He can be a little crazy from time to time." Lester Postal was speaking about Oswald Gilliam,

Spring Training in Miami

the Venezuelan firebrand who had already worn out his welcome as the manager of the Chicago Pantyhose and the Miami Minnows.

"Gilliam is really a good guy. Like I said, he knows the game. He doesn't care about law suits. I don't even think he cares that much about money. He only cares about winning baseball games. I can deal with that. He flat out told me that if I keep hitting the ball the way I have so far this Spring that I'll be the opening day right fielder. I can't ask for more than that."

"Yea, I sort of like Gilliam as well. He simply has a habit of saying whatever is on his mind and that gets him in trouble. I'm a bit surprised that he agreed to manage a team with so many floats, however."

"I think he just wants to get back in the game. I'm glad that he's the manager because I think he respects hard work."

The conversation was taking place in the open air with a lot of fans walking by. Several young fans came up to Crockett asking for his signature, and he obligingly signed his name as he conversed with the Postals. Georgette didn't bring up the lawsuit until later when they were all out to dinner together.

Nomar was an expensive restaurant and Sam Crockett was not yet making the kind of money that would warrant a meal at such an exclusive Miami Beach hotspot. Lester Postal wasn't a fan of Japanese food and it wouldn't have been his first choice either. But Georgette was making the big bucks and she was calling the shots so they continued their conversation over sushi, sashimi and shrimp tempura at the trendy South Beach eatery.

"So what can you tell me about the law suit? I must get asked about it dozens of times a day by reporters."

"Well to start with you should always tell them what I told you to say 'no comment.' You can always refer them to your attorneys and of course we'll tell them the same thing in a little more elaborate way."

"By the way how is your partner Tim doing? I thought I might see him down here today. I know he's a real big Mutts fan."

Flunking Chemistry Class

"Tim is getting over a personal problem. Evangeline has sent him out to the Beth Dodge Clinic to rehabilitate his drinking issues." Georgette gave Lester a sidelong glance which he sheepishly ignored as he silently disavowed any complicity in the problems of his little buddy. "But we expect that he'll be back at work by the end of next week."

"That's good. I like Tim. And Betsy Jo likes him also. Please say hi for us." Crockett then went back to his previous inquiry. "So what is new? I think I'm about to become a starting ballplayer instead of the 26th man. And we're still okay with that? The case still holds?"

"Yes absolutely. We are still arguing issues about the class structure and eligibility on both sides. It's getting quite complicated and expensive but there's very little doubt that we will win in the end."

"The newspaper articles that I've read on the topic say that it will never get to trial and that MBL will eventually settle with us out of court. Do you believe that this will go that way?"

"Maybe ... but we have to be prepared to take it all the way to the jury. In any case we will win. Right now we're still fighting the structural petitions. The MBLPA wants to sever itself from the defendant group and has sighted a laundry list of rationales. It claims that the franchise owners and MBL are the only parties that could reasonably conspire to juice up the game. MBL itself has taken the stance that it is totally innocent of any conspiracy and has taken a curious stance in its motions of not denying that there was a conspiracy, but rather by innuendo and insinuation suggesting that the players and the players union are solely responsible for the presence of floats in the game."

"It all sounds so confusing. But you think that I shouldn't do anything other than continue to play the game as best I possibly can."

"Exactly and sooner or later you'll get a big check for back pay for the years that you should have been in The Show. In fact, the better you play, the bigger the back pay check. We are all still astounded that they could be so short-sighted to ever let you back in the game. They dug their own grave and then just kept digging. But this all works quite well for us and no one ever thought that MBL was using MENSA to source its ownership group."

Spring Training in Miami

Lester Postal listened as his wife briefed his client. He wondered what happened to the days when a sportswriter wrote about pennant races and batting titles instead of PEDs and defendant groups. He looked at his attractive young wife and wondered if it might not soon be time to retire from his career as a writer and become a full time house husband.

XXXI

The *Myo-Nemesis* Mess

Summer of 2013

In addition to the 26th Man Class Action Law Suit there was another off field story that was also looming large for the game of baseball. MBL had finally gotten possession of the records of the *Myo-Nemesis* clinic and had secured the testimony and cooperation of Andrea Botch. The clinic's records included compelling evidence that Botch had provided PEDs to more than a dozen MBL players. Buzz Selout was fighting for the life of his legacy. In the process he had made a 180 degree turn with respect to the vigor with which he went after steroid cheats. Two floats in particular rankled Selout more than the others. The commissioner was gratified to learn that among the cheats that had been nailed in the *Myo* roundup were the Despicable Duo: A Dork and Brawny Glaun.

Selout had decided that he would wait until after the Parade of Stars Game to make the announcement ironically because he *didn't want to tarnish the game.* However in the interim he was issuing clandestine warnings to select team owners who would most likely be without the services of their floats for a period of time. One of these calls was answered over speaker phone by the principal owners of the Bronx Bloomers, the Little Hammers, Daryl and Darryl.

"Hello Darryl. Hey Daryl. How have you folks been?

"It's been a tough year. We've been playing without the left side of our infield with both A Dork and Jared Leader on the DL." said Daryl.

The Myo-Nemesis Mess

"Yeah ... a tough year," echoed Darryl.

"Well I thought that I might just tip you guys off about where we are with the *Myo* Mess. As I'm sure you suspect from all of the newspaper leaks, your third baseman, Alan Dorquez, is one of the players who will be hit with a suspension right after the break. In fact Mr. Dorquez may very well receive the stiffest penalty of any of the players that we suspend." The commissioner made his statement in a very formal sounding voice in order to hide the glee that he derived from making this announcement.

"Why is A Dork getting hit harder than the others?" Daryl Sledgehammer was now the spokesman for the Little Hammers, while Double R just listened in.

Because I hate his fucking guts, Selout thought. However his explanation into the phone was more reserved. "Mr. Dorquez has repeatedly violated the rules of our game and he has further demonstrated his total disregard for the covenants between the MBLPA and the league with respect to performance enhancing drugs. What I mean by that is that not only did he use the stuff but he attempted to impede our investigation into the matter."

"How did he do that?"

"First he tried to buy out all of Andrea Botch's records. Then when Heidi Hunt tried to put some pressure on your third baseman, he attempted to seduce her."

On the other end of the line both Sledgehammers recoiled at the very thought of that. They simultaneously affected a lemon sucking face at the notion of a sexual liaison with Heidi Hunt. Everyone knew that she was a two bagger. A Dork must have been getting really desperate.

"So what's the bottom line, Buzz? How long will he be out?"

"From the time I make the announcement until after the 2014 season ... altogether a little more than 200 games. Of course you won't have to pay him during that time so you'll probably save more than $30 million. And if this helps you guys get under the salary cap, it could potentially save you twice as much when you count luxury taxes for the next couple of years. I don't expect that this is bad news for you guys."

"Don't you think that he'll appeal? And how about the other floats? Won't they appeal as well? After Brawny Glaun beat the rap last year, these guys will probably be much more inclined to try to fight back."

"It may interest you to know that Glaun has already capitulated."

"What does that mean?"

"He and his agent and legal staff have all agreed that he will accept a suspension for the rest of this season."

"What did the Cheeseheads ownership have to say?"

"Not much … I think they realize that this isn't going to be their year. Since Vince Wielder left as a free agent before the 2012 season the Cheeseheads haven't been able to consider themselves true contenders. They'll save a few million in salary during a year that's lost anyway. Glaun is going to make some sort of personal statement tomorrow and then we're going to announce the other suspensions at the end of next week."

"This hasn't been the best of years so far for the Bloomers either. We're not going to make any public comment on the matter. But thanks for the heads up."

"Well I'll tell you this much. Your season might get a lot better if A Dork doesn't appeal. It will be one less distraction for you guys to put up with."

Daryl hesitated before replying and then simply said, "No comment on that, Buzz."

"Yeah, no comment, Buzz," echoed Double R.

XXXII
Never-Ever?

Fall of 2013

The Dominican Sugarlanders had a second straight good season. They were within shouting distance of making the postseason at the end of the regular schedule but fell two games short of a making the playoffs. They probably would have run away with the Native League's Southern Division if it hadn't been for injuries and suspensions. Their shortstop and two of their starting pitchers had been hit with 50 game suspensions as part of the *Myo-Nemeses* mess. Their big first baseman had spent two months on the DL with a pulled lat muscle injury and their manager Oswald Gilliam was fired mid season for naming his dog Fidel after one of his personal heroes.

Through all the turmoil, one Sugarlander player had a consistently solid year. In his first full year in The Show, Sam Crockett made a strong run at the Native League's Newbie of the Year Award. He batted .288 with 19 dingers and 90 RBI's. The only newbie position player who had a better year was the Hedgers' Cuban outfielder, Gazelle Tweeg. But there were a handful of pitchers who also had good years and the outcome wouldn't be known until after the Earth Series, because as everyone knew by now there was nothing more important than the Earth Series.

The voting for the Newbie Award was in the hands of the sportswriters. There was no longer anything that Crockett could do to influence

Flunking Chemistry Class

that vote. He would have to wait a few weeks on that tally. On the other hand, one thing that couldn't be taken away from him was his overwhelming election to the Parade of Stars Game during the season.

Although the sportswriters were generally supportive of Crockett because of his stance against steroids, they took their work seriously and supported players for awards and elections based upon their play on the field. *Fans* however elected the Parade of Stars Game participants and *fans* voted for whomever they damn well pleased. This year the fans had overwhelmingly stood behind Sam Crockett. He received the most votes ever for a write-in candidate and made the starting team for the Native league. He doubled in his one at bat and left the field to a standing ovation before as he was replaced by Clutch McAndrews of the Pittsburgh Pillagers. So as he looked back on his first full season, Sam Crockett was quite pleased.

Now in early October, Crockett was glad to be back in San Antonio with his wife and children. He had seen them less this season than in any season in the past. From March through September, he had not been back in San Antonio even for a single day. Betsy Jo had gone up to the Midsummer Masterpiece in New York and she and the children had spent two weeks with Sam for a long home stand in the Dominican during August. Other than that their relationship consisted of a lot of Face Time on their iPads. Sam only admitted it to himself and to Betsy Jo when he acknowledged that he was happy that the Sugarlanders didn't make the postseason. He might have been one of the few people in the game who understood that there were some things in life that truly were more important than the Earth Series.

Sam sat on the couch next to his two young sons as they watched the first game of the Earth Series, between the St Louis Scarlets and the Beantown Wallbangers. He had just put his three year old daughter Sally Ann to bed and Betsy Jo was out shopping with her mother.

"Who are you rooting for, Dad? The younger of Sam's two sons, Rory asked the question. Rory was now 10 years old and was a good bit

Never-Ever?

more outgoing than 11 year old JR. Both boys idolized their father, but JR was more tuned in to the sacrifices his mother made while his father was away playing ball.

"That's a good question, son. I'm not entirely sure who I like." The truth of the matter was that Sam Crockett didn't care for either team. The two franchises that were playing for the Earth Series championship were both promoters of steroid floats over the course of many years. Popeye Maloney had been the Scarlets most notorious float but there had been several others during the last decade. Manboy Ramendez had been the float who was the face of the Beantown team when they won their championships. "Who do you like Rory?"

"I think I'm going to root for the Wallbangers because they have Peppy Orbits. I like Big Popout because his popups just seem to float out of the park."

"I like the Scarlets because …" Sam Crockett never heard his eldest son's rooting preference because his thoughts were in another place. He had just read an article that said that that three steroid era managers, Joe Trophy of the Bronx Bloomers, Robby Dicks of the Atlanta Apaches and Timmy LaBamba of the St Louis Scarlets were probably going to be elected to the Corridor of Conceit by a special committee of the Corridor. He wondered whether that was fair. Weren't these men just as culpable as the floats they managed? How much did they know? Well maybe Joe Trophy should be admitted. After all they didn't call him 'Clueless Joe' for nothing. And now that he was working for Buzz Selout, the commissioner seemed to be getting tougher on the cheats. What about Robby Dicks? His teams won on the backs of soft tossing pitchers. What did he know? But surely LaBamba must have known something. And for all of these years he had been Popeye Maloney's biggest supporter. Were these guys part of the conspiracy? He just didn't know.

"Dad? Come on Dad watch. Big Popout is coming up. Dad?" Rory was disappointed that his father had gotten up from the couch.

"I'll be right back son. I just want to check on your sister."

Flunking Chemistry Class

After being suspended by MBL in early August A Dork immediately filed an appeal and was allowed to play for the Bloomers until the appeal went to a hearing before an arbitration panel. The Sledgehammers and the rest of the Bloomers management team privately wished that he hadn't appealed. His play was atrocious. He hit less than .250 and despite playing in a launching pad at the new Bloomers Stadium and hitting in the middle of an explosive lineup, A Dork had less than 20 RBI's in almost 50 games. The stench befouled the organization and the Bloomers had missed the playoffs entirely. Meanwhile the pending arbitration hearing loomed. The Commissioner did everything he could to stall the proceedings until after The Earth Series, because he believed nothing was more important than the Earth Series. Finally in early November the proceedings began to unfold.

The arbitration hearing didn't go well for A Dork. His lawyers were happy to take the ballplayer's money. However they had already informed A Dork that he didn't have a good chance at coming out of the hearing victorious. MBL put on its case in a very effective manner. Heidi Hunt and other persons from the commissioner's office made a compelling argument for a suspension of at least 200 games. They supported most of their testimony with records of emails and other correspondence between A Dork and Andrea Botch over a period of several years. The only testimony that the arbitrators found difficult to accept was Heidi Hunt's claim that A Dork tried to seduce her in order to get her to alter her findings. They thought that A Dork was much too vain to do a two bagger.

Buzz Selout knew that A Dork would try to create a circus atmosphere at the hearing. Therefore he let his underlings handle the whole procedure while he tended to other personal matters. The fact that Selout remained at his Wisconsin home while the third baseman's doping debacle unfolded in New York, infuriated the Bloomers' superfloat. After listening to more than a week's testimony about his transgressions A Dork stormed out of the hearing room. He claimed that he was going to sue everybody who was responsible for unfairly designating him as a float. His list included: the MBL; its commissioner, Buzz Selout; the players association and the Bronx Bloomers. He assumed none of the blame for any of the PEDs problems himself. Two of the

Never-Ever?

four lawyers who were part of his defense team came scurrying out of the hearing with him. The other two remained at the hearing that proceeded without A Dork. The lawyers weren't worried about A Dork's rash reaction. They were billing an average hourly rate of $875 regardless of the outcome.

Lead Counsel Bucky Wadsworth caught up with A Dork as he was making his way to the elevator after hurling a stream of obscenities at the arbitrators. They then made their way out of the building and onto Park Avenue. Both men had limousines and drivers waiting nearby. They decided to leave in A Dork's Escalade, together with the float's driver and body guard.

The studios for the radio station WNSS (W-Non-Stop Sports) were less than a five minute ride away from the hearing in MBL's midtown offices. Frank Poinsettia the talk show host better known as Frank the Fanatic was a shameless sycophant, or what the players referred to as a "jock sniff." Without the slightest smidgeon of his own athletic ability, Poinsettia made a living by talking as though he was a sports expert. In reality he never laced on a pair of spikes to play anything. He was an unapologetic Bloomers supporter and one of the few talk show hosts who had the requisite nasal blockage to put up with the stench of A Dork's narcissism. In fact he reveled in it and was regarded by many of his listeners as an A Dork toady of the first order.

At A Dork's behest, Bucky Wadsworth called the WNSS studio on the short ride downtown. They were coming by unannounced to appear on Poinsettia's drive time show.

"So you think this guy Poinsettia will help us out." The attorney had never listened to the *Frank the Fanatic Show*.

"Absolutely. He'll know just how to do it. He'll ask the right questions ... lots of hanging curve balls. He'll make it come out looking like Selout has tried to lynch me."

"This could be a little risky. If he asks any question that you don't want to answer just hesitate for a second and move the index finger on your right hand. Then I'll jump in and be the bad guy by saying that as your attorney I can't let you answer that. And I may do that even if you don't signal for help."

"Alright that will work. But I'm not too worried. This guy loves me. In fact I only have one problem with him."

"What's that?

"He may *love* me but he absolutely *worships* Jared Leader."

"Well look who is coming see us at WNSS!" Even as he pronounced their arrival over the airwaves, the corpulent commentator was stunned to see A Dork and his attorney right there in the studio. Poinsettia had only received word that the wilting Bloomer was showing up two minutes earlier. Frank the Fanatic also knew that the hearing had been taking place across town over the past few days but he didn't know any of the details.

The studio was small but the afternoon drive time show had a large audience. Not only was it a live show on the radio but it was also being simulcast on television throughout the greater NY/NJ metropolitan area

"Hi Frank. Thanks for having us on your show."

"Sure, A Dork, any time. So I understand that you just left your arbitration hearing. What's the story? Are we going to continue to see you playing third base for the Bloomers next year and beyond?

"That's my fervent hope Frank. As you know we didn't make the playoffs this year and because I was on the DL for most of year I wasn't able to contribute the way that I would have liked to. And of course I was playing with the shadow of Selout's absurd suspension threat hanging over my head."

Poinsettia was half listening to A Dork and half listening to what the production team was whispering into his earpiece. He was just now coming to understand that Dorquez had actually walked out on the arbitration process without testifying, basically without rebuttal.

"So A Dork, tell us what happened today at the hearing."

Never-Ever?

"I can't give you the details because I have to respect the process. Both sides are sworn to secrecy and have agreed not to go public with the details. But I will tell you this much. All of their evidence is based upon the lies of Andrea Botch a person who has a hard enough time determining her own gender, let alone what her business is all about."

"And what was the nature of your business dealings with Ms. Botch?

"She supplied me with vitamins and weight loss pills. That's all."

"That's it? You're being persecuted for vitamins and diet pills? No wonder you're so pissed off! Can you tell us what evidence they're trying to put forward? Can you tell us how they're trying to railroad you?

"As I said Frank, I want to respect the process. I've agreed not to go into those details.

Even the pathetically pandering Poinsettia was unable to put up with this pitiable pathos. If A Dork wasn't going to attack Selout and MBL than why had he come to the station? But Poinsettia humored his guest and continued to pitch him nice underhanded lobs.

"Sure A Dork we all understand that. And as you know I have been in your corner through all of this. I've had your back all along."

"Yes Frank, you and the millions of Bloomers fans here in New York have always supported me."

Throughout the city of New York people were listening to A Dork make an absolute fool of himself, while the witless commentator offered a camera lens and a microphone for the tragically comical farce to unfold. While it might be true that Frank Poinsettia adored A Dork, the "millions of fans" that the float referenced mostly despised the deceitful numbskull as a wretched liar and a petty cheat. But the prattle kept coming.

"Not only have the fans been great but my teammates also supported me through this troubling period." A Dork wasn't kidding himself on this one. He knew that he was the most vilely detested man in the clubhouse.

But the beat went on. "Even players on other teams have been very sympathetic to my case. Look at Peppy Orbits. Big Popout's nearly forty years old and still going strong. He called me the other day and offered his support ... Same thing with my teammate, Randy Elfin.

Flunking Chemistry Class

He'll tell you this is all a public lynching." A Dork was totally oblivious to the fact that his argument sounded a lot like Jesse James citing Pretty Boy Floyd and Willie Sutton as character references.

"So tell us why you left the hearing without testifying in your own defense."

"Selout decided that he wouldn't testify. So neither will I." For one reason or another, the absurdity of this logic did not register right away with Poinsettia. So he ended up asking a straight forward question that reflected that lack of understanding.

"So this is supposed to be *your appeal* of the ruling by MBL. But you walked out on your own appeal. What happens now?" For a brief moment Poinsettia and A Dork stared at each other anesthetized in some sort of muted mutual consternation as though they were auditioning for a remake of the movie "Numb and More Numb." Meanwhile counsel sat in respectful silence also – at nearly a thousand dollars an hour. Bucky Wadsworth, the lawyer spoke first.

"We are going to go back to my office and then we'll examine our options." Apparently, not everyone in the studio was an idiot.

Poinsettia then picked up the interview once again. "So anyway A Dork, you said that you couldn't talk about this while the proceedings were going on, but now that they have stopped or at least have been interrupted for a while, can you tell us on this program what you have done and what you didn't do?"

"Sure Frank, I can do that. I can tell you that I didn't do any of the things that they accused me of doing."

"So you didn't take any performance enhancing drugs?"

"Correct, I never took any PEDs whatsoever. Definitely. I never did that."

"Never?"

"Yes, Never."

"Never – except those times with the Drillies in 2001 through 2003 – the times that you have previously acknowledged. Right?"

"That's right … never… except then. I'm not counting those years as part of *never*. Never means *now* never… not *then* never."

"So *then* is not part of *now?*

Never-Ever?

"No, not now, and *never* has been!"

"Let me see if I've got this right. *Never* ... was not *then* and never has been."

"Yes, ... except now."

"So *now*, ... never means 'never now.' But it doesn't mean; 'never then.' "

"Exactly!"

"There you have it sports fans. A Dork right here on the Frank the Fanatic show has told all of us that he *never ever* took PEDs ... except in the irrelevant *never then* of the distant past."

Stan Laurel and Oliver Hardy rolled over in their respective graves.

The baseball season took longer to wind down than usual after the Earth Series, which the Scarlets lost to the Wallbangers in six games. To sooth their deflated egos, the Scarlets went right out and signed the most egregious float available on the free agent market, shortstop Pteer Jibralta, whose dyslectic parents still called him Petey. Jibralta had swallowed a 50 game suspension at the end of the 2013 season and that infamy enabled him to score a 4 year contract worth well in excess of $50 Million. Pteer Jibralta's signing reaffirmed the Scarlets position as one of the most blatantly skuzzy organizations in all of MBL. This was later underlined in early December when former manager Timmy LaBamba was in fact elected to the Corridor of Conceit. And yes Clueless Joe and Robby Dicks were voted in also.

Sam Crockett missed out on the Newbie of the Year award but still garnered votes on multiple ballots from the sportswriters. The NOY Award was won by a Cuban pitcher from the Miami Minnows who in turn narrowly defeated a Cuban outfielder from the Hedgers. The Hedgers responded by dropping advertising leaflets from a drone over the beaches of Cuba about a baseball tryout to be held in Haiti. They then signed eleven players who would soon escape from the island. Seven of the eleven were shortstops that the Magician believed he could turn into second basemen.

Back in New York Georgette Postal and Tim Burr were still readying their firm for the Trial of the Century. They had every confidence that they would ultimately be victorious and every day they gathered new evidence that the Steroid Era of MBL was an ongoing travesty. Any suggestion that the Steroid Era was a thing of the past was viewed as patently absurd. While the A Dork example was still playing out, they pointed to the contract of Brawny Glaun as the most heinous miscarriage of justice and they wanted some of his dollars for their clients. They also wanted A Dork's money and the Sledgehammers' money and they especially wanted some of Buzz Selout's money. In fact they were even bigger fans of redistribution than the Slumdog Running Bear himself, President Baroque O. Brahman!

XXXIII
The Beginning of the End

January 2014

Normally January is a football month. The playoffs leading up to Wonder Bowl are the mainstay of all sports news reporting during the first month of most years. There is an occasional Hot Stove story that gives baseball a little air time. But in a normal year it's ninety per cent football on the back pages of the tabloid press. However on the morning of the division football championships the biggest story in sports suddenly became the arbiters ruling on Alan Dorquez appeal. The ruling reduced A Dork's suspension to one full year or 162 games. The sanction also included the 2014 postseason, should the Bloomers make it that far. This announcement caused two rapid reactions. The first result was that A Dork immediately cried foul and filed seven different law suits including one against Buzz Selout and the MBL. The second immediate reaction was that The Little Hammers were ecstatic that they didn't have to pay A Dork for a whole year. They were so elated in fact that they went out and signed the best pitcher in all of Asia, Tabasco Molasses to a seven year nine figure contract. These two news stories actually edged the Wonder Bowl out of the headlines for a few days and ignited baseball fever in the middle of a snowy winter in New York.

Flunking Chemistry Class

Evangeline Burr had told her husband to take the day off. After all it was Saturday. More importantly Tim Burr's law partner Georgette Postal had agreed with Burr's wife. Tim needed a day off. He had been working diligently on the "26th Man Law Suit" for several months, stopping only briefly to celebrate Christmas Day. In addition to the fact that everyone seemed to agree that Tim needed to take a day off, Evangeline and Georgette had plans to go out shopping together while their husbands watched the football playoff games.

Tim Burr had agreed to meet Lester Postal in *The Morning After* for the first time since completing his alcohol rehab at the Beth Dodge Clinic. He needed to be able to visit his old haunts without letting them haunt him. He was sure he could count on Lester's support.

They sat at the end of the bar in their familiar seats. In fact Lester Postal actually *owned* both seats in which they were now sitting. Two years earlier *The Morning After* had come up with the idea of selling PSL's or Personal Seat Licenses to the 22 seats that lined the bar. This meant that the seat owners could oust other patrons from these perches during any televised sporting event that was being shown on the tavern's TV's. The seat owners naturally still had to pay for any alcohol and food that they consumed but they were treated like club members in that they were able to bill these charges to their seat license account and get a monthly statement for their purchases. One of the long time owners of the tavern, Joey Dee thought that this was a fabulous idea – mainly because he thought of it. His partner thought Joey was crazy and immediately sold his interest in the seats to Joey for a total of $6,000.00 or a little less than $300 per seat – thinking that this was the easiest six grand he had ever made. Joey Dee then turned around and put the PSL's on sale to his patrons for an absurdly high price of $5,000.00 a seat. Incredibly Dee actually sold fourteen of the 22 seats. The seats were more than just a good vantage point to watch a game. They were also status symbols in some bizarre way. There weren't a lot of people around who could plunk down 10 grand for two seats for the right to bullshit with a buddy every time a ballgame came on the tube. But everyone had different value systems these days. Lately Lester Postal was flush with cash. He looked at the 10 grand as

The Beginning of the End

the difference between his Cadillac and a low end Mercedes Benz. He kept his Caddy, eschewed the Benz and grabbed the two PSL's at *The Morning After*. The PSL's came with a lifetime warranty.

"So you're really going to do it, Lester? You're really going to pack it in?"

"Yeah, f*** that s***. I've been doing the same thing for more than forty years, Tim. I'll be turning 65 this year, so I've had enough. Why should I want to keep working? I've got a beautiful young wife. Georgette is quite successful and I have no financial worries in the world. My only regret is that I never had any kids."

The pregame show for one of the AFC conference games was winding down and it was only a few minutes before kickoff. The bar was getting quite crowded. However Postal and Burr were sitting with their arms on the bar and leaning in as they talked. This gave the grizzled sportswriter and his thirty something lawyer friend some sort of mob-shrouded privacy in their conversation. They were able to blot out all the loud crowd noise around them and tune into their own private tête-à-tête. There was an empty shot glass in front of Postal next to his half empty beer mug. Burr was drinking a ginless tonic with a twist.

"Funny you should say that Lester. I'm not supposed to tell anyone yet, but Evangeline and I are expecting a child."

"That's great Tim. When's she due?"

"August.

"August, huh? That's great. I'm happy for you guys. Evangeline hasn't told Georgette yet. Has she?"

"No not yet. But she was planning on telling her today while they're out shopping. Frankly I'm a little worried about how Georgette will react. At the current course and speed of things we could be in court on the 26th Man thing about that time. I'm sure she's not going to like the idea of my taking any paternity leave."

"Don't be ridiculous Tim. Georgette won't need you to be there." They both realized how that sounded but neither tried to mitigate

Flunking Chemistry Class

the statement at first. After the reply sat out there for a second or two Lester finally followed up with a qualifying bit of additional verbiage. "Georgette doesn't really need anybody. And I know you guys need to be ready by August, but Georgette thinks this could drag on well past that, probably into 2015."

Now it was Tim Burr's turn to comment but he chose to take the conversation in a slightly different direction. "I've known you for what ... about a fourteen or fifteen years?"

"I guess it's about that long."

"Do you ever find it strange that we have become good friends after a while but that in the beginning we were just kind of using one another?"

"Where are you going with this Tim?"

"It's interesting. That's all. You once told me that for a long time you simply considered me a 'rental friend' someone you could buy a few drinks for and get a lot of information from ... kind of the way you do with people like Ryan McGhee." He sipped his ginless tonic and then continued. "You know, things didn't change for a few years and then I introduced you to Georgette. Then after you asked Georgette to marry you, she then asked me to be her law partner. After we were law partners she introduced me to Evangeline and then we got married."

"And the point of all this is what?"

"The point is none of this would have happened if it weren't for steroids."

"What the fuck are you talking about, Tim? Did you start drinking again? None of that has anything to do with steroids other than we both were interested in getting the juice out of baseball. And frankly if that was our mutual mission, we've failed miserably. The fact of the matter is that we've become friends in spite of our common failure, not because of it."

The kickoff on TV was returned to midfield and the partisan viewers around the tavern reacted vocally according to their rooting interests. Postal tapped his shot glass as a signal for a refill and was so served. He had some minor bets on both games but truly wasn't that interested.

The Beginning of the End

"All I was saying is that people do things for different reasons. We repudiated steroid use together because it served our mutual interests to do so. These guys who were juicing up were doing so for their own interests also."

"You're getting way too philosophical for me, Tim. And don't put me in the same boat with those useless cheating assholes." He shook his head in dismay. "Do you have a point you're trying to make? Because if you do, it's lost on me."

"Yes I have a point. And it comes from all of the research I've been doing as a part of the 26th Man Law Suit."

"And?"

"What I was surprised to find out was that most of the ballplayers, who took steroids when they were playing, continued to take them well after they retired. They weren't cheating anybody at that point. They just wanted to look good ... or feel good ... or help themselves recover faster from minor injuries ... or something else along those lines ..."

"And so?"

"And so they must feel that whatever drugs, steroids, HGH ... or whatever it is that they want to take ... they must feel like these things are good for them, good for their health, I mean ... even beyond baseball."

"I don't know where you're going with this, but don't let Georgette hear you talk like that. She'll think you're going nutso on us."

"I've already had this discussion with Georgette and we've determined that it won't change our position on the 26th Man stuff at all. However she believes that it's much better to understand some of the arguments that we could be up against then to ignore them entirely."

"Alright then where are you going with this other stuff?"

"Here's the deal. While we both agree that certain players broke the rules of MBL and in many cases broke the law as well, these guys don't view themselves as doing anything wrong. They think that what they're doing is also what's best for their careers and their families."

"That's bullshit. What about the other guys' careers and their families?"

"Of course I know that and I'll get to that in a minute. For now I just want to say how these floats are feeling and thinking. Humor me for a second or two will you Lester?"

"Ok but get to the point, we want to watch this game don't we?"

"Alright, I'll get to the point. Many of the places that dispense HGH and other steroids claim to be *anti-aging* clinics. They claim that the various treatments that they prescribe are very beneficial to a person's health not just to his athletic performance. And my research has indicated that there is a lot of evidence supporting these claims. Take human growth hormone as an example. Some rather prestigious medical people have said that HGH can deliver a whole laundry list of benefits. Here look at this paper from the Columbian Clinic in Ohio. It's part of their anti-aging brochure."

Tim Burr took a six sided folded brochure from the inside pocket of the sports jacket he was wearing. He handed the brochure to Postal. There was a picture of a smiling young man and woman on the cover. Both were wearing shorts and sleeveless T's. Both had gorgeous bodies. The brochure also quoted a research report on nutrition, medication and longevity. Several paragraphs in the middle of a report had been highlighted by Burr:

> *"HGH is the crucial hormone which the body produces through the pituitary gland. This is a small gland with a big job. The pituitary gland secretes HGH which in turn is responsible for the acceleration of cell development. The pituitary gland is the body's smallest gland. However it is regarded as the master of all the other glands in the human body."*

Postal looked up for a second from the brochure he was reading, but before he could say anything, Burr put his finger right back on the printout nonverbally indicating that he wanted Postal to continue reading, right at the paragraphs to which he was now pointing.

> *"Recent scientific breakthroughs have provided strong evidence that the body's naturally produced HGH can be effectively supplemented with artificially produced HGH to achieve some significant benefits. HGH injections have long been effectively used to fight Chrone's Disease; for children with Renal*

The Beginning of the End

Disease; and in a variety of Osteoporosis Treatments. But now HGH is being utilized more frequently as a wellness enhancer or as an anti-aging agent."

Lester skipped down a few more paragraphs as the first touchdown of the game was shown up on the TV. He looked up for only a moment and then continued reading amidst a raucous atmosphere inside the tavern.

"It has been sufficiently documented that concurrent with the aging process the level of HGH in our bodies drops dramatically from peak levels of HGH and growth at puberty. Many researchers believe that it is the drop in HGH levels that causes all the symptoms that our bodies experience in the aging process. These indicators of aging include some of the following: fatigue, deteriorating eyesight; hair loss; dry and or wrinkled skin; weight gain and redistribution; sexual dysfunction (including impotence in men and vaginal dryness in women); sleeplessness; joint problems and a weakened immune system.

"As such benefits of controlled treatments can yield a wide variety of anti-aging benefits including: restoration of hair growth and color; stimulation of ellastin and collagen growth to reduce wrinkles; decrease body fat; improve sleep patterns; improve memory, vision and stamina; enhance immunity and increase sex drive. It is now widely accepted that such controlled use of HGH may not only retard the aging process but could possibly reverse certain symptoms of the process. In short, HGH supplementation may be looked at by many as the fountain of youth ... "

Postal handed the brochure articles back to Burr and finally gulped the shot of bourbon that was sitting next to his beer glass.

"Interesting perspective."

"Yeah and this is the Columbian Clinic. It's the place in Ohio that Baroque O. Brahman is always talking about when he pushes his healthcare reform."

"Yeah right. And how's that working out for him lately?"

"Touché"

Flunking Chemistry Class

Postal simply shook his head and looked up at the TV screen. He saw a commercial for an upcoming televised runway special featuring angelic models from the lingerie catalog *Vickie's Quickie*.

"Now there are some great bodies," he finally spoke with some enthusiasm.

"And you can be sure they didn't get that way solely by attending a couple of Pilates classes a week at the local gym." Even as he spoke the commercial went to a close up shot that briefly filled the wide screen TV with a bejeweled bra covering two mammary glands and some deep cleavage. "You see Lester? The thing is before too long everyone will be doing steroids and HGH, not just athletes and other celebrities. And if drugs like HGH can really reverse the aging process; then sign me up."

"Are you sure you had this conversation with Georgette? And you said the same things you're saying to me?"

"Yes in fact we've discussed this frequently of late. None of the potentially beneficial properties of steroids and HGH change the fact that the floats we are suing cheated. And those that sponsored them cheated also. Besides, there is a whole laundry list of negative side effects of PEDs. Some of these side effects could potentially kill you. Like all drug use, steroid use has to be appropriately controlled in a legal environment. Heroin ... or diamorphine as it is referred to medically... is used in hospitals to control pain all the time, but it also kills people on the streets of our cities every day. Just because hospitals use it effectively doesn't mean we should allow some junkies to enjoy the high they get from it. And just because some players hit more homeruns with HGH doesn't mean we should allow that either. And when these floats misuse this stuff they only encourage its misuse by other young athletes. Unfortunately some of them have died."

"Now you're sounding more like Georgette. That's better."

"Still there will come a future day, when these things are better controlled, and the use of these drugs will be more widespread in society and they will naturally be accepted in sports. But we're still a long way from then. Maybe at that time people will look back at the so-called Steroid Era of baseball a little differently."

The Beginning of the End

"Well I'm retiring this year so I won't be able to vote any more for the C of C candidates. But I'm happy that we shut out the cheating superfloats like Harry Bombs, Popeye Maloney and Jelly Rogers again this year. I certainly hope that the MBLWA continues to shut them out forever. Do you think they'll ever get in?"

"I don't know, Lester. I just don't know."

"Enough of this bull shit. Let's watch the game. He tapped his shot glass again. He found it hard to believe that his little buddy Tim Burr was drinking ginless tonic. What was the world coming to?

Later that evening as he was taking his cab ride home after the second football game, snow was beginning to fall in earnest all around the city. Postal heard the news report on the cab radio, first the weather and then the sports. The rapid recap of the playoff games was followed by a baseball story. A statement from Alan Dorquez' attorney said that the Bloomers third baseman was not accepting results of the arbitration process and that they were going to file suit in Federal Court.

What a total asshole this guy is, thought Lester. Everyone listening to this knows that Dorquez will never follow through on the law suit. That would mean that he would eventually have to testify in court which would then probably lead to perjury charges. A Dork is an asshole but he isn't an idiot. He saw the government go after Bombs and Rogers on perjury charges. They'd probably enjoy another shot at a float like A Dork. For that matter A Dork's attorneys probably wouldn't mind collecting additional legal fees either. It's amazing how much money this conceited clown will spend on trying to repair his irreparable image. But he's not going to risk going to jail so in a few weeks we'll hear that he dropped his suit.

The snow continued to fall and Lester thought back on his conversation with Tim Burr earlier in the afternoon. As the snow began to accumulate the streets of the city seemed much quieter than usual as people went inside to get out of the elements.

So Tim and Evangeline are going to have a baby. Good for them. It certainly would be nice to be young and virile again. He thought about Georgette

Flunking Chemistry Class

and wondered what it would be like to have a child with her. *Would it be that crazy to become a first time father as a senior citizen? After all, Georgette is still only 37 years old. What if the fountain of youth really is out there waiting for me?*

The snow was now nearly blinding. The driver slowed down as Lester continued musing. The road ahead was now suddenly icy and uncertain. He just shook his head to clear his thoughts and simply muttered to himself, "Fuck that shit."

Postscript

July 2018

Following his publication of the Dunn Wright Report, MBL Commissioner, Abner Doubledown, had struck a compelling deal with the MBLPA. The new drug agreement called for random blood testing administered up to twelve times a year. If a player failed a drug test, he was immediately suspended without pay for one full year and the team that held his contract would have the right to void the agreement. The player's future annual earnings would be capped at the major league minimum if the player did decide to return to the game after serving his suspension. In any case a second violation would cause a player to be banned for life from the MBL. Most of the new minor leagues that were forming around the world were signaling that they would honor the potential suspensions and additional sanctions imposed by the MBL.

In the wake of the settlement of the 26th Man law suit in 2016 – which included the MBL's forfeiture on its US antitrust exemption – college baseball had become a much bigger sport and was now the primary American grooming ground for the MBL. First year players out of the university were signing large contracts with major league teams before they even played a day in The Show. The minor leagues outside of the United States flourished and were more heavily scouted than ever before but the minor leagues inside the United States were atrophying rapidly. In the past American high school star players – like

Flunking Chemistry Class

Sam Crockett – were given bonuses to labor for years at the minor league level before making MBL minimum salaries. Now exposure at one of the top colleges for a year or two could earn a player an eight figure contract right out of college.

Of course no one was crying for Sam Crockett these days. After winning the MVP award with the Metropolitan Mutts, Crockett signed a record shattering three year extension. This new contract would take him through the 2021 season at which time he would be 37 years old. More importantly in 2021 his two sons JR and Rory would be out of high school and in college or maybe even in The Show. Both boys had recently generated significant interest in their baseball skills from their high school teams on Long Island where the Crockett family had lived for the last three years. Money was no longer a concern for Sam Crockett. In addition to his current MBL earnings he had received the largest single financial apportionment from the $1.15 Billion settlement of the "26th Man law suit." His piece of that pie totaled a little over $38 Million. And of course coming to agreement with the Mutts was a lot easier now that Crockett's friend Tim Burr was part owner of the team.

Meanwhile, after the acquisition of two other law firms, the firm of Postal and Burr now had more than 200 attorneys in seven cities around the United States and in three cities in Asia. They had several different specialties, and a growing sports representation business based out of Tokyo. Georgette and Lester Postal had moved to Florida shortly after the settlement of the 26th man lawsuit and were now active members of at *Beautiful and Bodacious Bodies*. They were expecting their first child in December and Lester Postal felt younger than ever.

Acknowledgements

My process for finishing a book includes giving a first draft to several readers who give me important feedback in order to shape the final product. <u>Flunking Chemistry Class</u> followed that process as well. Therefore I'd like to thank Maria Ditmar and George Silver for their editorial advice; my brother Tom Lynch for his legal insights and plotline critique; and my brother Larry Lynch for his character and content analysis. My daughter, Kieran Rafter, also provided encouragement and editorial pick-ups from her first draft review. My brother Don Lynch also gave me one piece of advice after my last novel and that was to toughen up my women. I have tried to follow his advice. Thanks to each of you for your contributions.

I would also like to acknowledge the professionalism of the publication staff at Amazon's CreateSpace subsidiary. They have helped me through the interior formatting and cover design process in a very responsive way and I have always felt confident that my finished work would be enhanced by their expertise.

www.ingramcontent.com/pod-product-compliance
Lightning Source LLC
Chambersburg PA
CBHW061633040426
42446CB00010B/1395